Betty Crocker's ITALIAN
c o o k i n g

RECIPES BY ANTONIO CECCONI

WILEY

Wiley Publishing, Inc.

Published by Wiley Publishing, Inc., Hoboken, NJ

For general information on our other products and services or to obtain technical support please contact our Customer Care Department within the U.S. at   800-762-2974, outside the U.S. at 317-572-3993 or fax 317-572-4002.

Wiley also publishes its books in a variety of electronic formats. Some content that appears in print may not be available in electronic books.

ISBN: 0-7645-6078-6

Library of Congress Cataloging-in-Publication Data is available upon request.

GENERAL MILLS

Betty Crocker Kitchens
DIRECTOR, BOOK and ONLINE PUBLISHING: Kim Walter
MANAGER, COOKBOOK PUBLISHING: Lois L. Tlusty
EDITOR: Lois L. Tlusty
RECIPE DEVELOPMENT: Antonio Cecconi
RECIPE TESTING: Betty Crocker Kitchens
FOOD STYLISTS: Cindy Lund, Cindy Syme, Carmen Bonilla

Photographic Services
PHOTO ART DIRECTOR: Cathy Spengler
PHOTOGRAPHERS: Nanci Doonan Dixon, Val Bourassa
AUTHOR PHOTOGRAPHS: John Gairy
Photographs of Italy on pages 7, 8, 9, 10, 13, 14, 15, 17, 18, 20, 21, 23, 47, 89, 149, 181, 243 and 283 by Antonio Cecconi

WILEY PUBLISHING, INC.

PUBLISHER: Natalie Chapman
EXECUTIVE EDITOR: Anne Ficklen
COVER DESIGN: Michele Laseau
INTERIOR DESIGN AND LAYOUT: Michele Laseau and Edwin Kuo
MANUFACTURING MANAGER: Kevin Watt

For consistent baking results, the Betty Crocker Kitchens recommend Gold Medal Flour.

Find more great ideas and shop for name-brand housewares at *BettyCrocker.com*

Manufactured in the United States of America

10 9 8 7 6 5 4 3

Third Edition

Cover photo: Risotto with Zucchini and Bell Peppers

Dear Italian food lovers,

For thousands of years, the world's people and cultures have flourished, and food traditions, such as the Italian cuisine, have never stopped evolving. While visiting Italy's local markets and sampling the flavors of freshly prepared foods and fragrant herbs, I find the inspiration for creating new recipes to share with students and friends upon my return to the States.

This cookbook celebrates the distinctive dishes and flavors that reflect the many regions of Italy. You'll discover fragrant risottos, polentas and sauces rich with cream and butter from northern Italy to the pizzas and zesty seafood dishes created with fresh tomatoes and olive oil from southern Italy. My recipes for the dishes of Italy will provide convenience and the reward of homemade, wholesome meals for you to share with family and friends.

True to Betty, these recipes reflect a practical approach to preparation, plus a wealth of enlightening information. I enjoyed sharing my knowledge about the recipes in *Parola di Antonio,* which means "a word from Chef Antonio." Please join me as I guide you through a culinary tour of Italy. If you like, you can contact me at tiga@uswest.net.

Buon Appetito,

Antonio Cecconi

CONTENTS

Vallé D'Aosta

Trentino-Alto Adige

Lombardy

Friuli-Venezia Giulia

Piedmont

Veneto

Liguria

Emilia-Romagna

Italia

Tuscany

Marche

Umbria

Lazio

Abruzzo

Molise

Sardinia

Campagnia

Apulia

Basilicata

Calabria

Sicily

A TASTE OF ITALY

A Culinary Tour of the Twenty Regions

With its simple preparation and fresh ingredients, Italian food has become a familiar part of

American cooking. Many people now know Italy as much for its delicious food as for its natural

beauty and cultural heritage. Twenty regions compose the Italian mosaic of flavors, ranging from

the spicy Middle Eastern foods of the warm southern islands to the Bavarian-style cuisine of the

northern regions high in the Alps.

Costa Verde beach

NORTHERN ITALY

Northern Italy includes the regions of Valle d'Aosta, Piedmont, Lombardy, Veneto, Trentino-Alto Adige, Friuli-Venezia Giulia, Liguria and Emilia-Romagna. Piedmont and Valle d'Aosta border France and Switzerland and are nestled between the Alps and the great Po Valley.

Valle d'Aosta

Valle d'Aosta is entirely mountainous, and its cooking was influenced by the Bavarian-style cuisine of Switzerland, one of its border countries. Peculiar to this region is the absence of pasta and vegetable oils, for which dark oat bread, butter or beef render are substituted. Hearty soups are the main staple, prepared with large floating dumplings called *canederli* (German noodles), made of oats or potatoes to which cheese is added. Chamois, or mountain ram, is the meat specialty of this region and is usually stewed with wine and herbs, accompanied by bread or polenta made from white or yellow cornmeal. Fontina cheese and several types of cured meats such as prosciutto are typical of this region.

Hot coffee drinks prepared with espresso, *grappa* brandy and caramelized lemon peel are very popular throughout the many skiing resorts in the area.

Piedmont

Immediately to the south of Valle d'Aosta spreads the wealthy region of Piedmont, which literally means "at the foot of the mountains." Well known for its gastronomic traditions and the vitality of its inhabitants, this agriculturally rich region prides itself on naming, inventing and influencing various styles of cooking that have evolved in other regions of Italy as well as in other countries. This is the home of *fonduta*, known elsewhere as "fondue," and veal and chicken Marengo. Turin, Piedmont's capital, was the seat of the former Italian kings of Savoy, and its cooking reflects the most regal way of preparing breads and pastries. Elaborate sauces and excellent sparkling wines such as Asti Spumante come from this region.

Lombardy

Lombardy is the most affluent Italian region, with a booming economy and prosperous agriculture. Stretching from the Alps in the north to the Po Valley in the south, it is a land of hill towns, ski resorts and peaceful, beautiful lakes. Milan, near the center of Lombardy, is the business capital of Italy; like New York, it is something of a melting pot for different cultures and cuisines. Yet Lombard cuisine can easily be identified by its rich sauces, risottos and polenta dishes. It is also renowned for its beef and veal dishes. Some of the cheeses from this region have become world famous, among them Gorgonzola, Parmigiano Grana Padano (the local version of Parmigiano-Reggiano), Taleggio and Bel Paese. From this region also comes *panettone*, the Christmas bread enjoyed by Italian families.

Veneto

Stretching from the great lakes of Lombardy to the shores of the Adriatic Sea is the region of Veneto, which includes Trentino-Alto Adige and Friuli-Venezia Giulia. Veneto is particularly dear to many that have seen the beauty of its capital, Venice. In the Dolomite Mountains to the north is the enchanting hill town of Verona, where one can sit under a starry sky in the Roman arena and fall under the spell of an opera.

The stunning art of the Veneto region is equally matched by its cuisine. The cooking can be divided into three dominant styles, each from a different province: Veneto, the main province; Friuli, and the Trentino-Alto Adige, a very independent province, where the customs and language are quite separate from Italy, resembling those of other Bavarian regions.

The majestic architecture of Venice and its countryside exhibit its importance and power. For centuries, Venice was the crossroads for European trading and crusades to the Middle East. The influence of then-exotic spices brought into Italy by merchants is still evident today in the use of saffron in risotto and nutmeg in cream sauces.

Mild weather, an influence of the warm Adriatic Sea, makes the agriculture prosperous, especially around the numerous rivers that flow from the Alps. Fish from fresh waters, lagoons and the sea are fundamental to Venetian cuisine and are frequently prepared with combinations of spices and wine. The lowlands are primarily used for cultivating rice and cornmeal, from which risotto and polenta are made. The use of rice and corn in Veneto overshadow the use of pasta as a staple in the local diet.

The wines and cheeses that come from the mountains and hills near the Alps are highly valued. One can find flavorful cheeses such as Asiago d'Allevo, Mascarpone and Parmesan, and wines such as Soave white, Valpolicella, Bardolino and Pinot. Radicchio was first grown in the little town of Treviso, and later, radicchio di Verona, a much milder type, was developed and is now popular in the United States. Under Austrian rule for several decades, Venetian chefs were influenced by the Austrians and created pastries that are quite exuberant and sophisticated, including Christmas *pandoro* and liqueur-laced *fugazza* pastries.

Sugar Loaf Island

Emilia-Romagna

A combination of two regions, Emilia-Romagna's wonderful cuisine is rooted in two glorious cities: Parma and Bologna. Both regions have distinctive styles. Emilia is known for its lasagna, tortellini and Parmesan dishes. In Romagna, cooks use more fish and olive oil and not as many butter-based sauces. The traditional Bologna hams and the Parmigiano-Reggiano cheese have inspired other countries to duplicate them, but nothing can match the genuine flavor of the foods manufactured here. Emilia-Romagna exports the world's biggest wheels of *Parmigiano-Reggiano* cheese, as well as meat-stuffed tortellini and prosciutto hams. And it was in Bologna that the classic ragú sauce was invented.

Another specialty of this region are the wines, such as Lambrusco, which complement the region's rich food since they are light, refreshing and have a low alcohol content. Pork and veal are cooked with vegetables and wine, and are frequently deep-fried. From this practice comes Bologna's nickname, *Grassa*, meaning "the fat one." Only recently have local restaurants begun to cook with the more healthful olive oil. However, butter remains the base for sauces and desserts.

Liguria

In a crescent between the Alps and the Appennine Mountains and the Mediterranean lies Liguria, forming the beautiful Italian Riviera. The land along the coast is densely cultivated with flowers, herbs and olive and pine groves. The most traditional version of pesto sauce comes from this region.

The warmth of the sea and the protection of the mountains fosters the growth of the high-altitude grapes, which produce robust red wines. Rivaling the culinary splendor of Venice on Italy's other coast is Genoa, the ancient city that was the home of Christopher Columbus. A seaport for more than two thousand years, Genoa has influenced many other regions, particularly in the Middle East. It was Genovese sailors who introduced potato and tomato plants to Italy.

Also from its seaside setting comes the rainbow of seafood delicacies that characterize the cuisine of Liguria. Classic dishes include *cappon magro* (a vegetable and seafood salad), the world-famous cioppino fish stew and minestrone soup laced with pesto. Another distinctive

Jumbo caper pods

product of the region is *farinata pizza*, a pancakelike pizza that originally came from the Orient, prepared by stir-frying pea flour (made from ground, dried peas) with tomato sauce and spices. *Focaccia Genovese*, another delicious specialty, is a stuffed pizza.

CENTRAL ITALY

Central Italy encompasses Tuscany, Umbria, Marche and Lazio and includes Rome and Florence.

Tuscany

Just as Latin was once the language of the Romans and their empire, the Tuscan dialect is considered to be the "proper" Italian spoken throughout Italy by many. A land of pleasant hills and small, refined towns, Tuscany holds many surprises, both cultural and gastronomical. The most brilliant example of its bounty is the capital, Florence, with its stunning Renaissance architecture, art collections and world-famous cuisine. The cuisine of Tuscany is noted for its classic simplicity and the purity of its fresh ingredients. The scents of fresh herbs and other aromas provide an enticing invitation for tourists, a charming introduction to the artistry of Tuscan kitchens.

Herbs such as sage and rosemary, leeks and garlic give a rustic character to the food and are usually incorporated in the main portion of the dish rather than in the sauce. Pasta dishes are not a mainstay of Tuscan cuisine; those that are served have unpretentious, flavorful sauces. Instead, rice is common. Much of the simple, modest Tuscan cuisine has influenced the French and the English. Sometimes one even finds such terms as *béchamel* (from the Italian *Balsa Melia*) and *pâte á choux* (from the Italian *Pasta Calda*) appearing in their original Italian on restaurant menus in other countries as a nod to their Tuscan heritage.

Tuscany offers a substantial variety of foods such as *tortelli di zucca* (pumpkin-filled ravioli), spit-roasted meats with little fat used in their cooking, exotic crisp-fried zucchini flowers, dozens of fresh-cooked vegetables and crunchy desserts frequently made with a variety of nuts.

Tuscany is famous for its wines, many of which have won prizes around the world. Foremost is the Chianti, from a district of only thirty square miles. In Tuscany, olive trees mingle with the grapevines; both are intrinsically linked to Tuscany's economy and cuisine.

Workers at medieval castles and villas continue planting and harvesting grapes and olives as they have for centuries, though modern technology has made some inroads. The combination of ancient agricultural methods with detailed attention to the planting and new innovations such as mechanical harvesting provides quality exports of wines and olive oils known throughout the world.

Wines are incorporated in several desserts and fruitcakes, and these sweets are usually eaten on separate occasions rather than served as part of a regular meal. This is particularly true for the delicious nut-based cakes and breads, which, when accompanied by a glass of strong Vinsanto (holy dessert wine), can be particularly luscious.

Umbria

Small in size, Umbria is the only region of the Italian peninsula not bordered by the sea. It is tucked between Lazio and Marche, with small cities scattered through its many mountains. The food found in Perugia, Assisi and Spoleto rivals the arts, opera, crafts and architecture that make these towns famous.

Although Umbria doesn't have access to the open sea, mountain streams provide tasty trout and carp, which are marinated and cooked with fresh herbs, notably marjoram. Traditional pasta dishes are prepared, baked and then served as timbales, which are sliced and often served cold. Mountain mushrooms such as *porcini* and *tartufi* are the main ingredients of Umbrian pies, which give them an exquisite earthy flavor and a lovely appearance. Producing tantalizing wine such as Orvieto and liqueurs is an ancient tradition of the numerous monasteries of the region. Wild boar and aged mountain beef are also renowned.

Marche

Marche, on the mid-Adriatic coast, is one of the most appealing though lesser-known regions of the entire peninsula. Its four major cities, almost overlooking one another, sit atop the pleasant Appennine foothills, with Ancona, its capital, facing the Adriatic shore from high cliffs. The reliably mild climate is reflected in the cuisine, where subtle spicing is the norm and seafood stews are common. From Marche departs one of the largest fishing fleets of the country, which consistently provides the local markets with an abundant selection of fresh fish. In the countryside towns of Urbino, Recanati and Pesaro, cattle and hogs have been raised since the days of the Renaissance. This is reflected in the role that cured meats such as salami and prosciutto play in its cuisine.

A giant type of green olive grown in the area of Ascoli Piceno becomes a delicacy when filled with Parmesan, ground meats, eggs and spices and then deep-fried; this treat is found in no other region of Italy. Peaches and apples are the predominant fruits grown in Marche. Also noteworthy is the white truffle, found during the fall months. Particularly renowned is the sauce known as *salso del Duca D'Urbino*, similar to English Worcestershire sauce. In fact, local legend has it that in the Middle Ages, after the Duke of Urbino lost a battle, he had to surrender his recipe to the Saxon victor, which explains how the sauce traveled to England.

Lazio

Lazio is known for its capital, Rome. Its simple cuisine is similar to that of Tuscany. Pasta is favored in Lazio, especially bucatini and penne. Rome was the birthplace of *spaghetti carbonara*, and outside of Naples it is the best place to eat pizza, baked in its traditional form with wood fires. Toppings are simple; sometimes just one is used, and it can be one of many vegetables, such as tomatoes, zucchini or mushrooms.

SOUTHERN ITALY

Southern Italy is composed of Abruzzi, Molise, Campania, Puglia, Basilicata and Calabria. Naples is the major city.

Abruzzi

Abruzzi is a region of rugged mountains, sunny plateaus and a rocky seacoast bordering the Adriatic Sea. Sparsely populated, the region is primarily agricultural. Some of the finest pastas come from Fara San Martino—due to excellent wheat grown in the region—and are a prime source of exports to other countries. Olive oils are also of excellent quality and are commonly used for deep-frying the seafood that comes from the coastal waters.

Molise

Smaller than Abruzzi, Molise is in many ways similar in both cuisine and geography. Campobasso is the main city of Molise. Fresh seafood and short-cut pasta, made from soft wheat and served with hot pepper and tomato sauce, dominate the cuisine. Lamb and baby goat are traditionally served in most restaurants and are usually spit-roasted. Seafood appetizers are also a specialty of this region, served simply with olive oil and lemon.

Campania

Campania is one of the most fascinating and complex regions of Italy, with densely populated cities, a beautiful coast and ancient ruins. Blessed by the Mediterranean sun most of the year, the great valley around Naples is shaded by the ever-towering volcano Vesuvius, and its rich volcanic ash makes the region the most fertile in the world for cultivating tomatoes. Similar to California in climate, it produces an overwhelming array of vegetables still grown in small family plots, without pesticides.

From this bounty, a local cuisine has evolved that uses many spices and has created flavor combinations that are famous throughout Italy.

Campania also produces fresh mozzarella cheese, made from the milk of a local breed of water buffalo. Seafood from coastal waters makes up more than half of the food consumed in the region. Pizza was invented in Naples by creative housewives, providing a use for the newly imported tomatoes, mysterious newcomers that were originally used only as ornamental plants because they were thought to be poisonous.

Puglia

Puglia is the "heel" of the Italian boot, a long strip of land that forms its own peninsula. Italians regard it as the vegetable garden of the country, where the freshest greens, seafood and light meats provide a dazzling combination. Foods are generously basted, fried, marinated or drizzled with olive oil, which is the staple of all the local recipes.

It is interesting to note that this is the region from which the majority of boats come and go to Greece, Turkey and most other Middle Eastern countries. The interchange of traffic dates back to pre-Roman times, and it is no surprise to see Egyptian or Arab foods—such as fava beans, lentils and sweet-and-sour ratatouille salads—at the heart of this region. Lamb, rabbit and chicken acquire an exotic tang from the cumin, hot pepper and saffron that season them. Another interesting tradition is a tomato and horsemeat stew slowly cooked in clay pots over hot coals.

These Eastern hints are also found in the desserts, prepared mainly with honey and nuts. A curiously sweet cheese (considered a dessert) is the *manteca*, an apple-size fresh cheese with sweet butter in the center. It is accompanied by large homemade loaves of crusty bread. Often the bread is imprinted with a family seal because bread is brought by the local housewives to their neighborhood baker to be baked, and it is later identified by its seal. Calzone and *panzarotti* foldovers of this region are prepared in two versions, sweet and savory, and are deep-fried rather than baked, in contrast to the Neapolitan version.

Calamosca Harbor lighthouse

Basilicata

Flanked by Calabria on the west and Apulia on the east, Basilicata is a small region with ancient culinary traditions. Both neighboring regions influence its cooking, and here again there is a hint of exotic spices. Because the region is at the center of the Ionic gulf, seafood plays a major role, as do olive oil and tomatoes. Strong goat cheese—dark and chewy with a pleasant stringiness—is made in the shape of animals; the shapes vary from one little town to the next, so locals can tell the origin of the cheese just from its shape. In the district of Lucania, legend has it that the Roman garrisons used to demand provisions from the people of Lucania in the form of a special mix of ground and spiced meats that had a very long shelf life, the precursor of modern sausages.

Calabria

Calabria, right at the "toe" of Italy, shares the Eastern heritage of Sicily, colonized first by the Greeks, then by the Arabs. It is one of the few regions where hot peppers are commonly used. As in Apulia, lamb, game and

seafood play a major role in the diet. *Capozello* and *cervellata* (head meat) are important meat dishes. Very hard wheat also provides excellent short-cut pasta, which is frequently prepared with special vegetables. Eggplant is the most prized vegetable and is used liberally as an appetizer, first course or main dish. It is spread on bread as *metanzane a scapece* (pickled eggplant). Some of Calabria's robust red wines are also noteworthy.

ITALIAN ISLANDS

Italy's two islands, Sicily and Sardinia, offer a wide range of attractions from their distinctive cuisines to their scenic coastlines.

Sicily

The southernmost Italian region, the island of Sicily has seen many different cultures. Phoenicians, followed by Greeks, Romans, Normans, Spaniards and Arabs, all colonized Sicily. It became part of Italy in the middle of the nineteenth century and has preserved a little of each of these cultures. Couscous, saffron rice, eggplant and olive dishes, seafood and desserts can also be found in several other Mediterranean countries. With its sunny, warm weather most of the year, Sicily has always attracted tourists as well as settlers. Over the past fifty years, modern industry has revolutionized outdated irrigation systems, projecting Sicily into full-scale export of citrus fruits, grapes and vegetables.

Wines and the business of fishing are also important to the economy of the island and rival those of the northern Italian regions. Desserts from Palermo and Catania, such as cannoli pastries, cassata cakes and ices, are known worldwide. Typical pasta dishes have seafood and hot peppers featured in their sauces, and tangy olives are present in many dishes.

Sardinia

Sardinia is Italy's smaller island, to the north of Sicily. The combination of rugged mountains and a spectacular coastline accounts for its popularity with tourists. Though invaded and colonized over the centuries by the Spanish and others, Sardinia has preserved its independent culture, language and gastronomy. The pride of its inhabitants is reflected in its cuisine, which has achieved a well-defined identity.

The staples of the Sardinian cuisine are fish, lamb and hard-wheat pastas. Shellfish is served as an appetizer, and fish is grilled, fried or served with succulent tomato and wine sauces. Sardinia grows excellent durum wheat, from which semolina is produced and used to prepare unusual pasta dishes such as ravioli filled with spinach or ricotta cheese and nuts, a type of porridge with lentils and tomato sauce, and tiny gnocchi, much smaller than the ones of the mainland.

From the island's interior come suckling pigs, boar and game; these are usually cooked on open-flame grills and flavored with fragrant herbs such as wild fennel, myrtle, rosemary, bay leaves, basil and saffron, all of which grow wild on the island. *Pecorino Romano*, a pungent cheese, is made from goat milk. Vegetables are fewer than on the mainland due to frequent droughts, but are quite flavorful. Some very strong local wines and Sassari olive oil have won national attention.

Desserts are simple and usually include honey and nuts. Desserts are traditionally eaten only on special occasions, and sugary desserts have a special role at weddings, funerals and baptisms.

Almond Tree

Flavors of Italian Cooking

Many of the flavors associated with Italian cooking are familiar to us. During the first centuries after the discovery of the New World, several new foods were brought to Italy, among them herbs, vegetables and fruits.

The tomato, of course, has become something of a symbol for Italian cooking—sliced fresh with basil, cooked to make sauces or sun-dried for soups, pizza, pasta and long-term storage. The herbs most commonly used to enhance the flavor of the tomato are basil and oregano, often paired with garlic and onion. These two herbs are essential to many Italian sauces, particularly in southern Italy. In the north, olive oil and tomato sauces give way to butter and cream sauces with more subtle and exotic flavors.

Venetian merchants introduced spices to their fellow Italians in the Middle Ages, and the use of spices slowly spread throughout the country. Foods that would otherwise have spoiled before the days of refrigeration were spiced with pepper to retard spoilage or hide the flavor of spoilage. Today, salt and pepper are still the basic ingredients used to cure meat such as prosciutto and pancetta. Cinnamon, cloves, nutmeg and other Eastern spices, once a luxury of the wealthy, slowly became available to cooks in humbler kitchens as the transportation and storage of

spices improved. These spices are still used in many meat dishes and desserts, especially in the northern regions.

In southern Italy, the sunny climate fosters the cultivation of caper bushes, bay leaves, rosemary, basil and thyme, which, along with a hint of hot pepper, spice meats and seafoods. Italian food isn't spiced to be burning hot; if hot peppers are called for in a dish, only the pulp is used, which is not as hot as the seeds and inner core. Citron, or candied fruit, is used in the breads and sweets of northern Italy, and nuts, cinnamon and raisins are more commonly used in the south.

The hills and plains around the Mediterranean are thick with small groves of picturesque gnarled olive trees. A popular olive used in Italy for both cooking and pure eating pleasure is the Kalamata (or Calamata) olive. These plump, purplish black Greek olives are the easiest to find, and the flavor is powerful yet balanced. Two other olives often found are the large green Greek olive, Ionian, and from France, Niçoise olives. The Niçoise is small in stature but has a pungent taste; its color ranges from gray green to charcoal. Olives usually are sold with their pits, for the increased flavor. Large crocks of olives in various colors and sizes, in brine or flavorful marinades, are plentiful in the markets and shops throughout Italy.

Herbs are the hallmarks of Italian culinary identity, giving a world of unique taste sensations and flavor combinations. Due to the favorable climate, most commonly used herbs are found fresh at the local markets in the regions where they can be cultivated or gathered wild. The herbs described below appear most frequently in Italian recipes.

BASIL can be seen growing in small pots on Italian balconies. It is a sweet, aromatic herb that can be a flavor powerhouse. It is the preferred herb for tomato recipes and is a flavorful addition when tossed with fresh greens in a salad. It should be torn into pieces rather than cut because the cut edges darken quickly and some claim the flavor is altered.

BAY LEAVES are pungent and aromatic. Dried leaves are the most widely used form; however, Italians often use fresh bay leaves. The assertive flavor goes well with grilled meats, soups and stews.

MARJORAM is moderately aromatic with a slightly bitter undertone and is closely related to oregano. It can be added to most meat dishes, soups and vegetables and to robust salad dressings. It is used both fresh and in dried form.

MINT has a distinctive sweet aroma and flavor and a cool aftertaste. Wild mint is used in Roman cooking, and in Naples, mint is used with fried eggplant and zucchini.

OREGANO is strong and aromatic with a pleasantly bitter undertone. It grows wild everywhere in the countryside close to the sea. It is the most popular herb that is used dried.

PARSLEY is by far the most popular herb in Italian cooking. It is available in two forms, curly leaf and flat leaf. The flat-leaf variety, also known as Italian parsley, is widely used. In fact, Italians assume everyone uses the flat-leaf parsley, which is more strongly flavored, so they don't specify it in recipes.

ROSEMARY is a perennial bush whose leaves resemble pine needles. It grows wild near the sea and its name, in fact, means "sea dew." More popular in northern and central Italy than it is in the south, it has a fresh, sweet flavor that can be very strong.

SAGE is an aromatic and slightly bitter herb used widely in the north. It is well suited for bread and meat stuffings, poultry, sausages and soups.

Marina Piccola at Poetto Beach

TARRAGON is known for its distinctive, slightly sweet aniselike flavor. It should be used with care because its strong flavor can easily overpower other flavors.

THYME is aromatic and pungent; a little goes a long way. It is excellent with poultry, fish, seafood, bread and meat stuffings and tomatoes.

ITALIAN VINEGARS

Used in Italy for centuries for both medicinal and culinary purposes, vinegar, or *aceto*, has been a familiar staple in Italian cuisine since Roman times.

Both red and white wines are used to make vinegar, as well as grape juice, as is the case with balsamic vinegar. Wine vinegar often serves as the base of herb- and fruit-flavored vinegars such as tarragon and raspberry. They are favored for use in salad dressings and classic sauces.

Balsamic (bal-SAH-mihk) vinegar, or *aceto balsamico*, (ah-CHEH-toh bahl-SAH-mee-koh), dates from the eleventh century, when it was considered a luxury for the royal families of Europe. Balsamic vinegar originated in the Emilia-Romagna provinces of Modena and Reggio,

the only area that can produce the traditional balsamic vinegars, which are very expensive. Labels of traditional balsamics have the letters API MO, indicating Modena, or API RE, for Reggio. Commercial balsamics from this region are more reasonably priced and are very good-quality vinegar for cooking. Only in the early 1900s did it become readily available for sale.

The characteristic flavor of balsamic vinegar is obtained through a long process of aging and the reduction of the white Trebbiano grape juice. The juice is stored and transferred through a succession of wooden barrels. Aging takes up to fifteen years, during which each barrel is closely monitored. The vinegar is usually transferred to smaller barrels every two years. At each interval, the vinegar is filtered and tested for sweetness and flavor development. The specific wood of the barrels contributes to refining the vinegar's flavor during the aging process. The overall result is a dark brown vinegar with a rich, mellow, smooth and slightly sweet flavor. A little brown sugar added to a commercially made balsamic vinegar will provide the smooth sweetness that resembles the traditionally made vinegars.

Scuba diving off Sardina

Balsamic vinegar can be used to add flavor to meats, seafood, poultry, sauces, salad dressings and freshly cooked vegetables. For a unique appetizer or first course, offer bite-size chunks or shavings of *Parmigiano-Reggiano* cheese to dip into balsamic vinegar (or sprinkle vinegar on the cheese), and serve with crusty Italian bread. For a simple dessert, combine fresh, sweet strawberries with a splash of balsamic vinegar.

THE ITALIAN MARKET

Many Italians still shop daily at small specialty shops, which are peppered throughout the neighborhoods in cities, as well as in small towns and villages. The Italian passion for food is reflected in the desire to use only the freshest and best seasonal ingredients.

A daily marketing excursion could start with a stop at the butcher or seafood shop to select the fresh catch of the day for the main course. Then on to the *frutta e verdura* where beautiful displays of fresh seasonal vegetables, fruits and herbs resemble still-life oil paintings. The knowledgeable shopkeeper will assist with selecting only the very best produce. At the bread shop, or *panetteria*, the shelves and display case are brimming with golden-crusted local breads and rolls baked fresh that day.

Traditional open-air markets are also very popular. On certain days, traveling vendors set up stalls or park refrigerated trucks in a *piazza* or on city streets to proudly display their wares. Not only is it a place to plan the family meals based on what is available, it is also a place to share greetings and news with friends and neighbors alike.

Shopping trips to the market may not be part of your daily schedule. For that reason, you may want to keep these items in your "Italian pantry" so you can prepare a tasty Italian recipe any day of the week. For some recipes, a quick stop at the market to pick up a few fresh ingredients may be all you need.

YOUR ITALIAN PANTRY

Anchovy fillets in oil (canned)

Anchovy paste

Artichoke hearts, marinated and plain

Beans, lentils, split peas, dried

Bread crumbs, Italian-style dry

Capers

Cheeses (Asiago, Gorgonzola, mozzarella, Parmesan, provolone, Romano)

Chicken broth

Cornmeal, yellow

Crushed red pepper

Flour (bread, semolina)

Garlic

Herbs, dried (basil, bay leaves, dill weed, marjoram, mint, oregano, rosemary, sage, tarragon)

Honey

Instant espresso coffee granules

Mushrooms, marinated

Mustard (Dijon, stone-ground)

Nuts (almonds, hazelnuts, pine nuts, walnuts)

Olive oils

Olives (Kalamata, Gaeta, Greek green, pimiento-stuffed, pitted ripe)

Pasta, dried (various shapes and sizes)

Rice (Arborio), long-grain regular)

Roasted red bell peppers, jarred

Spices (anise, cinnamon, nutmeg)

Tomatoes, Italian-style pear-shaped (plum), canned

Tomatoes, sun-dried

Vegetable broth

Vinegar (balsamic, red wine)

Wine (sparkling, red, white)

Gather Around the Table

*I*talians have been taking food seriously for more than two thousand years, and amazingly, most of the food eaten in Italy today remains roughly the same. Though the flavors and dishes may change from one region to the next, the love and appreciation of good food remains constant. Many people find the basic Italian diet—with its emphasis on olive oil; pasta, polenta and risotto dishes; sensible portions; and only occasional desserts—to be one of the most healthful ways to eat.

TRADITIONAL ITALIAN EATING

Traditionally, Italians respect regular mealtimes with the family gathering at the table every day, not just on special occasions. Instead of concentrating on one main dish flanked by side dishes, traditional meals consist of a series of courses served and eaten separately. This allows for more time to talk and enjoy the meal, and it aids digestion.

The variety of foods offered at traditional meals is frequently served on a sampling basis—small tastes of several dishes. In the past, the main meal of the day was served at lunch, frequently followed by an afternoon nap. Farmers started working very early in the morning and by noon had developed a hearty appetite. The hot afternoon was the ideal time to take a nap. Then the farmers returned to the fields and chores later in the day.

In urban areas, lunch was a time to close shops and offices to enjoy a leisurely meal at a local *trattoria* or at home. City workers, too, followed lunch with a nap or relaxing stroll. Of course, they worked later to recover the time, and dinner was usually served around nine o'clock. The Mediterranean dinner was a scaled-down version of lunch. The late evening meal also was an occasion for families to come together at the end of the day to relax in and enjoy one another's company.

A typical menu gives us insight into the traditional Italian meal. Large meals begin with a light *antipasto*, literally "before the pasta," that stimulates the appetite for the first course, or *prima*. These *antipasti* are generally cured meats or fresh seafood, depending on the region. Often olive oil and tangy lemon juice or vinegar highlight the food's flavor.

Next is the *prima*, the first course. It consists of pasta, soup, risotto, polenta or gnocchi. The first course is enjoyed in its own right, served in small portions to prevent overwhelming the other courses.

The second course, or *secondo*, is the main portion of the meal and is usually a meat, seafood or poultry dish. White meat is generally preferred to red, olive oil is favored in place of other fats and fresh herbs are used instead of a great deal of salt.

To complement the main dish, a *contorno* is served, which is either a salad or a raw or cooked vegetable, prepared simply. The purpose of this dish is to cleanse the palate, so heavy sauces or dressings are rare. The vegetables lead to the end of the meal; dessert, or *dolce*, can be either cheese with crusty bread or fresh fruit and on rare occasions a very sweet pastry. Some people drink espresso coffee as a "digestive" after a meal, though it is more commonly served for breakfast with a roll. An alcoholic beverage, such as *grappa*, is sometimes offered after coffee to aid the digestion and end the meal on a relaxing note.

ITALIAN EATING TODAY

Italians still cherish tradition, but because of today's changing lifestyles, their eating habits have also changed.

They do maintain their great passion for properly prepared meals using only the freshest and highest quality ingredients.

In some regions of Italy, the lunch period is shorter and no longer the main meal of the day due to longer workdays to remain competitive within the global economy. The evening meal, therefore, has become the main meal and is a little heartier than it had been in the past. It still is the time to gather with family or friends and enjoy good food together. For special occasions and holiday celebrations, however, the main meal is still served at noon rather than in the evening.

Although Italians have created luscious desserts known the world over, these are usually served only on special occasions. Italians serve dessert as a separate event, over which to socialize or celebrate, not as part of a meal. Sweets are generally served with coffee or a glass of wine.

Whether you take pleasure in a traditional Italian meal with several leisurely courses or in a lighter meal, you will always experience the wonderful aromas and flavors of fine Italian cooking. *Buon Appetito!*

Basil Toast, page 26

CHAPTER ONE

Antipasti

BEFORE THE MEAL

Formaggio— Cheeses of Italy

*I*taly's love of cheese is reflected in the multitude of cheeses that are produced throughout the county. Fresh or aged, soft or hard, the cheeses vary according to region, climate and soil. Many small farms and individual families still produce some of the country's finest cheeses. Cheese is used in various courses of an Italian meal, from the *antipasto* to a cheese course to cleansing the palate at the end of a meal. Here are some Italian cheeses that have gained popularity.

ASIAGO (ah-see-AH-goh) A semi-firm cheese with a rich, nutty flavor made from cow's milk. It is named after the area of Asiago. "Young" Asiago is used as a table cheese; when aged over a year, it becomes hard and is good for grating.

BEL PAESE (BELL pah-AY-zay) A semisoft cow's-milk cheese from Lombardy; literally translated, it means "beautiful country." This mild, buttery-flavored cheese is a great melting cheese and can be used in many dishes. Italians serve this as a dessert cheese, often with fresh fruit.

FONTINA (fahn-TEE-nah) A semi-firm yet creamy cow's-milk cheese from Valle d'Aosta in northern Italy, its name means "little spring fountain." Its mild, nutty flavor (similar to Swiss but without holes) and easy melting quality make it ideal for almost any use.

GORGONZOLA (gohr-guhn-ZOH-lah) A cow's-milk cheese named for a town outside of Milan in northern Italy. A rich, creamy, ivory-colored cheese, it can be lightly or thickly streaked with bluish-green veins. It has a slightly pungent yet savory flavor, and the aroma can be quite strong. This cheese can be crumbled on salads, added to creamy sauces for pasta or served for dessert with fresh pears.

MASCARPONE (mas-kar-POHN; mas-kahr-POH-nay) A buttery-rich, soft cow's-milk cheese from Italy's Lombardy region. Ivory in color, it ranges in flavor between rich clotted cream and soft butter. Because it is mild, it blends with other flavors.

MOZZARELLA (maht-suh-REHL-lah; moht-suh-REHL-lah) A fresh, soft cheese made from buffalo or cow's milk. The name comes from *mozzare*, referring to the process by which handfuls of cheese are torn off and twisted. Mozzarella can be shaped into rounds, braids or small balls called *bocconcini*. A smoked version is called *mozzarella affumicata*. Fresh mozzarella is usually available stored in water or whey. Regular mozzarella, which is factory produced, can be low-fat or nonfat. It is semisoft and has an excellent melting quality with a chewy, stringy texture.

PARMESAN (PAHR-muh-zahn); **parmigiano** (pahr-mee-J'YAH-noh) A hard, dry cow's milk cheese from the Emilia-Romagna region. This premier cheese is produced under strict regulations; it must contain no additives except rennet and salt. It is excellent for grating or finely shredding. Authentic cheese produced in Bologna, Mantua, Modena and Parma has the *Parmigiano-Reggiano* seal stenciled on its hard rind. The flaky, dry granular texture is excellent for grating, and it should melt in the mouth. Imported Parmesan has much more flavor and suitable texture than domestic varieties.

PECORINO (peh-kuh-REE-noh) A hard cheese made from sheep's milk. It has a sharp, robust flavor and can be used in place of Parmesan cheese if a stronger flavor is desired. The best known is *pecorino Romano*, commonly referred to as Romano cheese. This cheese is used primarily for grating and cooking.

PROVOLONE (proh-voh-LOH-neh) A cow's-milk cheese with a mild smoky flavor. This southern Italian cheese has a golden brown rind with a light yellow interior, and it comes in many forms. After it has aged, its flavor is more pungent, and the cheese can be used for grating. Its rich, nutty taste and excellent melting quality make it an ideal partner with mozzarella when topping pizzas.

RICOTTA (rih-KAHT-tuh) Fresh, soft, slightly grainy cheese that is similar to cultured cottage cheese. It has a slightly sweet flavor. *Ricotta* means "recooked" and is made by heating the whey from another cooked cheese.

Asiago

Gorgonzola

Parmesan

Provolone

Fontina

Ricotta

Bel Paese

Smoked Mozzarella

Fresh Mozzarella

Mozzarella

Pecorino

Mascarpone

BASIL TOAST
Crostini al Basilico

6 slices hard-crusted Italian bread
or 12 slices baguette, about
1/2 inch thick

1 large tomato, chopped (1 cup)

3 tablespoons chopped fresh
basil leaves

1 tablespoon capers

1/2 teaspoon salt

1/2 teaspoon pepper

1/4 cup extra-virgin olive oil

12 slices mozzarella cheese
(about 3/4 pound)

PREP: 10 MIN; BAKE: 8 MIN
12 appetizers

1. Heat oven to 375°. If using Italian bread, cut each slice in half. Place bread on ungreased cookie sheet.

2. Mix tomato, basil, capers, salt and pepper. Drizzle 1 teaspoon oil on each slice bread. Spoon half of the tomato mixture onto bread. Top each with cheese slice. Spoon remaining tomato mixture onto cheese.

3. Bake about 8 minutes or until hot and cheese is melted.

1 Appetizer: Calories 155 (Calories from Fat 90); Fat 10g (Saturated 4g); Cholesterol 15mg; Sodium 330mg; Carbohydrate 7g (Dietary Fiber 0g); Protein 9g
% Daily Value: Vitamin A 4%; Vitamin C 2%; Calcium 22%; Iron 2%
Diet Exchanges: 1/2 Starch, 1 Medium-Fat Meat, 1 Fat

Parola di Antonio

Crostini are a common type of appetizer that are easy to prepare and a delight to eat. All you need are small slices of crusty rustic bread and a little imagination for the toppings—meats, cheeses, seafood, vegetables, pâtés—whatever you like or have on hand. I like to serve this simple tomato-topped crostini on a platter along with thin slices of Genoa salami and sweet imported prosciutto.

ROASTED RED BELL PEPPER TOAST
Bruschetta Romana

8 slices hard-crusted Italian bread or
16 slices baguette, 1/2 inch thick

6 to 8 cloves garlic

1/4 cup extra-virgin olive oil

1 jar (7 ounces) roasted red bell
(sweet) peppers, drained and
cut into 1/2-inch strips

2 tablespoons chopped fresh parsley
or 1 teaspoon parsley flakes

2 tablespoons shredded imported
Parmesan cheese

1 tablespoon extra-virgin olive oil

1/4 teaspoon salt

1/4 teaspoon pepper

PREP: 15 MIN
16 appetizers

1. If using Italian bread, cut each slice in half. Toast or grill
   bread until golden brown on both sides.

2. Cut each garlic clove in half; rub cut sides over tops and
   sides of toast slices. Brush oil over tops of toast slices.

3. Mix remaining ingredients. Spoon onto toast.

1 Appetizer: Calories 145 (Calories from Fat 90); Fat 10g (Saturated 2g); Cholesterol 0mg;
Sodium 220mg; Carbohydrate 12g (Dietary Fiber 1g); Protein 3g
% Daily Value: Vitamin A 8%; Vitamin C 58 %; Calcium 4%; Iron 4%
Diet Exchanges: 1 Starch, 1 1/2 Fat

Parola di Antonio

The origin of bruschetta *in Italy began in ancient Rome when each winter
the first tasting of the freshly pressed green-olive oil took place. Slices of
grilled hearty bread were soaked with the oil and perhaps rubbed with
garlic. This frugal fare has now become popular in recent years in many
restaurants and homes alike. Actually, the name* bruschette *comes from the
word* bruscare, *which means "charcoal toasted" and is really a Roman
slang term. Today different toppings are added to the toast, and it is eaten
all over Italy.*

FRESH MOZZARELLA AND TOMATO
Insalata Caprese

4 medium tomatoes, cut into
1/4-inch slices

8 ounces fresh mozzarella cheese,
cut into 1/4-inch slices

2 tablespoons extra-virgin olive oil

2 tablespoons balsamic or
red wine vinegar

2 tablespoons chopped fresh
basil leaves

Freshly ground pepper

PREP: 10 MIN; STAND: 30 MIN
8 servings

1. Arrange tomatoes and cheese slices alternately on round plate. Drizzle oil and vinegar over tomatoes and cheese. Sprinkle with basil and pepper.

2. Let stand at room temperature 30 minutes to blend flavors. Cover and refrigerate any remaining cheese and tomatoes.

1 Serving: Calories 115 (Calories from Fat 70); Fat 8g (Saturated 4g); Cholesterol 15mg; Sodium 160mg; Carbohydrate 4g (Dietary Fiber 1g); Protein 8g
% Daily Value: Vitamin A 8%; Vitamin C 20%; Calcium 20%; Iron 2%
Diet Exchanges: 1 Lean Meat, 1 Vegetable, 1 Fat

Antipasto

There are three basics types of *antipasto*. *Freddi e crudi* includes raw vegetables and cold meats, fish and cheese. These can be served by themselves or in various combinations. *Affettati* includes cured meats that are sliced just before serving and are accompanied by crusty breads or breadsticks. *Prosciutto* is the most popular example of *affettati* and is served by itself or with fresh melon or figs. *Antipasti caldi* are fried or baked morsels, just large enough to take the edge off a diner's hunger without being filling. They range from batter fritters to seasoned bread tarts such as *bruschette* and *crostini*.

Fresh Mozzarella and Tomato

FRESH BASIL-WRAPPED CHEESE BALLS
Formaggio al Basilico

1/2 cup mascarpone cheese
    (4 ounces)*

1/2 cup crumbled Gorgonzola
    cheese (2 ounces)

2 tablespoons grated imported
    Parmesan cheese

1/8 teaspoon pepper

24 fresh basil leaves,
    2 to 2 1/2 inches long

*4 ounces cream cheese, softened,
can be substituted for the mascarpone.

PREP: 15 MIN; CHILL: 30 MIN
24 appetizers

1. Mix cheeses and pepper until blended. Cover and refrigerate about 30 minutes or until firm enough to shape into balls.

2. Shape 1 1/2 teaspoons cheese mixture into a ball. Roll slightly to form an oval, about 1 inch long. Place on wide end of basil leaf; roll up. Roll leaf and cheese between fingers to form an oval. Repeat with remaining cheese mixture and basil leaves.

3. Serve immediately, or cover with plastic wrap and refrigerate until ready to serve but no longer than 24 hours.

1 Appetizer: Calories 30 (Calories from Fat 25); Fat 3g (Saturated 2g); Cholesterol 10mg; Sodium 65mg; Carbohydrate 0g (Dietary Fiber 0g); Protein 1g
% Daily Value: Vitamin A 2%; Vitamin C 0%; Calcium 2%; Iron 0%
Diet Exchanges: 1/2 Fat

Parola di Antonio

I like to serve this refreshing treat when fresh basil is at its peak and its slightly spicy fragrance fills the air. If the basil leaves are not the correct size, I just chop them and roll the cheese balls in them rather than covering each ball with a whole leaf. To simplify the preparation even further, I sometimes roll the chilled cheese mixture into a rectangle between two sheets of waxed paper and then cut it into twenty-four strips. Place each strip on a large fresh basil leaf along with a thin strip of roasted red bell pepper. Or place coarse shavings of Parmesan cheese on large fresh basil leaves. Drizzle with a little extra-virgin olive oil, and dust with freshly ground pepper. Splendido!

MIXED-APPETIZER PLATTER
Antipasto Composto

12 slices hard-crusted round Italian bread or 24 slices French bread, 1/2 inch thick

2 cloves garlic

12 slices imported prosciutto or thinly sliced fully cooked ham (about 6 ounces), cut in half

12 slices provolone cheese (about 3/4 pound), cut in half

24 thin slices Genoa salami (about 3/4 pound)

24 marinated mushrooms

24 marinated artichoke hearts

24 imported Kalamata or Gaeta olives, pitted, or large pitted ripe olives

1/3 cup extra-virgin olive oil

1/2 medium lemon

1 tablespoon chopped fresh or 1/2 teaspoon dried oregano leaves

PREP: 15 MIN
24 appetizers

1. If using Italian bread, cut each slice in half. Cut each garlic clove in half; rub cut sides over both sides of bread. Arrange bread in single layer on serving platter.

2. Top each bread slice with prosciutto, cheese, salami, mushroom, artichoke heart and olive. Drizzle with oil. Squeeze juice from lemon over top. Sprinkle with oregano.

1 Appetizer: Calories 210 (Calories from Fat 135); Fat 15g (Saturated 5g); Cholesterol 30mg; Sodium 790mg; Carbohydrate 10g (Dietary Fiber 2g); Protein 11g
% Daily Value: Vitamin A 4%; Vitamin C 6%; Calcium 12%; Iron 8%
Diet Exchanges: 1/2 Starch, 1 Medium-Fat Meat, 1/2 Vegetable, 2 Fat

Parola di Antonio

Antipasto literally means "before the pasta" and is served as an appetizer. In Italy almost all antipasto dishes are prepared ahead and served at room temperature, although a few are served warm. Antipasto tempts the eater visually as well as with its taste, and a colorful antipasto not only stimulates the appetite but also reflects the creativity of the cook.

ROASTED GARLIC
Aglio Arrosto al Forno

6 medium bulbs garlic

2 tablespoons extra-virgin olive oil

Salt, if desired

Freshly ground pepper, if desired

12 to 18 slices hard-crusted
  Italian bread

PREP: 5 MIN; BAKE: 50 MIN
6 servings

1. Heat oven to 350°.

2. Carefully peel away papery skin around garlic bulbs, leaving just enough to hold garlic together. Cut 1/2-inch slice from top of bulbs to expose cloves. Place with stem end down on 12-inch square of aluminum foil. Drizzle each bulb with 1 teaspoon of the oil. Sprinkle with salt and pepper. Wrap securely in foil. Place in pie plate or shallow baking pan.

3. Bake 45 to 50 minutes or until garlic is very tender when pierced with a toothpick or fork. Cool slightly.

4. To serve, gently squeeze clove from bulb and spread on bread. Or place bulbs on serving plate with slices of bread and each person squeezes out his or her own cloves.

1 Serving: Calories 180 (Calories from Fat 55); Fat 6g (Saturated 1g); Cholesterol 0mg; Sodium 240mg; Carbohydrate 28g (Dietary Fiber 2g); Protein 5g
% Daily Value: Vitamin A 0%; Vitamin C 6%; Calcium 6%; Iron 8%
Diet Exchanges: 2 Starch, 1/2 Fat

Parola di Antonio

Since Roman times, garlic has also been used for therapeutic purposes, such as anesthetic for insect bites or the fresh-squeezed juice to cure the stomach flu. It is ironic that poor Italian immigrants at the turn of the century were scorned as "garlic heads" for their massive use of garlic. Despite its humble origins, roasted garlic is now seeing its moment of glory and has become a popular item on the menus of trendy restaurants. Roasting results in soft, spreadable cloves and a mellow, mild flavor. Add it to mayonnaise, spread it over crusty bread, toss it in salads or add it to mashed potatoes.

FRITTATA, GARDEN STYLE
Frittata Del Giardino

1 tablespoon olive oil

1/2 cup sliced mushrooms

2 tablespoons chopped drained
sun-dried tomatoes in oil

2 medium green onions, sliced
(2 tablespoons)

1 small yellow bell pepper, chopped
(1/2 cup)

8 eggs

1 tablespoon chopped fresh parsley
or 1 teaspoon parsley flakes

1 tablespoon chopped fresh or
1/2 teaspoon dried basil leaves

1 tablespoon freshly grated
imported Parmesan cheese

1/2 teaspoon salt

1/4 teaspoon pepper

PREP: 10 MIN; COOK: 15 MIN; BROIL: 3 MIN
6 first-course or 4 main-course servings

1. Heat oil in 10-inch ovenproof nonstick skillet over medium heat (if not using a nonstick skillet, increase oil to 2 tablespoons). Cook mushrooms, tomatoes, onions and bell pepper in oil 3 minutes, stirring frequently. Reduce heat to medium-low.

2. Beat remaining ingredients together until blended. Pour over vegetable mixture. Cover and cook 7 to 9 minutes or until eggs are set around edge and beginning to brown on bottom (egg mixture will be uncooked on top).

3. Set oven control to broil. Broil frittata with top about 5 inches from heat about 3 minutes or until eggs are cooked on top and light golden brown (frittata will puff up during broiling but will collapse when removed from broiler).

1 Serving: Calories 140 (Calories from Fat 90); Fat 10g (Saturated 3g); Cholesterol 280mg;
Sodium 310mg; Carbohydrate 3g (Dietary Fiber 0g); Protein 9g
% Daily Value: Vitamin A 10%; Vitamin C 22%; Calcium 6%; Iron 6%
Diet Exchanges: 1 Medium-Fat Meat, 1 Vegetable, 1 Fat

ARTICHOKE-BASIL FRITTATA

Frittata al Basilico e Carciofi

1 can (13 to 14 1/2 ounces)
    artichoke hearts, drained, or
    1 package (12 ounces) frozen
    artichoke hearts, thawed

1 tablespoon olive oil

1/2 cup chopped red onion

2 cloves garlic, finely chopped

2 tablespoons chopped fresh or
    2 teaspoons dried basil leaves

1 tablespoon chopped fresh parsley

6 eggs

1/2 teaspoon salt

1/4 teaspoon pepper

2 tablespoons freshly grated
    imported Parmesan cheese

PREP: 10 MIN; COOK: 12 MIN; BROIL: 3 MIN
6 first-course or 4 main-course servings

1. Cut artichoke hearts into quarters. Heat oil in 10-inch ovenproof nonstick skillet over medium heat (if not using nonstick skillet, increase oil to 2 tablespoons). Cook onion, garlic, basil and parsley in oil 3 minutes, stirring frequently, until onion is tender. Reduce heat to medium-low.

2. Beat eggs, salt and pepper until blended. Pour over onion mixture. Arrange artichokes on top of egg mixture. Cover and cook 7 to 9 minutes or until eggs are set around edge and beginning to brown on bottom (egg mixture will be uncooked on top). Sprinkle with cheese.

3. Set oven control to broil. Broil frittata with top about 5 inches from heat about 3 minutes or until eggs are cooked on top and light golden brown. (Frittata will puff up during broiling but will collapse when removed from broiler.)

Note: The cooked egg under the artichoke pieces may turn light green due to the acid in the artichoke hearts. This will not affect the eating quality or flavor of the frittata.

1 Serving: Calories 140 (Calories from Fat 70); Fat 8g (Saturated 2g); Cholesterol 215mg; Sodium 480mg; Carbohydrate 9g (Dietary Fiber 4g); Protein 10g
% Daily Value: Vitamin A 8%; Vitamin C 6%; Calcium 8%; Iron 8%
Diet Exchanges: 1 Medium-Fat Meat, 2 Vegetable, 1/2 Fat

Artichoke-Basil Frittata

EGGPLANT APPETIZER
Caponata

2 large eggplants
   (about 2 pounds each)

1 tablespoon salt

3 tablespoons olive oil

18 imported Kalamata olives, pitted,
   or large pitted ripe olives

4 medium tomatoes, chopped
   (3 cups)*

2 cloves garlic, finely chopped

1 tablespoon capers

1 tablespoon pine nuts

2 tablespoons balsamic or
   red wine vinegar

2 teaspoons sugar

1/2 teaspoon pepper

*1 can (28 ounces) Italian-style
pear-shaped (plum) tomatoes, well
drained and chopped, can be
substituted for the fresh tomatoes.*

PREP: 35 MIN; COOK: 20 MIN
12 servings

1. Peel eggplants; cut into 1/2-inch cubes. Spread eggplant on cutting board; sprinkle with salt. Tilt board slightly; let stand 30 minutes. Rinse eggplant; pat dry.

2. Heat oil in 12-inch nonstick skillet over medium-high heat. Stir in eggplant and remaining ingredients; reduce heat to medium. Cook uncovered about 20 minutes, stirring frequently until eggplant is tender.

3. Serve warm, or if desired, refrigerate at least 3 hours but no longer than 24 hours and serve cold.

1 Serving: Calories 70 (Calories from Fat 35); Fat 4g (Saturated 1g); Cholesterol 0mg; Sodium 530mg; Carbohydrate 11g (Dietary Fiber 3g); Protein 1g
% Daily Value: Vitamin A 4%; Vitamin C 8%; Calcium 2%; Iron 4%
Diet Exchanges: 2 Vegetable, 1/2 Fat

SPICY MEATBALLS
Polpettine Piccanti

1 pound lean ground beef

1 tablespoon grated imported
   Parmesan cheese

1 teaspoon dried oregano leaves

1/2 teaspoon dried basil leaves

1/2 teaspoon garlic salt

1/2 teaspoon pepper

1 egg

2 tablespoons fresh lemon juice

1/4 cup olive oil

1 clove garlic, finely chopped

1 red jalapeño chili, seeded
   and finely chopped

1 small onion, finely chopped
   (1/4 cup)

4 medium tomatoes, chopped
   (3 cups)*

1 tablespoon dry red wine,
   if desired

*1 can (28 ounces) Italian-style pear-
shaped (plum) tomatoes, well drained
and chopped, can be substituted for the
fresh tomatoes.

PREP: 20 MIN; COOK: 45 MIN
About 36 meatballs

1. Mix beef, cheese, oregano, basil, garlic salt, pepper, egg and lemon juice. Shape mixture into 1-inch balls.

2. Heat oil in 10-inch skillet over medium-high heat. Cook garlic, chili and onion in oil about 5 minutes, stirring frequently, until onion is tender. Add meatballs. Cook, turning meatballs, until meatballs are brown.

3. Stir in tomatoes and wine; reduce heat. Cover and simmer 30 minutes, stirring occasionally.

1 Meatball: Calories 45 (Calories from Fat 25); Fat 3g (Saturated 1g); Cholesterol 15mg; Sodium 25mg; Carbohydrate 1g (Dietary Fiber 0g); Protein 3g
% Daily Value: Vitamin A 0%; Vitamin C 2%; Calcium 0%; Iron 2%
Diet Exchanges: 1/2 High-Fat Meat

Parola di Antonio

These spicy little meatballs can also be used for a family Italian dinner. Serve the meatballs and fresh tomato sauce over plates of hot cooked spaghetti. If your family doesn't care for spicy meatballs, just leave out the chopped chili. Pass the shredded Parmesan cheese to sprinkle over the top.

SAUTÉED OLIVES FROM THE SOUTH
Olive Saltate del Sud

2 tablespoons olive oil

2 tablespoons chopped fresh parsley

1 medium green onion, chopped
   (1 tablespoon)

1 teaspoon crushed red pepper

2 cloves garlic, finely chopped

1 cup imported Kalamata olives
   (8 ounces), drained and pitted

1 cup imported Greek green olives
   (8 ounces), drained and pitted

1 cup imported Gaeta olives
   (8 ounces), drained and pitted

PREP: 20 MIN; COOK: 5 MIN
20 servings (6 olives each)

1. Heat oil in 10-inch skillet over medium heat. Cook parsley, onion, red pepper and garlic in oil about 4 minutes, stirring frequently, until garlic just begins to become golden brown.

2. Stir in olives. Cover and cook about 5 minutes, stirring occasionally, until olives are tender and skins begin to wrinkle.

1 serving: Calories 30 (Calories from Fat 25); Fat 3g (Saturated 0g); Cholesterol 0mg; Sodium 420mg; Carbohydrate 1g (Dietary Fiber 0g); Protein 0g
% Daily Value: Vitamin A 0%; Vitamin C 0%; Calcium 2%; Iron 2%
Diet Exchanges: 1/2 Fat

Parola di Antonio

A favorite appetizer throughout southern Italy, this recipe is usually accompanied by crusty bread slices and crisp, dry white wine. I like the color and texture combination of the three different types of olives. You can use just one type of olive, however, or any combination you like. The key to success for this appetizer is to use imported olives because they are usually sun ripened prior to curing, which gives them a richer flavor and color. Here is an easy way to pit the olives if you aren't able to find pitted ones. Place an olive on a cutting board, and press firmly with the side of a chef's knife; the pit will be easy to remove.

Sautéed Olives from the South

FILLED RICE FRITTERS
Suppli al Telefono

5 cups chicken broth

2 cups uncooked Arborio rice

2 eggs, beaten

1/4 cup freshly grated imported Parmesan cheese

1 tablespoon butter or margarine, softened

48 cubes (1/2 inch) mozzarella cheese

1/4 cup 1/4-inch cubes imported prosciutto or fully cooked ham (about 2 ounces)

1/4 cup 1/4-inch cubes mushrooms

1 cup Italian-style dry bread crumbs

Vegetable oil

PREP: 1 HR; FRY: 20 MIN
About 48 fritters

1. Heat broth and rice to boiling 3-quart saucepan; reduce heat. Cover and simmer about 20 minutes or until liquid is absorbed (do not lift cover or stir). Spread rice on ungreased cookie sheet; cool.

2. Mix rice, eggs, Parmesan cheese and butter. Shape into 1 1/2-inch balls. Press 1 cube mozzarella cheese, 1 cube prosciutto and 1 cube mushroom in center of each ball; reshape to cover cubes completely. Roll balls in bread crumbs to coat.

3. Heat oil (2 inches) in deep fryer or Dutch oven to 375°. Fry 5 or 6 fritters at a time about 2 minutes or until deep golden brown; drain on paper towels.

1 Fritter: Calories 75 (Calories from Fat 25); Fat 3g (Saturated 1g); Cholesterol 10mg; Sodium 160mg; Carbohydrate 9g (Dietary Fiber 0g); Protein 3g
% Daily Value: Vitamin A 0%; Vitamin C 0%; Calcium 2%; Iron 2%
Diet Exchanges: 1/2 Starch, 1 Fat

Parola di Antonio

When you break into these stuffed rice fritters, the melted cheese inside pulls into threads that look like telephone cords. That's how they got the name in Rome of suppli al telefono—*telephone cord.*

Filled Rice Fritters

SHRIMP WITH PROSCIUTTO

Gamberoni al Prosciutto

18 uncooked jumbo shrimp in shells

9 thin slices imported prosciutto
or fully cooked ham (about
5 ounces), cut crosswise in half

2 tablespoons butter or margarine

2 tablespoons olive oil

2 flat anchovy fillets in oil,
finely chopped

1 tablespoon chopped fresh parsley
or 1/4 teaspoon parsley flakes

2 cloves garlic, finely chopped

1/2 cup dry white wine or
chicken broth

1 to 2 tablespoons fresh lemon juice

PREP: 20 MIN; BAKE: 20 MIN
18 appetizers

1. Heat oven to 375°.

2. Peel shrimp, leaving tails intact. Make a shallow cut lengthwise down back of each shrimp; wash out vein. Wrap one half-slice prosciutto around each shrimp.

3. Heat butter and oil in square baking dish, 9 x 9 x 2 inches, in oven until butter is melted. Mix anchovies, parsley and garlic; spread evenly over butter mixture in baking dish. Place shrimp on anchovy mixture.

4. Bake uncovered 10 minutes. Pour wine and lemon juice over shrimp. Bake about 10 minutes longer or until shrimp are pink and firm.

1 Appetizer: Calories 40 (Calories from Fat 25); Fat 3g (Saturated 1g); Cholesterol 25mg; Sodium 115mg; Carbohydrate 0g (Dietary Fiber 0g); Protein 3g
% Daily Value: Vitamin A 2%; Vitamin C 0%; Calcium 0%; Iron 2%
Diet Exchanges: 1/2 Medium-Fat Meat

GOLDEN FRIED SQUID
Calamari Fritti

Vegetable oil

1 pound cleaned fresh squid tail
    cones (calamari) or squid rings
    and tentacles

1/2 cup all-purpose flour

1/2 teaspoon salt

1/4 teaspoon pepper

1 egg, slightly beaten

1 tablespoon fresh lemon juice

1 cup seasoned dry bread crumbs

1 lemon, cut into wedges

PREP: 10 MIN; COOK: 15 MIN
6 servings

1. Heat oil (2 inches) in deep fryer or Dutch oven to 375°.

2. Wash squid; pat dry. Cut squid into 1/4-inch slices. Mix flour, salt and pepper. Mix egg and lemon juice.

3. Coat squid with flour mixture; shake off excess. Dip squid into egg mixture, then coat with bread crumbs.

4. Fry about 1 minute or until golden brown; drain on paper towels. Serve with lemon wedges.

1 Serving: Calories 210 (Calories from Fat 80); Fat 9g (Saturated 2g); Cholesterol 190mg;
Sodium 370mg; Carbohydrate 19g (Dietary Fiber 1g); Protein 14g
% Daily Value: Vitamin A 2%; Vitamin C 2%; Calcium 6%; Iron 10%
Diet Exchanges: 1 Starch, 2 Medium-Fat Meat

STEAMED MUSSELS IN WINE SAUCE
Cozze al Vino

24 fresh large mussels (about
   2 pounds)

2 tablespoons olive oil

1/2 cup chopped fresh parsley

4 cloves garlic, finely chopped

2 roma (plum) tomatoes, chopped

1 cup dry white wine or
   chicken broth

1/2 teaspoon salt

1/2 teaspoon freshly ground pepper

PREP: 20 MIN; COOK: 15 MIN
4 servings

1. Discard any broken-shell or open (dead) mussels that do not close when tapped. Wash remaining mussels, removing any barnacles with a dull paring knife. Remove beards by tugging them away from shells.

2. Heat oil in 12-inch skillet over medium-high heat. Cook parsley and garlic in oil, stirring frequently, until garlic is lightly golden. Add tomatoes, mussels, wine, salt and pepper. Cover and cook about 10 minutes or until shells open.

3. Discard any unopened mussels. Spoon liquid from skillet over each serving.

1 Serving: Calories 140 (Calories from Fat 55); Fat 6g (Saturated 1g); Cholesterol 40mg;
Sodium 540mg; Carbohydrate 5g (Dietary Fiber 0g); Protein 16g
% Daily Value: Vitamin A 12%; Vitamin C 18%; Calcium 6%; Iron 96%
Diet Exchanges: 2 Lean Meat, 1 Vegetable

Parola di Antonio

Nestled in wine sauce, these succulent steamed mussels not only make a great appetizer but also a light dinner for two. I like to serve them with a crisp green salad dressed with a vinaigrette and topped with shavings of imported Parmesan cheese. Add chunks of crusty Italian bread for sopping up all that garlic-flavored wine sauce. Magnifico!

Steamed Mussels in Wine Sauce

Risotto with Asparagus and Chicken, page 53

CHAPTER TWO

RISOTTO, POLENTA, SOUPS AND MORE

CLASSIC RISOTTO

Risotto Classico Tradizionale

1 tablespoon butter or margarine

2 tablespoons olive oil

1 small onion, thinly sliced

1 tablespoon chopped fresh parsley

1 cup uncooked Arborio or regular long-grain rice

1/2 cup dry white wine or chicken broth

3 cups chicken broth, warmed

1/2 cup freshly grated or shredded imported Parmesan cheese

1/4 teaspoon coarsely ground pepper

PREP: 10 MIN; COOK: 25 MIN
4 first-course or 2 main-course servings

1. Heat butter and oil in nonstick 10-inch skillet or 3-quart saucepan over medium-high heat until butter is melted. Cook onion and parsley in oil mixture about 5 minutes, stirring frequently, until onion is tender.

2. Stir in rice. Cook, stirring, until edges of kernels are translucent. Stir in wine. Cook about 3 minutes, stirring constantly, until wine is absorbed.

3. Reduce heat to medium. Stir in 1 cup of the broth. Cook uncovered about 5 minutes, stirring frequently, until broth is absorbed. Stir in additional 1 cup broth. Cook about 5 minutes, stirring frequently, until broth is absorbed. Stir in remaining 1 cup broth. Cook about 8 minutes, stirring frequently, until rice is just tender and mixture is creamy.

4. Stir in cheese and pepper.

1 Serving: Calories 355 (Calories from Fat 135); Fat 15g (Saturated 6g); Cholesterol 15mg; Sodium 1040mg; Carbohydrate 43g (Dietary Fiber 1g); Protein 13g
% Daily Value: Vitamin A 4%; Vitamin C 2%; Calcium 20%; Iron 12%
Diet Exchanges: 3 Starch, 2 1/2 Fat

Parola di Antonio

The most classic risotto, Risotto alla Milanese, *is made with saffron and veal marrow. I find my version of classic risotto gratifying without the necessity of being prepared with marrow or saffron. The ingredients here are basic, and I keep them on hand so I can stir up a batch anytime I am in the mood.*

FOUR-CHEESE RISOTTO
Risotto ai Quattro Formaggi

2 tablespoons olive oil

1 medium onion, chopped (1/2 cup)

1 cup uncooked Arborio or regular long-grain rice

1 tablespoon dry white wine or chicken broth

3 1/2 cups chicken broth, warmed

1/2 cup ricotta cheese

1/4 cup shredded mozzarella cheese (1 ounce)

1/4 cup crumbled Gorgonzola or blue cheese (2 ounces)

1/4 cup grated or shredded imported Parmesan cheese

1 tablespoon chopped fresh parsley

PREP: 10 MIN; COOK: 30 MIN
4 first-course or 2 main-course servings

1. Heat oil in nonstick 10-inch skillet or 3-quart saucepan over medium-high heat. Cook onion in oil about 5 minutes, stirring frequently, until tender.

2. Stir in rice. Cook about 5 minutes, stirring occasionally, until edges of kernels are translucent. Stir in wine. Cook about 3 minutes, stirring constantly, until wine is absorbed.

3. Reduce heat to medium. Stir in 1/2 cup of the broth. Cook uncovered about 5 minutes, stirring frequently, until broth is absorbed. Stir in remaining broth, 1/2 cup at a time, cooking about 3 minutes after each addition and stirring occasionally, until broth is absorbed, rice is just tender and mixture is creamy.

4. Stir in cheeses. Sprinkle with parsley.

1 Serving: Calories 395 (Calories from Fat 145); Fat 16g (Saturated 6g); Cholesterol 25mg; Sodium 1000mg; Carbohydrate 45g (Dietary Fiber 1g); Protein 19g
% Daily Value: Vitamin A 6%; Vitamin C 2%; Calcium 28%; Iron 14%
Diet Exchanges: 3 Starch, 1 1/2 High-Fat Meat

The Art of Making Risotto

The key component of authentic risotto is rice itself, which—just like pasta—should be cooked until *al dente*, meaning "firm to the bite" yet tender in texture. Using warm broth is necessary when cooking risotto so the mixture continues to cook with each addition of broth. The trick is in the slow cooking of the rice, judicious stirring and regulating the amount of liquid added. Of course, parboiled or other types of rice may alter the recipe time and final performance.

RISOTTO WITH ZUCCHINI AND BELL PEPPERS
Risotto con Zucchini e Peperoni Dolci

1 tablespoon butter or margarine

1 tablespoon olive oil

2 medium zucchini (1 pound), cut into julienne strips

2 medium bell peppers, cut into julienne strips

1 medium onion, thinly sliced

2 cups uncooked Arborio or regular long-grain rice

1/3 cup dry white wine or chicken broth

3 1/3 cups chicken broth

1 cup whipping (heavy) cream or half-and-half

1/4 teaspoon coarsely ground pepper

2 tablespoons freshly grated or shredded imported Parmesan cheese

PREP: 15 MIN; COOK: 35 MIN
10 first-course or 5 main-course servings

1. Heat butter and oil in nonstick 12-inch skillet or Dutch oven over medium-high heat until butter is melted. Cook zucchini, bell peppers and onion in oil mixture about 5 minutes, stirring occasionally, until crisp-tender. Remove mixture from skillet; set aside.

2. Add rice to skillet. Cook about 5 minutes, stirring occasionally, until edges of kernels are translucent. Stir in wine. Cook about 3 minutes, stirring constantly, until wine is absorbed. Meanwhile, heat broth and whipping cream just to boiling; keep warm.

3. Reduce heat of rice to medium. Stir 1/2 cup broth mixture into rice. Cook uncovered about 5 minutes, stirring frequently, until liquid is absorbed. Stir in remaining broth mixture, 1/2 cup at a time, cooking about 3 minutes after each addition and stirring occasionally, until liquid is absorbed, rice is just tender and mixture is creamy.

4. Stir in zucchini mixture and pepper. Sprinkle with cheese.

1 Serving: Calories 130 (Calories from Fat 100); Fat 11g (Saturated 6g); Cholesterol 36mg; Sodium 390mg; Carbohydrate 5g (Dietary Fiber 1g); Protein 4g
% Daily Value: Vitamin A 8%; Vitamin C 22%; Calcium 4%; Iron 2%
Diet Exchanges: 1 Vegetable, 2 Fat

Risotto with Zucchini and Bell Peppers

RISOTTO WITH GORGONZOLA CHEESE
Risotto al Gorgonzola

2 tablespoons butter or margarine

1 medium onion, thinly sliced

1 medium carrot, thinly sliced
(1/2 cup)

2 cups uncooked Arborio or
regular long-grain rice

3 1/3 cups milk

1 1/3 cups whipping (heavy) cream

1/3 cup crumbled Gorgonzola or
blue cheese (3 ounces)

1/3 cup Bel Paese cheese or
1 package (3 ounces) cream
cheese, cut into cubes

1/4 teaspoon coarsely ground
pepper

PREP: 10 MIN; COOK: 35 MIN
8 first-course or 4 main-course servings

1. Melt butter in nonstick 12-inch skillet or Dutch oven over medium-high heat. Cook onion and carrot in butter about 7 minutes, stirring occasionally, until carrot is crisp-tender.

2. Stir in rice. Cook about 5 minutes, stirring frequently, until edges of kernels are translucent. Meanwhile, heat milk and whipping cream just until warm.

3. Reduce heat to medium. Stir 1/2 cup milk mixture into rice. Cook uncovered about 5 minutes, stirring occasionally, until liquid is absorbed. Stir in remaining milk mixture, 1/2 cup at time, cooking about 3 minutes after each addition and stirring occasionally, until liquid is absorbed, rice is just tender and mixture is creamy.

4. Stir in cheeses and pepper. Cook about 3 minutes, stirring constantly, until cheeses are melted.

1 Serving: Calories 340 (Calories from Fat 200); Fat 22g (Saturated 14g); Cholesterol 75mg; Sodium 190mg; Carbohydrate 28g (Dietary Fiber 1g); Protein 8g
% Daily Value: Vitamin A 32%; Vitamin C 2%; Calcium 20%; Iron 6%
Diet Exchanges: 1 Starch, 1 Vegetable, 1/2 Skim Milk, 4 Fat

Parola di Antonio

Several types of Gorgonzola are imported from Italy, and I prefer the more pungent Gorgonzola that is labeled naturale. *If you like a more delicate, mild-flavored cheese, select one that is* dolcelatte. *The flavor of hazelnuts pairs nicely with Gorgonzola cheese, so a generous sprinkling of toasted hazelnuts will add a wonderful finishing touch to this risotto.*

RISOTTO WITH ASPARAGUS AND CHICKEN
Risotto Al Pollo E Asparagi

1 pound asparagus or 1 package (10 ounces) frozen asparagus spears, thawed

2 tablespoons olive oil

1/2 cup chopped red onion

1 tablespoon chopped fresh parsley

2 cloves garlic, finely chopped

2 boneless, skinless chicken breast halves (about 3/4 pound), cut into 1-inch pieces

1 cup uncooked Arborio or regular long-grain rice

1/2 cup dry white wine or chicken broth

3 cups chicken broth, warmed

1/2 teaspoon coarsely ground pepper

1/4 cup grated or shredded imported Parmesan cheese

PREP: 10 MIN; COOK: 30 MIN
6 first-course or 3 main-course servings

1. Break off tough bottom ends of asparagus; cut spears into 1-inch pieces. Cover asparagus with cold water; set aside.

2. Heat oil in nonstick 10-inch skillet or 3-quart saucepan over medium-high heat. Cook onion, parsley and garlic in oil about 5 minutes, stirring frequently, until onion is tender.

3. Stir in chicken. Cook about 8 minutes, stirring occasionally, until chicken is lightly browned. Stir in rice and wine. Cook about 3 minutes, stirring constantly, until wine is absorbed.

4. Reduce heat to medium. Stir in 1 cup of the broth. Cook uncovered about 5 minutes, stirring frequently, until broth is absorbed. Stir in additional 1 cup broth. Cook about 5 minutes, stirring occasionally, until broth is absorbed.

5. Drain asparagus. Stir asparagus and remaining 1 cup broth into rice. Cook uncovered about 8 minutes, stirring occasionally, until rice is just tender, asparagus is crisp-tender and mixture is moist.

6. Stir in pepper and cheese.

1 Serving: Calories 260 (Calories from Fat 70); Fat 8g (Saturated 2g); Cholesterol 25mg; Sodium 620mg; Carbohydrate 31g (Dietary Fiber 1g); Protein 17g
% Daily Value: Vitamin A 4%; Vitamin C 8%; Calcium 8%; Iron 12%
Diet Exchanges: 1 Starch, 1 Lean Meat, 3 Vegetable, 1 Fat

THREE-MUSHROOM RISOTTO
Risotto ai Funghi Selvatici

1 package (about 1.25 ounces) dried porcini mushrooms (about 1 cup)

1/4 cup olive oil

2 tablespoons chopped fresh parsley

4 cloves garlic, finely chopped

2 medium green onions, sliced (2 tablespoons)

1 cup uncooked Arborio rice or regular long-grain rice

1 package (about 3.5 ounces) fresh shiitake mushrooms, thinly sliced

1 package (about 5.5 ounces) fresh crimini mushrooms, thinly sliced

3 1/2 cups chicken broth, warmed

1/2 cup freshly grated or shredded imported Parmesan cheese

1 tablespoon balsamic vinegar

STAND: 1 HR; PREP: 10 MIN; COOK: 25 MIN
6 first-course or 3 main-course servings

1. Cover porcini mushrooms with warm water. Let stand at room temperature about 1 hour or until tender; drain.

2. Heat oil in 10-inch nonstick skillet over medium-high heat. Cook parsley, garlic and onions in oil about 5 minutes, stirring frequently, until onions are tender.

3. Stir in rice. Cook, stirring, until edges of kernels are translucent. Stir in porcini, shiitake and crimini mushrooms. Cook uncovered about 3 minutes, stirring frequently, until mushrooms are tender.

4. Reduce heat to medium. Add 1 cup of the broth. Cook uncovered about 5 minutes, stirring frequently, until broth is absorbed. Stir in remaining broth, 1/2 cup at a time, cooking about 3 minutes after each addition and stirring occasionally, until broth is absorbed, rice is just tender and mixture is moist.

5. Stir in cheese and vinegar.

1 Serving: Calories 275 (Calories from Fat 115); Fat 13g (Saturated 3g); Cholesterol 5mg; Sodium 770mg; Carbohydrate 31g (Dietary Fiber 1g); Protein 10g
% Daily Value: Vitamin A 2%; Vitamin C 4%; Calcium 14%; Iron 12%
Diet Exchanges: 1 Starch, 3 Vegetable, 2 1/2 Fat

Parola di Antonio

Seeing the markets laden with mountains of fresh mushrooms of varying shapes and shades of brown is thrilling. I have selected three varieties mushrooms for this risotto; each brings its own character to the dish. The porcini mushroom, one of the greatest of Italy's mushrooms, has a soft texture and deep, bosky flavor that complements the quiet flavor of the shiitake. The crimini mushrooms add more flavor than the usual button mushroom would.

Three-Mushroom Risotto

RISOTTO WITH SHRIMP

Risotto ai Gamberi

2 tablespoons butter or margarine

1 medium onion, thinly sliced

1 pound uncooked medium shrimp in shells, peeled and deveined

1 1/2 cups uncooked Arborio or regular long-grain rice

1/2 cup dry white wine or chicken broth

3 cups chicken broth, warmed

1/4 teaspoon coarsely ground pepper

1/4 cup freshly grated or shredded imported Parmesan cheese

PREP: 15 MIN; COOK: 45 MIN
8 first-course or 4 main-course servings

1. Melt butter in nonstick 12-inch skillet or Dutch oven over medium-high heat. Cook onion in butter about 8 minutes, stirring frequently, until tender.

2. Reduce heat to medium. Stir in shrimp. Cook uncovered about 8 minutes, turning once, until shrimp are pink and firm. Remove shrimp from skillet; keep warm.

3. Add rice to skillet. Cook about 5 minutes, stirring occasionally, until edges of kernels are translucent. Stir in wine. Cook about 3 minutes, stirring constantly, until wine is absorbed.

4. Stir in 1/2 cup of the broth. Cook uncovered about 5 minutes, stirring occasionally, until broth is absorbed. Stir in remaining broth, 1/2 cup at a time, cooking about 3 minutes after each addition and stirring occasionally, until broth is absorbed, rice is just tender and mixture is creamy.

5. Stir in shrimp and pepper. Sprinkle with cheese.

1 Serving: Calories 220 (Calories from Fat 45); Fat 5g (Saturated 3g); Cholesterol 65mg;
Sodium 530mg; Carbohydrate 32g (Dietary Fiber 1g); Protein 12g
% Daily Value: Vitamin A 4%; Vitamin C 0%; Calcium 6%; Iron 12%
Diet Exchanges: 2 Starch, 1 Very Lean Meat, 1 Fat

POLENTA WITH SAUSAGE
Polenta con Salsiccia

Classic Tomato Sauce (page 140) or
  4 1/2 cups tomato pasta sauce
  (from 48-ounce jar)

4 cups water

1 1/2 teaspoons salt

1 1/2 cups yellow cornmeal

1 pound bulk Italian sausage

1 small onion, thinly sliced

1/2 cup freshly or shredded
  imported Parmesan cheese

Baked Polenta with Italian Sausage: Make polenta as directed; spread in ungreased square baking dish, 9 x 9 x 2 inches. Cover and refrigerate about 4 hours or until firm. Heat oven to 375°. Cut polenta into 1-inch cubes. Spread in baking dish. Spoon sausage over polenta; sprinkle with cheese. Bake uncovered about 20 minutes or until hot and bubbly.

PREP: 20 MIN; COOK: 1 HR 50 MIN
8 first-course or 4 main-course servings

1. Make Classic Tomato Sauce.

2. Heat water and salt to boiling in 3-quart saucepan. Gradually add cornmeal, stirring constantly with spoon or wire whisk to prevent clumping. Reduce heat to low. Cook uncovered about 30 minutes, stirring frequently, until mixture is very thick and smooth. Spread in ungreased square baking dish, 9 x 9 x 2 inches. Cover to keep warm.

3. Cook sausage and onion in 10-inch nonstick skillet over medium-high heat, stirring frequently, until sausage is no longer pink; drain. Stir in sauce. Heat to boiling; reduce heat. Simmer uncovered about 20 minutes, stirring occasionally, until slightly thickened.

4. Cut polenta into 8 pieces. Spoon sausage mixture over polenta. Sprinkle with cheese.

1 Serving: Calories 405 (Calories from Fat 170); Fat 18g (Saturated 6g); Cholesterol 35mg; Sodium 1640mg; Carbohydrate 48g (Dietary Fiber 4g); Protein 15g
% Daily Value: Vitamin A 12%; Vitamin C 18%; Calcium 12%; Iron 14%
Diet Exchanges: 3 Starch, 1/2 High-Fat Meat, 1 Vegetable, 2 Fat

Parola di Antonio

Since its introduction to Italy, corn has been a staple in the regions surrounding Venice (Veneto, Lombardy, Piedmont, Emilia and Romagna). Italians have eaten polenta, made from cornmeal, for centuries; it is a favorite substitute for bread or pasta and is served hot or cold. When warm, polenta is served with butter or cheese or with meats such as sausage, small game birds and even shellfish. Cold polenta is just as versatile; it can be baked, fried, grilled or broiled.

POLENTA WITH SAUTÉED SPINACH AND PINE NUTS
Polenta agli Spinaci Saltati e Pinoli

2 tablespoons olive oil

1 medium onion, thinly sliced

6 cups chicken broth or water

2 cups yellow cornmeal

1/4 cup freshly grated imported
   Parmesan cheese

1/2 teaspoon white pepper

2 tablespoons butter or margarine

4 cloves garlic, finely chopped

1 bag (12 ounces) ready-to-eat baby
   spinach or 1 package (12 ounces)
   frozen spinach leaves, thawed
   and squeezed to drain

1/2 cup coarsely chopped fresh
   basil leaves

1/2 teaspoon salt

1/4 teaspoon freshly grated or
   ground nutmeg

1/2 cup pine nuts

PREP: 10 MIN; COOK: 30 MIN
12 first-course or 6 main-course servings

1. Heat oil in 3-quart saucepan over medium heat. Cook onion in oil about 6 minutes, stirring occasionally, until tender. Stir in broth; heat to boiling.

2. Gradually add cornmeal, stirring constantly with spoon or wire whisk to prevent clumping. Reduce heat to medium-low. Cook 5 minutes, stirring constantly, until smooth and bubbly. Cook about 10 minutes longer, stirring occasionally, until thickened. Stir in cheese and white pepper; remove from heat. Pour into large serving platter and spread evenly; cover with plastic wrap or aluminum foil to keep warm.

3. Melt butter in 10-inch skillet over medium heat. Cook garlic in butter about 4 minutes, stirring occasionally, until garlic just starts to turn golden. Add spinach, basil, salt and nutmeg. Cover and cook about 5 minutes or until spinach is wilted. Stir in pine nuts. Spoon over polenta.

1 Serving: Calories 175 (Calories from Fat 70); Fat 8g (Saturated 2g); Cholesterol 0mg;
Sodium 680mg; Carbohydrate 22g (Dietary Fiber 3g); Protein 7g
% Daily Value: Vitamin A 26%; Vitamin C 6%; Calcium 6%; Iron 12%
Diet Exchanges: 3 Starch, 2 Vegetable, 1 Fat

Parola di Antonio

Here is another classic Italian first course—or even a complete meal in one dish. This simple preparation is a departure from the ancient image of a cook standing over a boiling pot of polenta for more than an hour. As long as there is a steady, low boil and frequent stirring, a delicious semisoft concoction is assured. For a vegetarian treat, use water or vegetable broth in place of the chicken broth.

Polenta with Sautéed Spinach and Pine Nuts

ROMAN-STYLE GNOCCHI
Gnocchi di Semola alla Romana

3 cups milk

1 cup yellow cornmeal

2 eggs, well beaten

1 tablespoon butter or margarine, softened

1 teaspoon salt

Dash of pepper

1/4 cup butter or margarine, softened

1 cup freshly grated or shredded imported Parmesan cheese

PREP: 10 MIN; COOK: 5 MIN; STAND: 1 HR; CHILL: 2 HR; BAKE: 30 MIN
8 first-course or 4 main-course servings

1. Grease rectangular pan, 13 x 9 x 2 inches. Heat milk just to boiling (small bubbles form around edges) in 2-quart saucepan; reduce heat medium-low. Gradually add cornmeal, stirring constantly with spoon or wire whisk to prevent clumping. Cook about 5 minutes, stirring constantly, until thickened (spoon will stand upright in mixture); remove from heat.

2. Stir in eggs, 1 tablespoon butter, the salt and pepper; beat until smooth. Spread in pan; cool about 1 hour or until room temperature. Cover and refrigerate 2 to 3 hours or until firm.

3. Heat oven to 350°. Cut cornmeal mixture into 1 1/2-inch squares or circles. (Dip knife in cold water to prevent sticking.) Place squares, overlapping, in ungreased rectangular baking dish, 13 x 9 x 2 inches. Dot with 1/4 cup butter. Sprinkle with cheese. Bake uncovered about 30 minutes or until crisp and golden.

1 Serving: Calories 175 (Calories from Fat 70); Fat 8g (Saturated 2g); Cholesterol omg; Sodium 680mg; Carbohydrate 22g (Dietary Fiber 3g); Protein 7g
% Daily Value: Vitamin A 26%; Vitamin C 6%; Calcium 6%; Iron 12%
Diet Exchanges: 1 Starch, 2 Vegetable, 1 Fat

Parola di Antonio

Every region of Italy has its own form of gnocchi. Some are made with potato, some with pumpkin, while others use bread crumbs or cornmeal. These easy baked cornmeal dumplings—the pride of Rome—are thought to date back to the days of the Caesars. They make a truly exciting side dish and are guaranteed to win applause. If you like, serve them Roman style as a separate course preceding the main course.

POTATO GNOCCHI WITH CLASSIC TOMATO SAUCE
Gnocchi di Patate al Sugo

1 1/2 cups Classic Tomato Sauce
(page 140) or 1 jar (14 ounces)
tomato pasta sauce

1 large baking potato (8 ounces)

1/2 teaspoon white pepper

1/4 teaspoon salt

1 egg, slightly beaten

1 to 1 1/2 cups all-purpose flour

4 quarts water

1 tablespoon salt

1/4 cup fresh grated or shredded
imported Parmesan cheese

Freshly grated or shredded imported Parmesan cheese, if desired

PREP: 25 MIN; COOK: 8 MIN
4 first-course or 2 main-course servings

1. Make Classic Tomato Sauce.

2. Heat potato and enough water to cover to boiling. Cover
   and boil about 30 minutes or until tender; drain and cool
   slightly. Peel potato and mash in medium bowl until
   smooth; cool.

3. Stir white pepper, 1/4 teaspoon salt, the egg and enough of
   the flour into mashed potato to make a stiff dough. Knead
   dough on lightly floured surface about 6 minutes or until
   smooth and springy. Cover and let stand 5 minutes.

4. Cut dough in half. Roll each half into 12 x 1-inch rope
   on lightly floured surface. Cut into 1-inch pieces. Shape
   each piece into oval-shaped balls. Cover and let stand
   10 minutes.

5. Heat 4 quarts water and 1 tablespoon salt to boiling in
   6- to 8-quart saucepan. Add about half of the gnocchi.
   After gnocchi rise to surface, boil uncovered 4 minutes.
   Remove with slotted spoon; drain. Repeat with remaining
   gnocchi.

6. Gently mix gnocchi, sauce and 1/4 cup cheese. Sprinkle
   with additional cheese.

1 Serving: Calories 300 (Calories from Fat 65); Fat 7g (Saturated 2g); Cholesterol 55mg;
Sodium 2000mg; Carbohydrate 52g (Dietary Fiber 3g); Protein 10g
% Daily Value: Vitamin A 10%; Vitamin C 16%; Calcium 12%; Iron 14%
Diet Exchanges: 3 Starch, 1 Vegetable, 1 Fat

POTATO GNOCCHI WITH PARSLEY SAUCE

Gnocchi in Salsa Verde

2 medium baking potatoes
(6 ounces each)

1 teaspoon salt

2 eggs

2 to 2 1/3 cups all-purpose flour

1 1/2 cups chopped fresh parsley

1/2 cup freshly grated imported
Parmesan cheese

1/2 cup extra-virgin olive oil

2 tablespoons capers

1/2 teaspoon pepper

2 cloves garlic, cut up

4 quarts water

1 tablespoon salt

PREP: 10 MIN; COOK: 40 MIN
6 first-course or 3 main-course servings

1. Heat potatoes and enough water to cover to boiling. Cover and boil about 30 minutes or until tender; drain and cool slightly. Peel potatoes and mash in large bowl until smooth; cool.

2. Stir 1 teaspoon salt, the eggs and enough of the flour into mashed potatoes to make a stiff dough. Shape into 1-inch oval balls.

3. Place remaining ingredients except water and 1 tablespoon salt in blender. Cover and blend on medium speed until smooth.

4. Heat 4 quarts water and 1 tablespoon salt to boiling in 6- to 8-quart Dutch oven or stockpot. Add about one-fourth of the gnocchi. After gnocchi rise to surface, boil uncovered 4 minutes. Remove with slotted spoon; drain. Repeat with remaining gnocchi.

5. Gently toss gnocchi and parsley sauce until gnocchi is coated.

1 Serving: Calories 405 (Calories from Fat 205); Fat 23g (Saturated 5g); Cholesterol 75mg;
Sodium 1050mg; Carbohydrate 41g (Dietary Fiber 2g); Protein 11g
% Daily Value: Vitamin A 10%; Vitamin C 20%; Calcium 14%; Iron 18%
Diet Exchanges: 2 Starch, 2 Vegetable, 4 1/2 Fat

Parola di Antonio

Until the sixteenth century, gnocchi were made with flour, eggs and water. However, after the discovery of the potato in America and its introduction to Italy, this nutritious vegetable become an integral part of gnocchi. Potatoes were easier to grow than grain and more tolerant of the cold climate in northern Italy, so they became a staple of the northern diet.

Potato Gnocchi with Parsley Sauce

SPINACH GNOCCHI WITH NUTMEG
Gnocchi di Spinaci alla Noce Moscata

1 medium baking potato (6 ounces)

1/2 teaspoon salt

1 teaspoon freshly grated nutmeg

1 egg

1 package (10 ounces) frozen chopped spinach, thawed and squeezed to drain

1 to 1 1/3 cups all-purpose flour

2 tablespoons butter or margarine

2 medium green onions, thinly sliced (2 tablespoons)

1 cup whipping (heavy) cream

1/4 teaspoon white pepper

4 quarts water

1 tablespoon salt

1/4 cup freshly grated or shredded imported Parmesan cheese

4 quarts water

1 tablespoon salt

PREP: 20 MIN; COOK: 45 MIN
4 first-course or 2 main-course servings

1. Heat potato and enough water to cover to boiling. Cover and boil about 30 minutes or until tender; drain and cool slightly. Peel potato and mash in medium bowl until smooth; cool.

2. Stir 1/2 teaspoon salt, the nutmeg, egg, spinach and enough of the flour into mashed potato to make a stiff dough. Shape into 1-inch oval balls.

3. Melt butter in 10-inch nonstick skillet over medium-high heat. Cook onions in butter about 5 minutes, stirring occasionally, until tender. Stir in whipping cream and white pepper. Heat to boiling; reduce heat. Simmer uncovered about 10 minutes or until thickened; keep warm.

4. Heat 4 quarts water and 1 tablespoon salt to boiling in 6- to 8-quart Dutch oven or stockpot. Add about half of the gnocchi. After gnocchi rise to surface, boil uncovered 4 minutes. Remove with slotted spoon; drain. Repeat with remaining gnocchi.

5. Gently mix gnocchi and cream sauce. Sprinkle with cheese.

1 Serving: Calories 435 (Calories from Fat 260); Fat 28g (Saturated 17g); Cholesterol 140mg; Sodium 1710mg; Carbohydrate 35g (Dietary Fiber 3g); Protein 11g
% Daily Value: Vitamin A 58%; Vitamin C 8%; Calcium 22%; Iron 14%
Diet Exchanges: 2 Starch, 1 Vegetable, 5 1/2 Fat

Parola di Antonio

To make traditional "grooved" gnocchi, roll each ball over the grooves of a wooden butter paddle, or pull the tines of a fork over each to form ridges. The grooved surfaces of gnocchi help collect sauce and cheese, and smooth gnocchi are surprisingly good when tossed with shredded cheese and melted butter.

EGGPLANT PARMIGIANA
Parmigiana di Melanzane

1 1/2 cups Classic Tomato Sauce
   (page 140) or 1 jar (14 ounces)
   tomato pasta sauce

2 medium eggplants
   (1 1/2 pounds each)

1 tablespoon salt

1/3 cup milk

1/2 cup Italian-style dry bread
   crumbs

1/2 cup olive oil

1 tablespoon chopped fresh or
   1 teaspoon dried basil leaves

1/2 cup grated or shredded
   imported Parmesan cheese

2 cups shredded mozzarella cheese
   (8 ounces)

2 tablespoons chopped fresh
   parsley, if desired

Chicken Parmigiana (Pollo alla Parmigiana): Substitute
4 boneless, skinless chicken breast
halves (about 1 1/4 pounds) for the
eggplant. Flatten each chicken
breast half to 1/4-inch thickness
between sheets of plastic wrap or
waxed paper. Continue as directed—
except cook coated chicken in oil
about 10 minutes, turning once,
until chicken is golden brown.

PREP: 55 MIN; COOK: 12 MIN; BAKE: 20 MIN
8 first-course or 4 main-course servings

1. Make Classic Tomato Sauce. While tomato sauce simmers, peel eggplant. Cut crosswise into 1/2-inch slices. Place slices on cutting board; sprinkle with salt. Tilt board slightly; let stand 30 minutes. Rinse eggplant; pat dry.

2. Heat oven to 400°. Dip eggplant slices into milk, then coat with bread crumbs.

3. Heat oil in 12-inch nonstick skillet over medium heat. Cook eggplant slices in oil about 2 minutes on each side or until tender and golden brown.

4. Mix sauce and basil. Spread 1 cup of the sauce in ungreased rectangular baking dish, 13 x 9 x 2 inches. Arrange half of the eggplant slices on sauce. Sprinkle with 1/4 cup of the Parmesan cheese and 1 cup of the mozzarella cheese. Top with 1/2 cup of the sauce and remaining eggplant slices. Top with remaining sauce; sprinkle with remaining cheeses.

5. Cover and bake about 20 minutes or until hot and bubbly. Uncover and bake about 10 minutes longer or until cheese is lightly browned. Sprinkle with parsley.

1 Serving: Calories 340 (Calories from Fat 205); Fat 23g (Saturated 7g); Cholesterol 20mg; Sodium 560mg; Carbohydrate 24g (Dietary Fiber 4g); Protein 13g
% Daily Value: Vitamin A 10%; Vitamin C 6%; Calcium 34%; Iron 8%
Diet Exchanges: 5 Vegetable, 5 Fat

HOMEMADE BEEF AND VEGETABLE SOUP
Minestrone Casereccio Classico

1 pound beef round, tip or chuck
   steak, about 3/4 inch thick

1 tablespoon olive oil

1 clove garlic, finely chopped

1 medium onion, chopped (1/2 cup)

2 large romaine leaves, torn into
   bite-size pieces

2 large red cabbage leaves, coarsely
   chopped

2 medium stalks celery, chopped
   (1 cup)

1 medium potato, chopped (1 cup)

1 medium tomato, chopped
   (3/4 cup)

1 medium carrot, chopped
   (1/2 cup)

1 bay leaf

4 quarts water

1/2 cup dried split peas

1 tablespoon salt

1/2 teaspoon pepper

1 cup uncooked rotini pasta
   (3 ounces)

PREP: 20 MIN; COOK: 1 HR 10 MIN
8 servings

1. Remove bone and excess fat from beef; set bone aside. Cut beef into 1-inch pieces.

2. Heat oil in 6-quart Dutch oven over medium-high heat. Cook beef, garlic and onion in oil about 15 minutes, stirring occasionally, until beef is brown.

3. Stir in bone and remaining ingredients except pasta. Heat to boiling; reduce heat. Cover and simmer about 45 minutes or until beef is tender.

4. Stir in pasta. Cover and simmer about 10 minutes or until pasta is tender. Remove bone and bay leaf before serving.

1 Serving: Calories 185 (Calories from Fat 35); Fat 4g (Saturated 1g); Cholesterol 25mg; Sodium 920mg; Carbohydrate 25g (Dietary Fiber 4g); Protein 16g
% Daily Value: Vitamin A 14%; Vitamin C 8%; Calcium 2%; Iron 12%
Diet Exchanges: 1 Starch, 1 Lean Meat, 2 Vegetable

Parola di Antonio

This vegetable-packed soup recalls the simplicity of old-fashioned country meals. All the ingredients in this soup, starting with the ever-ready bag of potatoes, were readily available in farm kitchens. And just outside the kitchen door, romaine, cabbage, carrots and tomatoes could be picked.

Homemade Beef and Vegetable Soup; White Bread, page 168

CHICKEN-SPAGHETTI SOUP
Minestra di Pasta e Pollo

2 tablespoons olive oil

2 cloves garlic, finely chopped

2 medium green onions, chopped
(2 tablespoons)

1 medium carrot, chopped
(1/2 cup)

1 pound boneless, skinless chicken
breast halves, cut into 1-inch
pieces

3 cans (14 1/2 ounces each)
chicken broth (5 1/2 cups)

1 cup 2-inch pieces uncooked
spaghetti

1/4 cup chopped fresh parsley or
1 teaspoon parsley flakes

1/2 teaspoon ground nutmeg

1/4 teaspoon pepper

1 bay leaf

PREP: 15 MIN; COOK: 20 MIN
4 servings

1. Heat oil in 3-quart saucepan over medium heat. Cook garlic, onions and carrot in oil about 4 minutes, stirring occasionally, until onion is tender.

2. Stir in chicken. Cook about 5 minutes, stirring occasionally, until chicken is lightly browned.

3. Stir in remaining ingredients. Heat to boiling; reduce heat. Cover and simmer about 15 minutes, stirring occasionally, until carrot and spaghetti are tender. Remove bay leaf.

1 Serving: Calories 355 (Calories from Fat 15); Fat 13g (Saturated 3g); Cholesterol 75mg; Sodium 1500mg; Carbohydrate 24g (Dietary Fiber 2g); Protein 37g
% Daily Value: Vitamin A 24%; Vitamin C 6%; Calcium 4%; Iron 16%
Diet Exchanges: 1 Starch, 4 Lean Meat, 2 Vegetable

Italian Soups

There are three types of soups in Italian cooking. Although they all begin with a meat, seafood or vegetable broth, their final flavors, appearances and textures are quite different.

Zuppe are the heartiest soups, in which vegetables and meat form a dense, chunky mixture. An excellent example of *zuppa* is Homemade Beef and Vegetable Soup on page 66. It is almost a complete meal in itself.

Minestre start with a light broth to which pasta, a vegetable or sometimes seafood is added to give it depth and a subtle flavor. This lighter soup, such as Egg Drop Soup Florentine on page 82, is an ideal first course or a prelude to a heartier *secondo*, or entrée.

Crème are smooth, creamy soups made with milk or a combination of milk and cream for a richer soup. Cream of Spinach Soup on page 86 is a deliciously creamy soup without being excessively rich. *Crème* soups are popular in northern Italy and can be very thick.

GARDEN-FRESH VEGETABLE SOUP
Minestrone Vegetale

2 tablespoons olive oil

2 cloves garlic, finely chopped

1 medium onion, coarsely chopped
(1/2 cup)

1 1/2 cups fresh lima beans or
1 package (10 ounces) frozen
lima beans, rinsed to separate

2 medium carrots, sliced (1 cup)

1 medium potato, peeled and cubed
(1 cup)

1 small tomato, diced (1/2 cup)

1/2 cup chopped red or green
cabbage

1 tablespoon chopped fresh parsley
or 1 teaspoon parsley flakes

1 tablespoon chopped fresh or
1 teaspoon dried basil leaves

2 teaspoons chopped fresh or
1/4 teaspoon dried dill weed

1 bay leaf

3 cans (14 1/2 ounces each)
vegetable broth (5 1/2 cups)

1/2 cup uncooked farfalle pasta or
medium pasta shells

PREP: 20 MIN; COOK: 35 MIN
6 servings

1. Heat oil in 3-quart saucepan over medium heat. Cook garlic and onion in oil about 5 minutes, stirring frequently, until onion is tender.

2. Stir lima beans and remaining ingredients except pasta into onion mixture. Heat to boiling; reduce heat. Cover and simmer 15 minutes.

3. Stir in pasta. Cover and simmer 10 to 15 minutes or until pasta is tender. Remove bay leaf.

1 Serving: Calories 165 (Calories from Fat 45); Fat 5g (Saturated 1g); Cholesterol 0mg; Sodium 940mg; Carbohydrate 29g (Dietary Fiber 5g); Protein 6g
% Daily Value: Vitamin A 48%; Vitamin C 16%; Calcium 4%; Iron 8%
Diet Exchanges: 1 1/2 Starch, 1 Vegetable, 1/2 Fat

Parola di Antonio

You can tell the part of Italy you are in by the vegetable soup that is served. The soups of the south rely on tomato, garlic and olive oil and may have pasta. Central Italians make their soups heartier by adding beans. The north uses rice for added fortification, and the Riviera takes advantage of the plentiful fresh herbs. My vegetable soup favors the south with a variety of vegetables plus the addition of pasta. Buon appetito!

ROASTED GARLIC AND ONION SOUP
Zuppa All'Aglio E Cipolla

2 medium bulbs Roasted Garlic
(page 32)

1 tablespoon olive oil

1/2 cup chopped imported prosciutto or fully cooked smoked ham
(about 4 ounces)

1/4 cup chopped fresh parsley

1/4 cup chopped fresh basil leaves

2 medium onions, coarsely chopped
(1 1/2 cups)

1 large baking potato, peeled and
shredded

2 cans (14 1/2 ounces) chicken
broth (3 1/2 cups)

1/4 teaspoon white pepper

1/4 cup freshly grated imported
Parmesan cheese

PREP: 10 MIN; COOK: 20 MIN
6 servings

1. Make Roasted Garlic. Remove 12 garlic cloves from the bulbs; mash with fork to make a paste.

2. Heat oil in 3-quart saucepan over medium-high heat. Cook prosciutto, parsley, basil and onions in oil about 5 minutes, stirring occasionally, until onions are tender.

3. Stir in potato and broth. Heat to boiling; reduce heat. Simmer uncovered 10 minutes.

4. Stir in roasted garlic paste, white pepper and cheese. Simmer uncovered about 10 minutes, stirring occasionally, until thickened.

1 Serving: Calories 150 (Calories from Fat 70); Fat 8g (Saturated 2g); Cholesterol 10mg;
Sodium 860mg; Carbohydrate 12g (Dietary Fiber 1g); Protein 9g
% Daily Value: Vitamin A 2%; Vitamin C 8%; Calcium 8%; Iron 6%
Diet Exchanges: 1/2 Lean Meat, 2 Vegetable, 1 Fat

Parola di Antonio

Heartwarming and surprisingly smooth textured, this old-time comfort food will help you make it through the coldest of winters. To make it a little more nourishing, I like to tear a piece of my hearty homemade bread into bite-size pieces and place some in each bowl before ladling in the hot garlicky soup. This is definitely a classic "antifreeze."

Roasted Garlic and Onion Soup

ONION AND POTATO SOUP
Zuppa di Patate e Cipolle

3 tablespoons butter or margarine

2 large white onions, thinly sliced

2 tablespoons chopped fresh parsley
   or 1/2 teaspoon parsley flakes

2 cloves garlic, finely chopped

2 bay leaves

1/2 cup diced imported prosciutto
   or fully cooked ham (about
   4 ounces)

1 carton (32 ounces) chicken broth
   (4 cups)

3 cups water

1/2 teaspoon pepper

4 large baking potatoes, shredded
   (4 cups)

1/4 cup freshly grated or shredded
   Romano, imported Parmesan or
   Asiago cheese

PREP: 15 MIN; COOK: 45 MIN
6 servings

1. Melt butter in 4-quart Dutch oven over medium-low heat. Stir in onions. Cover and cook about 10 minutes, stirring occasionally, until onions are tender.

2. Stir in parsley, garlic, bay leaves and prosciutto. Cook uncovered over high heat 5 minutes, stirring frequently. Stir in remaining ingredients except cheese.

3. Heat to boiling; reduce heat. Cover and simmer 30 minutes, stirring occasionally. Remove bay leaves. Serve with cheese.

1 Serving: Calories 230 (Calories from Fat 80); Fat 9g (Saturated 5g); Cholesterol 25mg; Sodium 950mg; Carbohydrate 30g (Dietary Fiber 3g); Protein 10g
% Daily Value: Vitamin A 6%; Vitamin C 12%; Calcium 6%; Iron 6%
Diet Exchanges: 2 Starch, 1/2 High-Fat Meat, 2 Fat

CHUNKY TOMATO SOUP
Pappa al Pomodoro

2 tablespoons olive oil

2 cloves garlic, finely chopped

2 medium stalks celery, coarsely chopped (1 cup)

2 medium carrots, coarsely chopped (1 cup)

2 cans (28 ounces each) Italian-style pear-shaped (plum) tomatoes, undrained

4 cups water

2 cans (14 1/2 ounces each) chicken broth (3 1/2 cups)

2 tablespoons chopped fresh or 1 teaspoon dried basil leaves

1/2 teaspoon pepper

2 bay leaves

8 slices hard-crusted Italian or French bread, 1 inch thick, toasted

PREP: 10 MIN; COOK: 1 HR 10 MIN
8 servings

1. Heat oil in 4-quart Dutch oven over medium-high heat. Cook garlic, celery and carrots in oil 5 to 7 minutes, stirring frequently, until carrots are crisp-tender.

2. Stir in tomatoes, breaking up tomatoes coarsely. Stir in remaining ingredients except bread.

3. Heat to boiling; reduce heat. Cover and simmer 1 hour, stirring occasionally. Remove bay leaves.

4. Place 1 slice toast in each of 8 bowls. Ladle soup over toast.

1 Serving: Calories 140 (Calories from Fat 45); Fat 5g (Saturated 1g); Cholesterol 0mg; Sodium 880mg; Carbohydrate 21g (Dietary Fiber 3g); Protein 6g
% Daily Value: Vitamin A 36%; Vitamin C 24%; Calcium 8%; Iron 10%
Diet Exchanges: 1 Starch, 1 Vegetable, 1 Fat

SPINACH-POLENTA SOUP
Minestra di Polenta e Spinaci

2 tablespoons olive oil

2 cloves garlic, finely chopped

1 medium onion, finely chopped
  (1/2 cup)

1 bag (16 ounces) frozen cut-leaf or
  chopped spinach

3 cans (14 1/2 ounces each) ready-
  to-serve vegetable broth
  (5 1/2cups)

1 tablespoon freshly grated imported Parmesan cheese

1 tablespoon chopped fresh parsley
  or 1 teaspoon parsley flakes

1/4 teaspoon pepper

1/2 cup yellow cornmeal

PREP: 15 MIN; COOK: 20 MIN
8 servings

1. Heat oil in 3-quart saucepan over medium heat. Cook garlic and onion in oil about 5 minutes, stirring occasionally, until onion is tender.

2. Stir in frozen spinach and broth. Heat to boiling; reduce heat. Stir in remaining ingredients except cornmeal. Gradually stir in cornmeal.

3. Cover and simmer about 15 minutes, stirring frequently, until soup is slightly thickened.

1 Serving: Calories 90 (Calories from Fat 35); Fat 4g (Saturated 1g); Cholesterol 0mg; Sodium 730mg; Carbohydrate 12g (Dietary Fiber 2g); Protein 3g
% Daily Value: Vitamin A 40%; Vitamin C 6%; Calcium 8%; Iron 6%
Diet Exchanges: 2 Vegetable, 1 Fat

Parola di Antonio

When adding the cornmeal, stir the soup constantly so the cornmeal won't clump together and make the soup grainy rather than thick and creamy. The cornmeal helps to thicken this hearty soup to just the right consistency.

Spinach-Polenta Soup; Italian Flatbread, page 169

LETTUCE SOUP
Zuppa di Lattuga

2 tablespoons butter or margarine

1 medium onion, finely chopped
  (1/2 cup)

1 tablespoon chopped fresh parsley

6 large iceberg lettuce leaves,
  torn into bite-size pieces

6 large Boston or Bibb lettuce
  leaves, torn into bite-size pieces

6 large romaine leaves, torn into
  bite-size pieces

1 can (49 1/2 ounces) chicken broth
  (6 cups)

1 egg yolk, slightly beaten

Juice of 1 lemon
  (2 to 3 tablespoons)

1 cup uncooked small pasta shells
  (4 ounces)

1/4 cup freshly grated or shredded
  imported Parmesan cheese

PREP: 15 MIN; COOK: 30 MIN
4 servings

1. Melt butter in 3-quart saucepan over medium-high heat. Cook onion and parsley in butter about 3 minutes, stirring occasionally, until onion is tender.

2. Stir in lettuces and romaine; cover and cook until wilted.

3. Stir in broth, egg yolk and lemon juice; heat to boiling. Stir in pasta; reduce heat to medium. Cover and cook about 20 minutes or until pasta is tender. Serve with cheese.

1 Serving: Calories 285 (Calories from Fat 110); Fat 12g (Saturated 6g); Cholesterol 75mg; Sodium 1730mg; Carbohydrate 31g (Dietary Fiber 3g); Protein 16g
% Daily Value: Vitamin A 16%; Vitamin C 12%; Calcium 14%; Iron 16%
Diet Exchanges: 1 Starch, 1 Medium-Fat Meat, 3 Vegetable, 1 Fat

Parola di Antonio

Lettuce isn't just for salads! You'll find the addition of three different lettuces—iceberg, Boston and romaine—adds a different twist to this soup. This is an excellent quick soup for busy days. In roughly half an hour, you will have the satisfaction of homemade soup, without the long cooking time.

TORTELLINI SOUP
Tortellini in Brodo

3 tablespoons butter or margarine

2 cloves garlic, finely chopped

2 medium stalks celery, chopped
(1 cup)

1 medium carrot, chopped
(1/2 cup)

1 small onion, chopped (1/4 cup)

2 cartons (32 ounces each) chicken
broth (8 cups)

4 cups water

2 packages (9 ounces each) dried
cheese-filled tortellini

2 tablespoons chopped fresh parsley

1/2 teaspoon pepper

1 teaspoon freshly grated nutmeg

Freshly grated imported Parmesan
cheese, if desired

PREP: 10 MIN; COOK: 45 MIN
8 servings

1. Melt butter in 6-quart Dutch oven over medium-low heat. Stir in garlic, celery, carrot and onion. Cover and cook about 10 minutes, stirring occasionally, until onion is tender.

2. Stir in broth and water; heat to boiling. Stir in tortellini; reduce heat. Cover and simmer about 20 minutes, stirring occasionally, until tortellini is tender.

3. Stir in parsley, pepper and nutmeg. Cover and simmer 10 minutes. Serve with cheese.

1 Serving: Calories 175 (Calories from Fat 80); Fat 9g (Saturated 5g); Cholesterol 65mg;
Sodium 1110mg; Carbohydrate 15g (Dietary Fiber 1g); Protein 10g
% Daily Value: Vitamin A 32%; Vitamin C 2%; Calcium 6%; Iron 8%
Diet Exchanges: 1 Starch, 1 Lean Meat, 1 Fat

BASIL-RICE SOUP
Minestra di Riso e Basilico

2 tablespoons olive oil

2 cloves garlic, finely chopped

2 medium stalks celery, chopped
  (1 cup)

1 medium onion, chopped (1/2 cup)

1 medium carrot, chopped
  (1/2 cup)

1/4 cup chopped fresh basil leaves

3/4 cup uncooked regular
  long-grain rice

2 medium tomatoes, chopped
  (1 1/2 cups)

1 carton (32 ounces) chicken broth
  (4 cups)

1 cup water

1 teaspoon salt

1/4 teaspoon pepper

1/4 cup freshly grated or shredded
  Romano or imported Parmesan
  cheese

PREP: 10 MIN; COOK: 40 MIN
6 servings

1. Heat oil in 4-quart Dutch oven over medium-low heat. Stir in garlic, celery, onion, carrot and basil. Cover and cook 10 minutes, stirring occasionally.

2. Stir in rice and tomatoes. Cook uncovered over medium heat 5 minutes, stirring occasionally. Stir in remaining ingredients except cheese.

3. Heat to boiling; reduce heat. Cover and simmer about 20 minutes or until rice is tender. Serve with cheese.

1 Serving: Calories 185 (Calories from Fat 65); Fat 7g (Saturated 2g); Cholesterol 5mg; Sodium 1170mg; Carbohydrate 26g (Dietary Fiber 2g); Protein 7g
% Daily Value: Vitamin A 18%; Vitamin C 8%; Calcium 8%; Iron 8%
Diet Exchanges: 1 Starch, 2 Vegetable, 1 Fat

Basil-Rice Soup

CLAM CHOWDER
Zuppa d'Arselle

1/4 cup olive oil

3 tablespoons chopped fresh parsley

4 cloves garlic, finely chopped

2 medium green onions, finely
chopped (2 tablespoons)

1 small red Fresno or jalapeño chili,
seeded and finely chopped

1 pound shucked fresh clams,
drained and chopped

1 can (28 ounces) Italian-style
pear-shaped (plum) tomatoes,
drained

8 cups water

1/2 cup dry white wine or
chicken broth

1 1/2 teaspoons salt

1/2 teaspoon pepper

1 cup uncooked ditalini pasta

PREP: 20 MIN; COOK: 55 MIN
6 servings

1. Heat oil in 4-quart Dutch oven over medium-high heat. Cook parsley, garlic, onions and chili in oil 3 minutes, stirring frequently. Stir in clams. Cover and cook 5 minutes.

2. Place tomatoes in food processor or blender. Cover and process until finely chopped. Stir tomatoes, water, wine, salt and pepper into clam mixture.

3. Heat to boiling; reduce heat. Cover and simmer 40 minutes, stirring occasionally. Stir in pasta. Cover and cook about 10 minutes or until pasta is tender.

1 Serving: Calories 220 (Calories from Fat 90); Fat 10g (Saturated 1g); Cholesterol 5mg; Sodium 800mg; Carbohydrate 28g (Dietary Fiber 3g); Protein 7g
% Daily Value: Vitamin A 16%; Vitamin C 32%; Calcium 6%; Iron 20%
Diet Exchanges: 1 Starch, 2 Vegetable, 2 Fat

Clam Chowder

EGG DROP SOUP FLORENTINE
Stracciatella

1 can (49 1/2 ounces) chicken broth (6 cups)

1/2 cup uncooked rosamarina (orzo) pasta

2 eggs

1 teaspoon freshly grated nutmeg

1/2 teaspoon white pepper

1/3 cup all-purpose flour

1/2 cup freshly shredded or grated imported Parmesan cheese

1 tablespoon chopped fresh parsley

PREP: 15 MIN; COOK: 20 MIN
6 servings

1. Heat broth to boiling in 4-quart Dutch oven. Stir in pasta; reduce heat to medium. Cook uncovered about 10 minutes or until pasta is tender.

2. Beat eggs, nutmeg and white pepper in small bowl with fork. Gradually stir in flour, beating until mixture is smooth. Slowly pour egg mixture into broth mixture, stirring constantly with wire whisk or fork to form shreds.

3. Cook uncovered 5 minutes, stirring occasionally. Top each serving with cheese and parsley.

1 Serving: Calories 160 (Calories from Fat 55); Fat 6g (Saturated 3g); Cholesterol 75mg; Sodium 1220mg; Carbohydrate 15g (Dietary Fiber 1g); Protein 13g
% Daily Value: Vitamin A 2%; Vitamin C 0%; Calcium 14%; Iron 8%
Diet Exchanges: 1 Starch, 1 1/2 Lean Meat

Parola di Antonio

Egg drop soup isn't found only in Asian cuisine. The Italian version was originally served when people were ill, because it is so easy to digest. It is generally made with semolina flour or some type of small pasta, as in this version, and herbs. In Rome, fresh marjoram is used and lemon juice is combined with the egg-broth mixture.

LENTIL SOUP
Zuppa di Lenticchie

2 tablespoons olive oil

2 cloves garlic, finely chopped

1 medium onion, finely chopped
(1/2 cup)

1 bay leaf

1/2 cup diced imported prosciutto
or fully cooked ham (about
4 ounces)

1/4 cup diced Genoa salami
(about 2 ounces)

1 1/2 cups dried lentils (12 ounces),
sorted and rinsed

1/2 teaspoon pepper

1 can (49 1/2 ounces) chicken broth
(6 cups)

PREP: 5 MIN; COOK: 1 1/4 HR
6 servings

1. Heat oil in 4-quart Dutch oven over medium-high heat.
   Cook garlic, onion and bay leaf in oil about 5 minutes,
   stirring frequently, until onion is tender.

2. Stir in prosciutto and salami. Cook uncovered over
   medium heat 10 minutes, stirring frequently.

3. Stir in remaining ingredients. Heat to boiling; reduce heat.
   Cover and simmer about 1 hour, stirring occasionally,
   until lentils are tender. Remove bay leaf.

1 Serving: Calories 225 (Calories from Fat 90); Fat 10g (Saturated 2g); Cholesterol 15mg;
Sodium 1000mg; Carbohydrate 24g (Dietary Fiber 9g); Protein 19g
% Daily Value: Vitamin A 0%; Vitamin C 2%; Calcium 4%; Iron 24%
Diet Exchanges: 1 Starch, 2 Lean Meat, 2 Vegetable

PASTA AND BEAN SOUP
Pasta e Fasuli

1/2 cup dried lima beans

1/2 cup dried kidney beans

2 tablespoons olive oil

1/2 cup chopped lean bacon

2 cloves garlic, finely chopped

2 medium stalks celery, finely
    chopped (1 cup)

1 medium carrot, finely chopped
    (1/2 cup)

1 medium onion, finely chopped
    (1/2 cup)

1/2 cup dried split peas

1 can (49 1/2 ounces) chicken broth
    (6 cups)

2 cups water

1 teaspoon salt

1/2 teaspoon pepper

2 bay leaves

1 cup uncooked rigatoni pasta

PREP: 20 MIN; STAND: 1 HR; COOK: 2 HR
8 servings

1. Cover lima and kidney beans with cold water in 2-quart saucepan; heat to boiling. Boil 2 minutes; remove from heat. Cover and let stand 1 hour; drain.

2. Heat oil in 6-quart Dutch oven over medium heat. Cook bacon, garlic, celery, carrot and onion in oil 10 minutes, stirring occasionally. Stir in beans mixture and remaining ingredients except pasta.

3. Heat to boiling; reduce heat. Cover and simmer 1 1/2 hours, stirring occasionally, until beans are tender.

4. Heat to boiling. Stir in pasta; reduce heat. Cover and cook about 12 minutes or until pasta is tender. Remove bay leaves.

1 Serving: Calories 175 (Calories from Fat 25); Fat 3g (Saturated 1g); Cholesterol 0mg;
Sodium 1120mg; Carbohydrate 31g (Dietary Fiber 7g); Protein 13g
% Daily Value: Vitamin A 12%; Vitamin C 2%; Calcium 4%; Iron 14%
Diet Exchanges: 2 Starch, 1 Very Lean Meat

Pasta and Bean Soup

CREAM OF SPINACH SOUP
Minestra di Spinaci

2 tablespoons olive oil

2 tablespoons butter or margarine

2 tablespoons chopped fresh parsley

4 cloves garlic, finely chopped

1 leek, thinly sliced

1 pound washed fresh spinach,
   torn into bite-size pieces

2 cups whipping (heavy) cream

2 cups milk

2 cups chicken broth

1 tablespoon fresh lemon juice

1 teaspoon freshly grated nutmeg

1 teaspoon salt

1/2 teaspoon white pepper

PREP: 15 MIN; COOK: 45 MIN
6 servings

1. Heat oil and butter in 4-quart Dutch oven over medium-high heat. Cook parsley, garlic and leek in oil mixture about 5 minutes, stirring occasionally, until leek is tender.

2. Reduce heat to low; stir in spinach. Cook uncovered about 10 minutes, stirring frequently, until spinach is wilted. Stir in remaining ingredients.

3. Heat to boiling; reduce heat. Cover and simmer 30 minutes, stirring occasionally. Serve with additional freshly grated nutmeg if desired.

1 Serving: Calories 385 (Calories from Fat 315); Fat 35g (Saturated 20g); Cholesterol 105mg; Sodium 880mg; Carbohydrate 10g (Dietary Fiber 2g); Protein 8g
% Daily Value: Vitamin A 72%; Vitamin C 18%; Calcium 22%; Iron 10%
Diet Exchanges: 1/2 High-Fat Meat, 1 Vegetable, 1/2 Skim Milk, 6 Fat

SUMMER COLD SOUP
Zuppa Estiva Fredda

2 tablespoons olive oil

4 roma (plum) tomatoes, chopped*

2 cloves garlic, finely chopped

4 slices imported prosciutto or
   fully cooked smoked ham
   (about 2 ounces), cut into
   1/4-inch strips

2 medium cucumbers, peeled, cut
   lengthwise into fourths and sliced

2 cups whipping (heavy) cream

1 cup chicken broth

1/2 teaspoon salt

1 teaspoon pepper

1/2 cup sliced pitted imported
   Greek green olives

1 medium green onion, thinly sliced
   (1 tablespoon)

4 ice cubes

*4 Italian-style pear-shaped (plum)
tomatoes (from 28-ounce can) can be
substituted for the fresh tomatoes.

PREP: 15 MIN; COOK: 45 MIN; CHILL: 4 HR
4 servings

1. Heat oil in 3-quart saucepan over medium-high heat. Cook tomatoes and garlic in oil, stirring frequently, 5 minutes. Stir in prosciutto and cucumbers. Stir in whipping cream, broth, salt and pepper.

2. Heat to boiling; reduce heat. Cover and simmer 40 minutes, stirring occasionally. Cover and refrigerate until chilled, about 4 hours but no longer than 48 hours.

3. Ladle soup into 4 chilled individual bowls. Top each with olives, onion and ice cube.

1 Serving: Calories 490 (Calories from Fat 425); Fat 47g (Saturated 25g); Cholesterol 140mg; Sodium 1110mg; Carbohydrate 10g (Dietary Fiber 2g); Protein 8g
% Daily Value: Vitamin A 34%; Vitamin C 14%; Calcium 12%; Iron 6%
Diet Exchanges: 1 Vegetable, 1/2 Skim Milk, 9 Fat

Parola di Antonio

Cold soups are traditionally associated with French cuisine, but they are also found in northern Italy. They are as refreshing as they are convenient and can be prepared ahead and served later—a boon on a busy day. For a special touch, add a fresh herb, such as dill weed, Italian parsley or oregano, to each ice cube before freezing.

Lover's-Style Pasta, page 104; Herbed Breadsticks, page 173

CHAPTER THREE

Pasta E Salse

AROMATIC PASTA AND SAUCES

Pasta—Its Many Shapes and Forms

ere are some shapes and forms of pasta, freshly made or dried, that are popular in Italian cooking.

Delicate pasta such as angel hair and vermicelli should be used with delicate sauces such as olive oil and light cream sauces. Hearty, robust tomato and meat sauces are best with a hearty pasta, such as rigatoni or mostaccioli, or a pasta with grooves that attract and hold the sauces, such as penne rigate.

BUCATINI (boo-kah-TEE-nee) A long, hollow tube of pasta, thicker than spaghetti, that originated in Naples. *Bucatoni* are even thicker.

CANNELLONI (kan-eh-LOH-nee) A large, tubular pasta usually stuffed and baked with a sauce.

CAPELLI D'ANGELO (ka-PELL-ee DAN-zheh-low) Italian for "angel hair." It is long, very thin strands of pasta.

CAPELLINI (ka-pel-LEE-nee) Thin-cut spaghetti that is slightly thicker than **capelli d'angelo**.

CAPPELLETTI (kah-peh-LEH-tee) "Little hats." Small stuffed pasta that resemble three-cornered hats. They are served in broth and are a specialty of Reggio.

CAVATAPPI (kah-vah-TAH-pee) A corkscrew-shaped pasta of southern Italy.

CONCHIGLIE (kohn-CHEE-l'yeh) Shell-shaped pasta that are available in several sizes and usually have ridges.

DITALINI (dee-tah-LEE-nee) "Little toes." A pasta cut into short segments that is typically cooked in soups.

FARFALLE (fahr-FAH-leh) Pasta shaped like butterflies or bow ties. *Farfalline* are the smallest butterflies, and *farfallone* are the largest.

FETTUCCINE (feht-tuh-CHEE-nee) Literally meaning "little strands," fettuccine are long, flat noodles, roughly 3/8 to 1/4 inch wide.

FUSILLI (foo-SEE-lee) A spiral pasta from southern Italy. *Fusilli lunghi* are the long strands.

GEMELLI (jeh-MEH-lee) "Twins." A pasta that resembles two strands of spaghetti twisted together.

LASAGNA (lah-ZAHN-yuh) Wide pasta strips layered with various ingredients and baked. The plural is *lasagne*.

Cannelloni

Rigatoni

Conchiglie

Manicotti

Ziti

Gemelli

Cappelletti

Rotini

Ditalini

Penne

Tortellini

Rosamarina

Mostaccioli

Tortelli

Cavatappi

Ravioli

Orecchiette

Fusilli

Orzo

Farfalle

LINGUINE (lihn-GWEE-nee) "Little tongues." A flat, thin noodle roughly 1/8 inch wide.

MANICOTTI (mah-nee-KOH-tee) A large, 4-inch-long, tubular pasta that is stuffed with a variety of fillings and baked with a sauce.

MOSTACCIOLI (mos-tah-chee-OH-lee) "Mustaches." A pasta tube about 2 inches long, cut on the diagonal. Its surface can be either smooth or ridged.

ORECCHIETTE (oh-rayk-kee-EHT-tay) "Little ears." Pasta shape that resembles a small human ear.

ORZO (OHR-zoh) A small rice-shaped pasta that is used in soups or in place of rice in some dishes.

PAPPARDELLE (pah-pahr-DEH-leh) "Gulp down." A long, flat homemade pasta about 1 inch wide and about 6 inches long.

PENNE (PEN-nay) A short-cut pasta about 1 1/4 inches long. Tubular in shape with slanted cuts at both ends, penne can be *lisce* (smooth) or *rigate* (with a grooved finish).

RAVIOLI (rav-ee-OH-lee) Pillow-shaped stuffed pasta popular in several Italian regions.

RIGATONI (rihg-ah-TOH-nee) Short-cut, wide tubular pasta, about 1 inch long, with lengthwise grooves.

ROSAMARINA (rohs-ah-mah-REE-nah) A tiny bead-shaped pasta, ideal for use in soups.

ROTINI (roh-TEE-nee) A short-cut pasta with a corkscrew shape.

SPAGHETTI (spuh-GEHT-ee) "Little strings." Long, thin strands of pasta that are round and solid. *Spaghettini* is very thin spaghetti.

TAGLIATELLE (tah-l'yah-TEH-leh) A flat pasta, about 1/4 inch wide.

TORTELLI (tohr-TEH-lee) "Little torte." A round variety of ravioli.

TORTELLINI (tohr-teh-LEE-nee) Little rings of pasta filled with cheese, originally from the city of Bologna.

VERMICELLI (ver-mih-CHEHL-ee) "Little worms." Very slender pasta strands, thinner than spaghetti.

ZITI (ZEE-tee) "Bridegrooms." A short-cut, thin, tubular pasta popular in southern Italy.

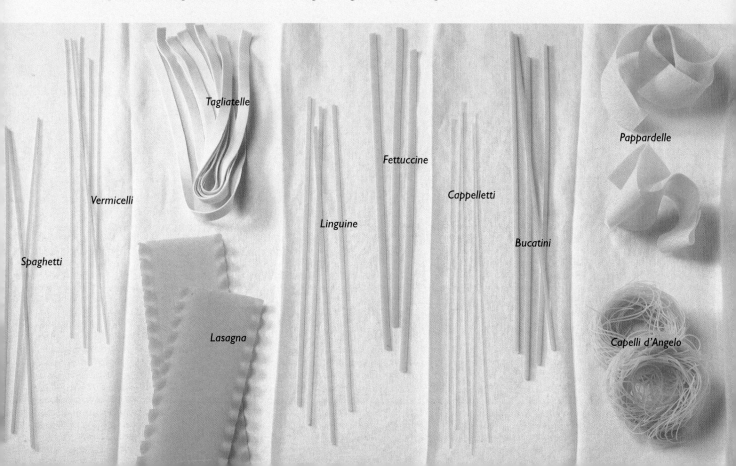

Tagliatelle

Vermicelli

Fettuccine

Cappelletti

Pappardelle

Linguine

Bucatini

Spaghetti

Lasagna

Capelli d'Angelo

HOMEMADE PASTA
Pasta all'Uovo

3 cups all-purpose or semolina flour

4 large eggs

1 teaspoon olive oil

1/4 teaspoon salt

4 quarts water

1 tablespoon salt

PREP: 30 MIN; REST: 45 MIN; COOK: 4 MIN
24 ounces uncooked pasta (8 servings, about 1 cup each)

1. Place flour in a mound on flat surface or in large bowl. Make a well in center of flour; add eggs, oil and 1/4 teaspoon salt. Mix ingredients in center thoroughly with fork, gradually bringing flour to center, until dough forms. (If dough is too sticky, gradually add flour when kneading; if dough is too dry, mix in enough water to make dough easy to handle.) Knead dough on lightly floured surface about 15 minutes or until smooth and springy. Cover with plastic wrap; let rest 15 minutes.

2. Divide dough into 4 equal parts. (Or tightly wrap unrolled dough and refrigerate up to 2 days; let stand uncovered at room temperature 30 minutes before rolling and cutting.) Roll dough as directed for Hand Rolling or Manual Pasta Machine; cut into desired width (see Cutting Pasta below).

3. Arrange pasta in single layer on lightly floured towels; sprinkle lightly with flour. (Or hang pasta on drying rack.) Let rest uncovered at room temperature 30 minutes.* Cook immediately as directed in step 4.

4. Heat water and 1 tablespoon salt to boiling in large kettle or stockpot; add pasta. Boil uncovered 2 to 4 minutes, stirring occasionally, until tender. Begin testing for doneness when pasta rise to surface of water. Drain pasta; do not rinse unless directed in recipe.

Hand Rolling: Roll one part dough on lightly floured surface with rolling pin into 1/8- to 1/16-inch-thick rectangle (keep remaining dough covered). Sprinkle dough lightly with flour. Loosely fold rectangle lengthwise into thirds. With sharp knife, cut crosswise into 1/8-inch strips for linguine,

Half-Recipe Homemade Pasta:
To make 12 ounces of uncooked pasta, use 1 1/2 cups flour, 2 eggs, 1/2 teaspoon olive oil and 1/8 teaspoon salt. Continue as directed.

Homemade Spinach Pasta (Pasta agli Spinaci Casereccio): Omit oil. Use 3 large eggs. Cook 1 package (10 ounces) frozen chopped spinach as directed on package; squeeze or press out excess liquid. Finely chop spinach, or place in food processor or blender and cover and process until smooth. Add spinach with eggs and salt in step 1. Continue as directed.

1/4-inch strips for fettuccine or 1 1/2- to 2-inch strips for wide pasta. Shake out strips. Repeat with remaining dough.

Manual Pasta Machine: Flatten one part dough on lightly floured surface with hands to 1/2-inch thickness (keep remaining dough covered). Feed dough through smooth rollers set at widest setting. Sprinkle with flour if dough becomes sticky. Fold lengthwise into thirds. Repeat feeding dough through rollers and folding into thirds 8 to 10 times or until firm and smooth. Feed dough through progressively narrower settings until dough is 1/8 to 1/16 inch thick. (Dough will lengthen as it becomes thinner; cut crosswise at any time for easier handling.) Feed dough through cutting rollers of desired shape. To cut by hand, sprinkle dough lightly with flour. With sharp knife, cut crosswise into 1/8-inch strips for linguine or 1/4-inch strips for fettuccine. Shake out strips. Repeat with remaining dough.

If not using pasta immediately, toss fresh pasta lightly with flour. Let stand until partially dry but still pliable. Loosely coil pasta into rounds for easier storage. Store in sealed plastic container or plastic bags for up to 3 days in refrigerator or up to 1 month in freezer. Cook as directed in step 4.

1 Serving: Calories 210 (Calories from Fat 35); Fat 4g (Saturated 1g); Cholesterol 105mg; Sodium 330mg; Carbohydrate 36g (Dietary Fiber 1g); Protein 8g
% Daily Value: Vitamin A 2%; Vitamin C 0%; Calcium 2%; Iron 14%
Diet Exchanges: 2 Starch, 1 Fat

Cutting Pasta

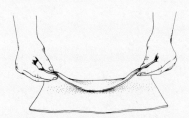

Fold one-third of dough lengthwise slightly over the center.

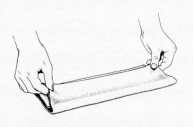

Bring remaining side over folded dough.

Cut crosswise into desired width.

ANGEL HAIR PASTA WITH SHRIMP
Capellini ai Gamberetti

1 package (16 ounces) capellini
(angel hair) pasta

1/4 cup olive oil

2 tablespoons chopped fresh parsley

2 cloves garlic, finely chopped

1 red jalapeño chili, seeded
and finely chopped

1/3 cup dry white wine or chicken
broth

1/2 teaspoon freshly grated nutmeg

3/4 pound uncooked fresh or
frozen (thawed) peeled deveined
small shrimp

PREP: 15 MIN; COOK: 15 MIN
6 main-course or 8 first-course servings

1. Cook and drain pasta as directed on package.

2. While pasta is cooking, heat oil in 12-inch skillet or 4-quart Dutch oven over medium-high heat. Cook parsley, garlic and chili in oil about 3 minutes, stirring frequently, until garlic is soft.

3. Stir in wine, nutmeg and shrimp; reduce heat. Cover and simmer about 5 minutes or until shrimp are pink and firm.

4. Add pasta to mixture in skillet; toss gently until pasta is evenly coated.

1 Serving: Calories 425 (Calories from Fat 100); Fat 11g (Saturated 2g); Cholesterol 80mg;
Sodium 100mg; Carbohydrate 62g (Dietary Fiber 3g); Protein 19g
% Daily Value: Vitamin A 10%; Vitamin C 14%; Calcium 4%; Iron 24%
Diet Exchanges: 4 Starch, 1 Very Lean Meat, 2 Fat

Angel Hair Pasta with Shrimp

ANGEL HAIR PASTA IN GARLIC SAUCE
Capelli d'Angelo

1 package (16 ounces) capellini
  (angel hair) pasta

1/4 cup olive oil

1/4 cup chopped fresh parsley

4 cloves garlic, finely chopped

1/2 cup freshly grated or shredded
  imported Parmesan cheese

Freshly ground pepper

PREP: 5 MIN; COOK: 15 MIN
6 main-course or 8 first-course servings

1. Cook and drain pasta as directed on package.

2. While pasta is cooking, heat oil in 12-inch skillet over medium heat. Cook parsley and garlic in oil about 3 minutes, stirring frequently, until garlic is soft.

3. Add pasta to mixture in skillet; toss gently until pasta is evenly coated. Sprinkle with cheese. Serve with pepper.

1 Serving: Calories 410 (Calories from Fat 115); Fat 13g (Saturated 3g); Cholesterol 5mg;
Sodium 160mg; Carbohydrate 62g (Dietary Fiber 3g); Protein 14g
% Daily Value: Vitamin A 2%; Vitamin C 2%; Calcium 14%; Iron 18%
Diet Exchanges: 4 Starch, 2 Fat

Cooking Pasta

Cook pasta until *al dente*, or "firm to the bite." Here are my simple steps for cooking the perfect pasta:

- Add salt to the water, about 1 tablespoon per gallon, to help keep pasta firm. This is important for fresh pasta, which is tender and fragile.
- Use a gallon of water per pound of pasta so the pasta cooks uniformly.
- The water should always be at a full boil when pasta is added, and it should remain boiling during the entire cooking time.
- When pasta is cooked, it floats to the top of the water, so test the pasta on top for doneness.

SPAGHETTI WITH MUSSEL SAUCE
Spaghetti al Sugo di Cozze

2 pounds mussels

1 package (16 ounces) spaghetti

2 tablespoons olive oil

2 tablespoons chopped fresh parsley

2 cloves garlic, finely chopped

2 cans (28 ounces each) Italian-style pear-shaped (plum) tomatoes, drained and chopped

1 medium red bell pepper, chopped (1 cup)

1 tablespoon freshly grated or shredded imported Parmesan cheese

Freshly ground pepper

PREP: 20 MIN; COOK: 10 MIN
6 main-course or 8 first-course servings

1. Discard any broken-shell or open (dead) mussels that do not close when tapped. Wash remaining mussels, removing any barnacles with a dull paring knife. Remove beards by tugging them away from shells.

2. Cook and drain spaghetti as directed on package.

3. While spaghetti is cooking, heat oil in 10-inch skillet over medium-high heat. Cook parsley and garlic in oil about 3 minutes, stirring frequently, until garlic is soft. Stir in tomatoes and bell pepper. Cook uncovered about 5 minutes, stirring frequently, until bell pepper is tender.

4. Add mussels. Cover and cook about 5 minutes or until mussels open. Discard unopened mussels. Remove mussels from shells; discard shells. Stir mussels into sauce.

5. Add spaghetti to mixture in skillet; toss gently until spaghetti is evenly coated. Sprinkle with cheese. Serve with pepper.

1 Serving: Calories 390 (Calories from Fat 65); Fat 7g (Saturated 1g); Cholesterol 15mg; Sodium 340mg; Carbohydrate 69g (Dietary Fiber 5g); Protein 18g
% Daily Value: Vitamin A 24%; Vitamin C 52%; Calcium 8%; Iron 56%
Diet Exchanges: 4 Starch, 2 Vegetable, 1 Fat

Enjoying Mussels

Mussels are an Italian seaside favorite. Scrub them thoroughly with a brush under running water. Before cooking them, soak them in salted water for an hour, using about 1 tablespoon salt to a gallon of water. To remove the "beard"—the anchor that holds the mussel shell to the rocks—hold the mussel in one hand, pull the beard firmly with the other.

SPAGHETTI OF THE NIGHT
Spaghetti alla Puttanesca

1/3 cup olive oil

2 cloves garlic, cut in half

1 tablespoon capers

4 flat anchovy fillets in oil, drained

2 cans (28 ounces each) Italian-style pear-shaped (plum) tomatoes, drained and chopped

1 red jalapeño chili, seeded and finely chopped

1/2 cup sliced imported Kalamata or large ripe olives

1 package (16 ounces) spaghetti

PREP: 20 MIN; COOK: 28 MIN
6 main-course or 8 first-course servings

1. Heat oil in large kettle or stockpot over medium-high heat. Cook garlic in oil about 5 minutes, stirring frequently, until garlic just begins to turn golden. Remove garlic and discard.

2. Stir capers, anchovy fillets, tomatoes and chili into oil in Dutch oven. Heat to boiling; reduce heat. Simmer uncovered about 20 minutes or until slightly thickened. Stir in olives; keep warm.

3. While tomato mixture is simmering, cook and drain spaghetti as directed on package. Add spaghetti to tomato mixture. Cook over high heat about 3 minutes, tossing gently, until spaghetti is evenly coated.

1 Serving: Calories 435 (Calories from Fat 135); Fat 15g (Saturated 2g); Cholesterol 2mg; Sodium 430mg; Carbohydrate 68g (Dietary Fiber 5g); Protein 12g
% Daily Value: Vitamin A 16%; Vitamin C 28%; Calcium 6%; Iron 24%
Diet Exchanges: 4 Starch, 1 Vegetable, 2 Fat

Parola di Antonio

The ladies of the night in Naples are credited with making this dish popular. They liked it because it was fast and easy to cook, and it used a few inexpensive ingredients. It became popular with people from all walks of life but kept the name "hooker's style" as a tribute to its origin. The captivating scent of this sauce still drifts through the narrow streets of Naples at dinnertime. And it's becoming popular in America as well, appearing on menus across the country under its Italian name Spaghetti alla Puttanesca.

COAL MINER'S SPAGHETTI
Spaghetti alla Carbonara

1 package (16 ounces) spaghetti

1 tablespoon olive oil

1 clove garlic, finely chopped

1 pound sliced lean bacon, cut into
   1-inch pieces

3 eggs

1/4 cup freshly grated or shredded
   imported Parmesan cheese

1/4 cup freshly grated Romano
   cheese

2 tablespoons chopped fresh parsley

1/4 teaspoon pepper

Freshly grated or shredded imported Parmesan cheese, if desired

Freshly ground pepper, if desired

PREP: 10 MIN; COOK: 10 MIN
6 main-course or 8 first-course servings

1. Cook spaghetti as directed on package.

2. While spaghetti is cooking, heat oil in 2-quart saucepan over medium-high heat. Cook garlic and bacon in oil about 5 minutes, stirring frequently, until bacon is crisp; drain.

3. Mix eggs, 1/4 cup Parmesan cheese, the Romano cheese, parsley and 1/4 teaspoon pepper; set aside.

4. Drain spaghetti; immediately return to saucepan over very low heat. Add egg mixture; quickly toss with spaghetti. Add bacon mixture; toss. Sprinkle with Parmesan cheese. Serve with pepper.

1 Serving: Calories 495 (Calories from Fat 170); Fat 19g (Saturated 7g); Cholesterol 130mg; Sodium 490mg; Carbohydrate 61g (Dietary Fiber 3g); Protein 23g
% Daily Value: Vitamin A 6%; Vitamin C 0%; Calcium 12%; Iron 20%
Diet Exchanges: 4 Starch, 1 Medium-Fat Meat, 2 Fat

Parola di Antonio

The Italians have several theories regarding the origin of the expression alla carbonara. *One theory maintains that coal miners invented it, and the dish became a favorite of the laborers working near Rome. Others claim that the dish was originally prepared outdoors over a coal fire. Whatever the true history,* spaghetti alla carbonara *has long been a Roman favorite. It is said that American soldiers popularized it after Rome was liberated at the end of World War II.*

SPAGHETTI IN PARCHMENT
Spaghetti in Cartoccio

2 tablespoons olive oil

2 tablespoons chopped fresh parsley

2 cloves garlic, finely chopped

2 cups chopped roma (plum) tomatoes or tomatoes

1/2 cup dry white wine or chicken broth

1/2 package (16-ounce size) spaghetti

1/2 cup finely shredded or grated imported Parmesan cheese

2 tablespoons chopped fresh basil leaves

1 tablespoon capers

PREP: 15 MIN; COOK: 15 MIN; BAKE: 30 MIN
4 main-course or 6 first-course servings

1. Heat oven to 350°. Heat oil in 10-inch skillet over medium-high heat. Cook parsley and garlic in oil about 3 minutes, stirring occasionally, until garlic is soft. Stir in tomatoes and wine. Heat to boiling; reduce heat. Cover and simmer about 15 minutes, stirring occasionally, until slightly thickened; keep warm.

2. While tomato mixture is simmering, cook spaghetti as directed on package. Drain spaghetti; return to saucepan. Add tomato mixture; toss until spaghetti is evenly coated.

3. Place double-thickness cooking parchment paper or aluminum foil, 24 x 15 inches, on ungreased cookie sheet. Spread spaghetti mixture lengthwise down center of parchment paper. Sprinkle with cheese, basil and capers. Bring 24-inch sides of parchment paper together up over spaghetti; fold down and roll over to seal; twist ends securely.

4. Bake 30 minutes to blend flavors. To serve, carefully cut open center of parchment paper, leaving ends twisted.

1 Serving: Calories 370 (Calories from Fat 110); Fat 12g (Saturated 4g); Cholesterol 10mg; Sodium 300mg; Carbohydrate 51g (Dietary Fiber 3g); Protein 14g
% Daily Value: Vitamin A 8%; Vitamin C 16%; Calcium 20%; Iron 16%
Diet Exchanges: 3 Starch, 1 Vegetable, 2 Fat

Parola di Antonio

Cooking food al cartoccio—*in parchment paper—seals in the essence and moisture of the sauce. It gives the spaghetti in this recipe added flavor and allows it to remain moist and al dente (firm). The dish is also easy to serve: Carefully open the sealed top of the parchment paper and you have your own "serving bowl."*

VERMICELLI WITH FRESH HERBS
Vermicelli alle Erbe Crude

1 package (16 ounces) vermicelli

1/4 cup olive oil

1/4 cup pine nuts

1 tablespoon chopped fresh parsley

1 tablespoon capers, chopped

2 teaspoons chopped fresh rosemary leaves

2 teaspoons chopped fresh sage
leaves

1 teaspoon chopped fresh basil
leaves

1 pint (2 cups) cherry tomatoes,
cut into fourths

Freshly ground pepper

PREP: 10 MIN; COOK: 15 MIN
6 main-course or 8 first-course servings

1. Cook and drain vermicelli as directed on package.

2. While vermicelli is cooking, mix oil, pine nuts, parsley, capers, rosemary, sage and basil in large bowl. Mix in tomatoes.

3. Add vermicelli to tomato mixture; toss gently until vermicelli is evenly coated. Serve with pepper.

1 Serving: Calories 415 (Calories from Fat 125); Fat 14g (Saturated 2g); Cholesterol 0mg; Sodium 50mg; Carbohydrate 65g (Dietary Fiber 4g); Protein 11g
% Daily Value: Vitamin A 4%; Vitamin C 10%; Calcium 2%; Iron 20%
Diet Exchanges: 4 Starch, 1 Vegetable, 2 Fat

Draining Pasta

Draining pasta is an important step in preparing pasta dishes because it instantly stops the cooking. Drain pasta quickly to prevent it from sticking together or cooling down too much. If a recipe calls for it, you can add some Parmesan cheese while mixing the pasta and sauce to help the sauce cling to the pasta. Don't add oil or rinse the pasta in cold water (unless you are making a cold pasta dish) because this will cool the noodles and make them too slippery to receive a sauce. After draining, immediately toss warm pasta gently with the sauce.

Vermicelli with Fresh Herbs

LOVER'S-STYLE PASTA
Bucatini all'Amatriciana

2 tablespoons olive oil

1 tablespoon chopped fresh parsley

1 teaspoon chopped fresh thyme
    leaves

1 medium onion, thinly sliced

1 red jalapeño chili, seeded and
    finely chopped

1/4 pound sliced bacon, cut into
    1-inch pieces

1 tablespoon balsamic vinegar

4 cups chopped roma (plum)
    tomatoes*

1 package (16 ounces) bucatini pasta

*2 cans (28 ounces each) Italian-style
pear-shaped (plum) tomatoes, drained
and chopped, can be substituted for the
fresh tomatoes.

PREP: 20 MIN; COOK: 35 MIN
6 main-course or 8 first-course servings

1. Heat oil in 4-quart Dutch oven or 12-inch skillet over medium-high heat. Cook parsley, thyme, onion and chili in oil about 3 minutes, stirring frequently, just until onion is soft.

2. Stir in bacon. Cook about 8 minutes, stirring occasionally, until bacon is crisp. Drain off fat and reserve 2 tablespoons; discard remaining fat.

3. Stir vinegar into mixture in Dutch oven; cook until evaporated. Stir in tomatoes and reserved bacon fat. Heat to boiling; reduce heat. Cover and simmer 20 minutes, stirring occasionally.

4. While tomato mixture is simmering, cook and drain pasta as directed on package. Add pasta to tomato mixture in Dutch oven. Cook over high heat about 3 minutes, tossing gently, until pasta is evenly coated.

1 Serving: Calories 380 (Calories from Fat 80); Fat 9g (Saturated 2g); Cholesterol 5mg; Sodium 100mg; Carbohydrate 67g (Dietary Fiber 5g); Protein 13g
% Daily Value: Vitamin A 14%; Vitamin C 32%; Calcium 2%; Iron 20%
Diet Exchanges: 4 Starch, 1 Vegetable, 1 Fat

Parola di Antonio

Commonly called Lover's-Style Pasta, this dish actually originated in the town of Amatrice, near Rome, a heritage that is reflected in its name. Every summer, Amatrice holds a celebration where this luscious dish is cooked and served for free to tourists, residents and other lovers of Bucatini all'Amatriciana.

LINGUINE WITH BASIL-GARLIC SAUCE
Linguine al Pesto

Basil-Garlic Sauce (page 146) or
1 1/2 cups purchased basil pesto

1 package (16 ounces) linguine

PREP: 10 MIN; COOK: 20 MIN
6 main-course or 8 first-course servings

1. Make Basil-Garlic Sauce.

2. Cook linguine as directed on package. Drain linguine; return to saucepan. Add sauce; toss gently until linguine is evenly coated.

1 Serving: Calories 560 (Calories from Fat 260); Fat 29g (Saturated 5g); Cholesterol 5mg; Sodium 560mg; Carbohydrate 64g (Dietary Fiber 4g); Protein 15g
% Daily Value: Vitamin A 6%; Vitamin C 6%; Calcium 14%; Iron 22%
Diet Exchanges: 4 Starch, 5 1/2 Fat

LINGUINE WITH CLASSIC TOMATO SAUCE
Linguine al Sugo

Classic Tomato Sauce* (page 140)

1 package (16 ounces) linguine

2 tablespoons freshly grated or shredded imported Parmesan cheese

1 jar (28 ounces) plus 1 jar (14 ounces) tomato pasta sauce can be substituted for the Classic Tomato Sauce.

PREP: 15 MIN; COOK: 50 MIN
6 main-course or 8 first-course servings

1. Make Classic Tomato Sauce; keep warm.

2. While sauce is simmering, cook linguine as directed on package. Drain linguine; return to saucepan. Add sauce; toss gently until linguine is evenly coated. Sprinkle with cheese.

1 Serving: Calories 360 (Calories from Fat 45); Fat 5g (Saturated 1g); Cholesterol 0mg; Sodium 240mg; Carbohydrate 70g (Dietary Fiber 5g); Protein 13g
% Daily Value: Vitamin A 30%; Vitamin C 34%; Calcium 8%; Iron 22%
Diet Exchanges: 4 Starch, 2 Vegetable

LINGUINE WITH SPICY CHICKEN SAUCE
Linguine con Pollo al Pepe

1/2 package (16-ounce size) linguine or 1/2 recipe Homemade Pasta for linguine (page 92)

2 tablespoons olive oil

2 cloves garlic, finely chopped

2 teaspoons anchovy paste

1 red jalapeño chili, seeded and finely chopped

2 tablespoons chopped sun-dried tomatoes packed in oil

1 tablespoon chopped fresh or 1 teaspoon dried oregano leaves

2 boneless, skinless chicken breasts (about 1/2 pound), cut into 1-inch pieces

1 medium yellow bell pepper, cut into 1 x 1/4-inch strips

1 medium red bell pepper, cut into 1 x 1/4-inch strips

1/2 cup dry red wine or chicken broth

1/2 cup freshly grated or shredded imported Parmesan cheese

PREP: 10 MIN; COOK: 20 MIN
4 main-course or 6 first-course servings

1. Cook and drain linguine as directed on package.

2. While linguine is cooking, heat oil in 12-inch skillet over medium-high heat. Cook garlic, anchovy paste, chili and tomatoes in oil about 5 minutes, stirring frequently, until garlic just begins to turn golden.

3. Stir in oregano, chicken, bell peppers and wine. Cover and cook about 10 minutes, stirring occasionally, until chicken is no longer pink in center.

4. Add linguine and 1/4 cup of the cheese to mixture in skillet; toss until linguine is evenly coated. Sprinkle with remaining 1/4 cup cheese.

1 Serving: Calories 420 (Calories from Fat 125); Fat 14g (Saturated 4g); Cholesterol 35mg; Sodium 490mg; Carbohydrate 52g (Dietary Fiber 3g); Protein 24g
% Daily Value: Vitamin A 30%; Vitamin C 100%; Calcium 20%; Iron 18%
Diet Exchanges: 3 Starch, 2 Lean Meat, 1 Vegetable, 1 Fat

Parola di Antonio

This is a good recipe for using up leftover cooked chicken and is fairly simple to make. People in southern Italy prefer their dishes with "bite," hence the combination of anchovies and chili. Remember, the smaller the chili, the hotter the bite. A red Thai chili will be hotter than a red jalapeño chili, so you decide how hot you want it. The sweetness of the red and yellow bell peppers imparts a nice flavor contrast and color to the dish.

Linguine with Spicy Chicken Sauce

LINGUINE WITH CLAM SAUCE
Linguine alle Vongole

1 pint shucked small clams, drained and liquid reserved

1/4 cup olive oil

3 cloves garlic, finely chopped

1 can (28 ounces) Italian-style pear-shaped (plum) tomatoes, drained and chopped

1 red jalapeño chili, seeded and finely chopped

1 tablespoon chopped fresh parsley

1/2 teaspoon salt

1 package (16 ounces) linguine

Chopped fresh parsley, if desired

PREP: 10 MIN; COOK: 40 MIN
6 main-course or 8 first-course servings

1. Chop clams; set aside. Heat oil in 10-inch skillet over medium-high heat. Cook garlic in oil about 3 minutes, stirring frequently, until soft. Stir in tomatoes and chili. Cook uncovered 3 minutes; stir in clam liquid. Heat to boiling; reduce heat. Simmer uncovered about 10 minutes or until slightly thickened.

2. Stir in clams, 1 tablespoon parsley and the salt. Cover and simmer about 30 minutes, stirring occasionally, until clams are tender.

3. While clam sauce is simmering, cook linguine as directed on package. Drain linguine; return to saucepan. Add clam sauce; toss gently until linguine is evenly coated. Sprinkle with parsley.

1 Serving: Calories 430 (Calories from Fat 100); Fat 11g (Saturated 2g); Cholesterol 15mg; Sodium 420mg; Carbohydrate 69g (Dietary Fiber 4g); Protein 18g
% Daily Value: Vitamin A 20%; Vitamin C 34%; Calcium 8%; Iron 60%
Diet Exchanges: 4 Starch, 2 Vegetable, 1 1/2 Fat

STRAW AND HAY PASTA
Paglia e Fieno

1 tablespoon butter or margarine

1 1/2 cups sliced mushrooms
(4 ounces)

4 ounces imported prosciutto or
fully cooked ham, cut into 1 x 1/4
inch strips (about 1/2 cup)

2 tablespoons chopped fresh parsley

2 tablespoons chopped onion

1/4 cup brandy or chicken broth

1 cup whipping (heavy) cream

1/4 teaspoon salt

1/4 teaspoon pepper

1/2 package (16-ounce size)
fettuccine

1/2 package (16-ounce size) spinach
fettuccine

1/2 cup freshly grated or shredded
imported Parmesan cheese

Freshly ground pepper

PREP: 15 MIN; COOK: 25 MIN
6 main-course or 8 first-course servings

1. Melt butter in 10-inch skillet over medium-high heat. Cook mushrooms, ham, parsley and onion in butter about 5 minutes, stirring occasionally, until mushrooms are tender. Stir in brandy. Cook uncovered until liquid has evaporated.

2. Stir in whipping cream, salt and pepper. Heat to boiling; reduce heat. Simmer uncovered about 15 minutes, stirring frequently, until thickened.

3. While sauce is simmering, cook plain and spinach fettuccine together as directed on package. Drain fettuccine; return to saucepan. Add mushroom sauce; toss gently until fettuccine is evenly coated. Sprinkle with cheese. Serve with pepper.

1 Serving: Calories 475 (Calories from Fat 190); Fat 21g (Saturated 11g); Cholesterol 130mg; Sodium 460mg; Carbohydrate 54g (Dietary Fiber 3g); Protein 17g
% Daily Value: Vitamin A 12%; Vitamin C 2%; Calcium 16%; Iron 20%
Diet Exchanges: 3 1/2 Starch, 1 Lean Meat, 3 Fat

Parola di Antonio

The "straw" in this delightful dish is the egg noodles; the "hay," the green spinach noodles. Its birthplace is Bologna in northern Italy, which is known throughout the country as a bastion of glorious foods. It's hard to believe that the dish, topped with a creamy, brandy-laced mushroom sauce, is so simple to prepare.

FOUR-CHEESE FETTUCCINE
Fettuccine ai Quattro Formaggi

1 package (16 ounces) fettuccine or Homemade Pasta for fettuccine (page 92)

2 tablespoons olive oil

2 tablespoons butter or margarine

4 medium green onions, chopped (1/4 cup)

1 tablespoon chopped fresh parsley

1/2 cup ricotta cheese

1/2 cup crumbled feta cheese (2 ounces)

3/4 cup shredded Asiago cheese

3/4 cup freshly grated or shredded imported Parmesan cheese

1/2 teaspoon pepper

Chopped fresh parsley, if desired

PREP: 10 MIN; COOK: 15 MIN
6 main-course or 8 first-course servings

1. Cook and drain fettuccine as directed on package.

2. While fettuccine is cooking, heat oil and butter in 12-inch skillet over medium heat. Cook onions and 1 tablespoon parsley in oil mixture about 4 minutes, stirring occasionally, until onions are tender.

3. Stir in ricotta and feta cheeses; reduce heat to low. Cook about 2 minutes, stirring frequently, until cheeses are melted.

4. Add fettuccine, Asiago and Parmesan cheeses and pepper to mixture in skillet. Cook about 4 minutes, tossing gently, until cheeses are melted and fettuccine is evenly coated. Sprinkle with parsley.

1 Serving: Calories 500 (Calories from Fat 205); Fat 23g (Saturated 10g); Cholesterol 115mg; Sodium 470mg; Carbohydrate 52g (Dietary Fiber 2g); Protein 23g
% Daily Value: Vitamin A 12%; Vitamin C 2%; Calcium 44%; Iron 20%
Diet Exchanges: 3 1/2 Starch, 1 1/2 High-Fat Meat, 2 Fat

Parola di Antonio

Amazingly simple to prepare, this dish has a sophisticated taste because of the four cheeses. It is important not to overcook the cheeses in the skillet, however, because they could stick and burn. You may want to use Italian flat-leaf parsley instead of curly-leaf parsley for this dish. The slightly strong flavor of the flat-leaf complements the cheeses.

Four-Cheese Fettuccine

FETTUCCINE PRIMAVERA
Fettuccine con Primizie

Alfredo Sauce* (below)

1/2 package (16-ounce size)
    fettuccine or linguine

1 tablespoon olive oil

1 cup broccoli flowerets

1 cup cauliflowerets

2 medium carrots, thinly sliced
    (1 cup)

1 cup fresh or frozen (rinsed to
    separate) green peas

1 small onion, chopped (1/4 cup)

1 tablespoon freshly grated
    imported Parmesan cheese

1 tablespoon butter or margarine

1/2 small onion, thinly sliced

2 cups whipping (heavy) cream

1 tablespoon freshly grated
    imported Parmesan cheese

1/2 teaspoon freshly grated nutmeg

1/4 teaspoon salt

1/4 teaspoon pepper

*1 container (10 ounces) refrigerated
Alfredo sauce can be used for the
Alfredo Sauce.*

PREP: 25 MIN; COOK: 30 MIN
4 main-course or 6 first-course servings

1. Make Alfredo Sauce; keep warm. While sauce is simmering, cook and drain fettuccine as directed on package.

2. Meanwhile, heat oil in 12-inch skillet over medium-high heat. Cook broccoli, cauliflowerets, carrots, peas and onion in oil about 8 minutes, stirring frequently, until vegetables are crisp-tender. Stir in sauce.

3. Add fettuccine to mixture in skillet; toss gently until fettuccine is evenly coated. Sprinkle with cheese.

Alfredo Sauce

Melt butter in 3-quart saucepan over medium heat. Cook onion in butter about 5 minutes, stirring occasionally, until tender. Stir in remaining ingredients. Heat to boiling; reduce heat. Simmer uncovered about 20 minutes, stirring frequently, until thickened.

1 Serving: Calories 665 (Calories from Fat 425); Fat 47g (Saturated 26g); Cholesterol 190mg; Sodium 330mg; Carbohydrate 53g (Dietary Fiber 6g); Protein 14g
% Daily Value: Vitamin A 84%; Vitamin C 32%; Calcium 18%; Iron 18%
Diet Exchanges: 3 Starch, 2 Vegetable, 8 Fat

ANTONIO'S FETTUCCINE ALFREDO

Fettuccine Alfredo

2 tablespoons butter or margarine

1 small onion, thinly sliced

4 cups whipping (heavy) cream

2 tablespoons freshly grated
   imported Parmesan cheese

2 teaspoons freshly grated nutmeg

1/2 teaspoon salt

1/2 teaspoon pepper

1 package (16 ounces) fettuccine

2 tablespoons freshly grated or
   shredded imported Parmesan
   cheese

Freshly ground pepper

PREP: 10 MIN; COOK: 35 MIN
6 main-course or 8 first-course servings

1. Melt butter in 10-inch skillet over medium heat. Cook onion in butter about 5 minutes, stirring frequently, until tender. Stir in whipping cream; 2 tablespoons cheese, 1 teaspoon of the nutmeg, the salt and 1/2 teaspoon pepper. Heat to boiling; reduce heat. Simmer uncovered about 30 minutes, stirring frequently, until thickened.

2. While sauce is simmering, cook fettuccine as directed on package. Drain fettuccine; return to saucepan. Add cream sauce; toss gently until fettuccine is evenly coated. Sprinkle with 2 tablespoons cheese, remaining 1 teaspoon nutmeg and the pepper.

1 Serving: Calories 730 (Calories from Fat 515); Fat 57g (Saturated 35g); Cholesterol 255mg; Sodium 370mg; Carbohydrate 55g (Dietary Fiber 3g); Protein 15g
% Daily Value: Vitamin A 42%; Vitamin C 0%; Calcium 20%; Iron 18%
Diet Exchanges: 3 Starch, 1 Skim Milk, 10 Fat

Parola di Antonio

Alfredo's was a popular restaurant in Rome, where the chef's fresh pasta was served at the table and topped with sauces prepared before the diners' eyes. Cream and Parmesan form one of the most versatile sauces for pasta, and this sauce from Alfredo's, served over fettuccine, has become known as Fettuccine Alfredo. My variation of this classic is an adagio *version, where the sauce is cooked at a slower pace, giving the cook time to prepare the noodles as the sauce simmers. The freshly grated nutmeg gives the dish a subtle flavor.*

BRAVO! FETTUCCINE

Fettuccine alla Bravo!

Classic Tomato Sauce* (page 140)

1 tablespoon butter or margarine

1 cup sliced mushrooms (3 ounces)

1/2 cup chopped imported prosciutto or fully cooked ham (about
4 ounces)

2 medium green onions, thinly sliced
(2 tablespoons)

1 cup whipping (heavy) cream

1/2 teaspoon freshly grated nutmeg

1/4 teaspoon pepper

1 package (16 ounces) fettuccine

1/2 cup freshly grated or shredded
imported Parmesan cheese

*1 jar (28 ounces) plus 1 jar
(14 ounces) tomato pasta sauce can
be substituted for the Classic Tomato
Sauce.*

PREP: 20 MIN; COOK: 1 HR 10 MIN
6 main-course or 8 first-course servings

1. Make Classic Tomato Sauce.

2. While sauce is simmering, melt butter in 3-quart saucepan over medium-high heat. Cook mushrooms, prosciutto and onions in butter about 5 minutes, stirring frequently, until onions are tender.

3. Stir in whipping cream, nutmeg and pepper. Heat to boiling; reduce heat. Simmer uncovered about 20 minutes, stirring frequently, until thickened.

4. Stir in sauce. Heat to boiling; reduce heat. Simmer uncovered about 15 minutes, stirring occasionally, until thickened.

5. While sauce is simmering, cook fettuccine as directed on package. Drain fettuccine; return to saucepan. Add sauce; toss gently until fettuccine is evenly coated. Sprinkle with cheese.

1 Serving: Calories 510 (Calories from Fat 205); Fat 23g (Saturated 12g); Cholesterol 125mg; Sodium 570mg; Carbohydrate 62g (Dietary Fiber 5g); Protein 19g
% Daily Value: Vitamin A 42%; Vitamin C 36%; Calcium 22%; Iron 26%
Diet Exchanges: 4 Starch, 1 High-Fat Meat, 2 Fat

Parola di Antonio

I served this signature pasta dish at my restaurant, Bravo!, and it soon became a favorite with many of my guests. It began as an experiment when I combined the assertive flavor of sugo sauce, a favorite of pasta lovers, with the smoothness of cream. The addition of prosciutto and mushrooms makes this pasta a very satisfying meal.

Bravo! Fettuccine; "Slipper" Bread, page 164

TAGLIATELLE PASTA WITH ASPARAGUS AND GORGONZOLA SAUCE

Tagliatelle Agli Asparagi & Gorgonzola

1 package (8 ounces) tagliatelle pasta*

1 pound asparagus, cut into 1-inch pieces

2 tablespoons olive oil

4 medium green onions, sliced (1/4 cup)

1/4 cup chopped fresh parsley

1 clove garlic, finely chopped

1 cup crumbled Gorgonzola cheese (4 ounces)

1/2 teaspoon freshly cracked pepper

*1/2 package (16-ounce size) fettuccine can be substituted for the tagliatelle.

PREP: 15 MIN; COOK: 10 MIN
4 main-course or 6 first-course servings

1. Cook and drain pasta as directed on package—except add asparagus 5 minutes before pasta is done.

2. While pasta is cooking, heat oil in 12-inch skillet over medium-high heat. Cook onions, parsley and garlic in oil about 5 minutes, stirring occasionally, until onions are tender. Reduce heat to medium.

3. Add pasta, asparagus and cheese to mixture in skillet. Cook about 3 minutes, tossing gently, until cheese is melted and pasta is evenly coated. Sprinkle with pepper.

1 Serving: Calories 370 (Calories from Fat 155); Fat 17g (Saturated 7g); Cholesterol 70mg; Sodium 410mg; Carbohydrate 42g (Dietary Fiber 3g); Protein 15g
% Daily Value: Vitamin A 12%; Vitamin C 18%; Calcium 20%; Iron 18%
Diet Exchanges: 2 Starch, 1/2 High-Fat Meat, 2 Vegetable, 2 1/2 Fat

Parola di Antonio

This recipe is a flavor powerhouse made with minimum effort. Cooking asparagus in the pasta pot saves one major step. The Gorgonzola would provide plenty of flavor if tossed in uncooked, but tossing it with the pasta and asparagus mellows its pungency and contributes to a subtle, balanced blend of flavors.

Tagliatelle Pasta with Asparagus and Gorgonzola Sauce

CHEESE AND SPINACH PASTA ROLLS
Rotolini di Pasta Agli Spinaci

Classic Tomato Sauce* (page 140)

18 uncooked dried lasagna noodles
(from 16-ounce package)

1 container (15 ounces) ricotta
cheese

1 package (10 ounces) frozen
chopped spinach, thawed and
squeezed to drain

2 cloves garlic, finely chopped

1 medium green onion, chopped
(1 tablespoon)

1 cup chopped fresh basil leaves

1/2 cup freshly grated or shredded
imported Parmesan cheese

1/2 teaspoon salt

1/2 teaspoon pepper

*1 jar (28 ounces) plus 1 jar
(14 ounces) tomato pasta sauce can
be substituted for the Classic Tomato
Sauce.*

PREP: 50 MIN; BAKE: 50 MIN
6 main-course or 9 first-course servings

1. Make Classic Tomato Sauce.

2. While sauce is simmering, cook noodles as directed on package.

3. Heat oven to 350°. Grease rectangular baking dish, 13 x 9 x 2 inches.

4. Mix remaining ingredients. Spread 2 tablespoons of the cheese mixture down center of noodle. Roll up gently, starting with narrow edge. Place seam side down in baking dish. Repeat with remaining noodles and cheese mixture. Spoon sauce evenly over noodles.

5. Cover and bake 45 to 50 minutes or until sauce is thickened and bubbly and noodles are hot.

1 Serving: Calories 430 (Calories from Fat 110); Fat 12g (Saturated 6g); Cholesterol 30mg;
Sodium 670mg; Carbohydrate 63g (Dietary Fiber 6g); Protein 23g
% Daily Value: Vitamin A 66%; Vitamin C 38%; Calcium 42%; Iron 24%
Diet Exchanges: 3 Starch, 1 1/2 Medium-Fat Meat, 3 Vegetable

Parola di Antonio

Parmigiano-Reggiano is a favorite Italian cheese used in many dishes. It comes from the district of Parma in northern Italy and is usually aged for more than a year before it is sold. Parmesan has a dense texture and flakes easily when grated or shaved. True Parmigiano-Reggiano is identifiable by the red Italian government stamp that appears on the rind. By the way, don't throw away the rind after using the cheese. It adds amazing flavor depth when cooked in soups and sauce.

ITALIAN SAUSAGE LASAGNA
Lasagne al Forno

1 tablespoon olive oil

4 cloves garlic, finely chopped

3/4 pound bulk Italian sausage

1 medium onion, chopped (1/2 cup)

1 medium carrot, chopped
(1/2 cup)

2 cans (28 ounces each) Italian-style
pear-shaped (plum) tomatoes,
drained

1/4 cup fresh basil leaves

1/4 teaspoon salt

1/2 teaspoon pepper

1/2 recipe Homemade Pasta*
(page 92)

3 cups shredded mozzarella cheese
(12 ounces)

1/2 cup freshly grated or shredded
imported Parmesan cheese

*12 dried lasagna noodles can be sub-
stituted for the 1/2 recipe Homemade
Pasta. Cook noodles as directed on package. Assemble lasagna as directed—
except use 4 cooked dried noodles for
2 fresh pasta rectangles.

PREP: 25 MIN; COOK: 30 MIN; BAKE: 40 MIN; STAND: 15 MIN
8 main-course servings

1. Heat oil in 10-inch skillet over medium-high heat.
Cook garlic, sausage, onion and carrot in oil, stirring
occasionally, until sausage is no longer pink; drain.

2. Place tomatoes and basil in food processor or blender. Cover
and process until smooth. Stir tomato mixture,
salt and pepper into sausage mixture. Heat to boiling; reduce
heat. Simmer uncovered 30 minutes, stirring occasionally.

3. While sauce is simmering, make Homemade Pasta; divide
dough into 6 parts. Roll each part into 12 x 4-inch rectangle.
(Cover rectangles with plastic wrap until ready to use.)

4. Heat oven to 375°. Grease rectangular baking dish,
13 x 9 x 2 inches. Mix cheeses. Place 2 rectangles in baking
dish; top with half of the sausage mixture and one-third of
the cheese mixture. Repeat with 2 rectangles, remaining
sausage mixture and one-third of the cheese mixture. Top
with remaining rectangles and cheese mixture. Cover and
bake about 40 minutes or until hot and bubbly. Let stand
15 minutes before cutting.

1 Serving: Calories 315 (Calories from Fat 110); Fat 12g (Saturated 6g); Cholesterol 30mg;
Sodium 710mg; Carbohydrate 36g (Dietary Fiber 4g); Protein 20g
% Daily Value: Vitamin A 30%; Vitamin C 24%; Calcium 46%; Iron 14%
Diet Exchanges: 2 Starch, 2 Medium-Fat Meat, 1 Vegetable

Parola di Antonio

*Until the nineteenth century, Italian noodles were always manufactured
during the summer and dried in the sun. When natural gas became available, hundreds of pasta factories throughout Italy began using gas-fired
machines to dry dough, and pasta became available year-round. With the
increased production, pasta was inexpensively exported to other countries.*

LASAGNA WITH TWO SAUCES
Lasagne al Due Sapori

1 1/2 cups Classic Tomato Sauce*
   (page 140)

Alfredo Sauce* (page 112)

12 uncooked dried lasagna noodles

1 tablespoon olive oil

3 cups thinly sliced mushrooms
   (8 ounces)

2 medium carrots, thinly sliced
   (1 cup)

1 medium onion, chopped (1/2 cup)

2 cloves garlic, finely chopped

2 cups shredded mozzarella cheese
   (8 ounces)

1 container (15 ounces) ricotta
   cheese

1/2 cup grated imported Parmesan
   cheese

1 package (10 ounces) frozen
   chopped spinach, thawed and
   squeezed to drain

1/2 cup chopped fresh basil leaves

1/4 cup grated or shredded
   imported Parmesan cheese

*1 jar (14 ounces) tomato pasta sauce
can be substituted for the Classic
Tomato Sauce, and 1 container (10
ounces) refrigerated Alfredo sauce can
be substituted for the Alfredo Sauce.

PREP: 30 MIN; COOK: 10 MIN; BAKE: 50 MIN; STAND: 15 MIN
8 main-course servings

1. Make Classic Tomato Sauce and Alfredo Sauce. Heat oven to 375°. Cook and drain noodles as directed on package.

2. While noodles are cooking, heat oil in 10-inch skillet over medium-high heat. Cook mushrooms, carrots, onion and garlic in oil 8 to 10 minutes, stirring frequently, until carrots are crisp-tender; drain.

3. Mix mozzarella, ricotta and 1/2 cup Parmesan cheese. Mix spinach and basil. Spread 1 cup of the tomato sauce in ungreased rectangular baking dish, 13 x 9 x 2 inches. Top with 4 noodles, 1 cup of the cheese mixture, one-third of the vegetable mixture and remaining tomato sauce.

4. Top with 4 noodles, 1 cup of the cheese mixture, one-third of the vegetable mixture and the spinach mixture. Top with remaining noodles, cheese mixture and vegetable mixture. Top with Alfredo sauce. Sprinkle with 1/4 cup Parmesan cheese.

5. Cover and bake 30 minutes. Uncover and bake 15 to 20 minutes longer or until hot and bubbly. Let stand 15 minutes before cutting.

1 Serving: Calories 510 (Calories from Fat 245); Fat 27g (Saturated 15g); Cholesterol 75mg; Sodium 810mg; Carbohydrate 44g (Dietary Fiber 4g); Protein 27g
% Daily Value: Vitamin A 64%; Vitamin C 12%; Calcium 64%; Iron 16%
Diet Exchanges: 2 Starch, 2 High-Fat Meat, 3 Vegetable, 2 Fat

Parola di Antonio

Be sure to squeeze the moisture out of the thawed spinach thoroughly so the lasagna will not be too moist and saucy. If fresh basil isn't available, mixing 1 1/2 teaspoons dried basil leaves with the spinach is also tasty.

Lasagna with Two Sauces

ZITI WITH ASPARAGUS SAUCE
Ziti agli Asparagi

2 tablespoons butter or margarine

2 cloves garlic, finely chopped

1 leek, thinly sliced

1 1/2 pounds asparagus

1 cup chicken broth

1/2 cup dry white wine or chicken broth

1/2 teaspoon pepper

1 package (16 ounces) ziti pasta

1/4 cup freshly grated or shredded imported Parmesan cheese

PREP: 10 MIN; COOK: 30 MIN
6 main-course or 8 first-course servings

1. Melt butter in 10-inch skillet over low heat. Stir in garlic and leek. Cover and cook 10 minutes. Add asparagus, broth, wine and pepper. Heat to boiling; reduce heat. Cover and simmer about 10 minutes or until asparagus is tender.

2. Remove 12 asparagus spears; cut tips from asparagus and set aside. Place asparagus stalks and remaining asparagus mixture in food processor or blender. Cover and process until smooth.

3. Cook pasta as directed on package. Drain pasta; return to saucepan. Add asparagus sauce; toss gently until pasta is evenly coated. Top with asparagus tips. Sprinkle with cheese.

1 Serving: Calories 360 (Calories from Fat 65); Fat 7g (Saturated 4g); Cholesterol 15mg;
Sodium 370mg; Carbohydrate 63g (Dietary Fiber 4g); Protein 15g
% Daily Value: Vitamin A 8%; Vitamin C 14%; Calcium 10%; Iron 20%
Diet Exchanges: 3 Starch, 3 Vegetable, 1 Fat

Parola di Antonio

Leeks look like large, straight green onions. To prepare them, trim the long, green leaves to about 2 inches from the top of the white part. Use the trimmed leaves in soups and stews to add flavor. The white bulb is made up of layers, which create the perfect traps for sand to hide in. After peeling off the outer layer and discarding it, wash the leeks several times in cold water to remove any hidden sand.

PENNE WITH RADICCHIO
Penne al Radicchio

2 tablespoons olive oil

2 tablespoons butter or margarine

1 medium onion, thinly sliced

1 head radicchio, cut into 1/4-inch strips

1/2 cup dry white wine or chicken broth

1 cup whipping (heavy) cream

1/2 teaspoon pepper

1 package (16 ounces) penne rigate pasta

1/2 cup freshly grated or shredded imported Parmesan cheese

PREP: 20 MIN; COOK: 45 MIN
6 main-course or 8 first-course servings

1. Heat oil and butter in 10-inch skillet over medium-high heat. Cook onion in oil mixture about 5 minutes, stirring occasionally, until tender. Stir in radicchio. Reduce heat to low. Cover and cook about 5 minutes or until radicchio is tender.

2. Stir in wine. Cook uncovered until liquid has evaporated. Stir in whipping cream and pepper. Heat to boiling; reduce heat. Simmer uncovered about 30 minutes, stirring frequently, until thickened.

3. While radicchio mixture is simmering, cook and drain pasta as directed on package. Add pasta and 1/4 cup of the cheese to radicchio mixture; toss gently until pasta is evenly coated. Sprinkle with remaining 1/4 cup cheese.

1 Serving: Calories 530 (Calories from Fat 225); Fat 25g (Saturated 13g); Cholesterol 60mg; Sodium 200mg; Carbohydrate 63g (Dietary Fiber 3g); Protein 15g
% Daily Value: Vitamin A 12%; Vitamin C 0%; Calcium 16%; Iron 18%
Diet Exchanges: 4 Starch, 1 Vegetable, 4 Fat

PENNE WITH SPICY SAUCE
Penne All'Arrabbiata

1 package (16 ounces) penne rigate
  pasta

1 can (28 ounces) Italian-style
  pear-shaped (plum) tomatoes,
  undrained

2 tablespoons olive oil

2 cloves garlic, finely chopped

1 teaspoon crushed red pepper

2 tablespoons chopped fresh parsley

1 tablespoon tomato paste

1/2 cup freshly grated or shredded
  imported Parmesan cheese

PREP: 10 MIN; COOK: 20 MIN
6 main-course or 8 first-course servings

1. Cook and drain pasta as directed on package.

2. While pasta is cooking, place tomatoes with juice in food processor or blender. Cover and process until coarsely chopped; set aside.

3. Heat oil in 12-inch skillet over medium-high heat. Cook garlic, red pepper and parsley in oil about 5 minutes, stirring frequently, until garlic just begins to turn golden.

4. Stir in chopped tomatoes and tomato paste. Heat to boiling; reduce heat. Cover and simmer about 10 minutes, stirring occasionally, until slightly thickened.

5. Add pasta and 1/4 cup of the cheese to mixture in skillet. Cook about 3 minutes, tossing gently, until pasta is evenly coated. Sprinkle with remaining 1/4 cup cheese.

1 Serving: Calories 390 (Calories from Fat 80); Fat 9g (Saturated 2g); Cholesterol 5mg;
Sodium 380mg; Carbohydrate 66g (Dietary Fiber 4g); Protein 15g
% Daily Value: Vitamin A 10%; Vitamin C 18%; Calcium 16%; Iron 22%
Diet Exchanges: 4 Starch, 1 Vegetable, 1 Fat

Parola di Antonio

A signature dish of Roman cuisine, arrabbiata *sauce stands for "prepared in the angry way," referring to its fiery dose of hot pepper. Not limited to pasta, the sauce is also appreciated as an accompaniment to robust meat dishes, such as pork chops and* spezatino di maiale, *and crustacean dishes, such as shrimp and lobster. Whatever the dish, small morsels of meat, pasta or seafood are penetrated by the pungent, redolent power of the pepper. Have a refreshing glass of chilled Frascati wine by your side—you will need it. It is important to keep the cooking heat on the high side to achieve the best release of potency from the hot pepper, as is serving the pasta at once while piping hot.*

Penne with Spicy Sauce

MOSTACCIOLI WITH VODKA SAUCE
Mostaccioli alla Vodka

3 tablespoons butter or margarine

1 tablespoon olive oil

2 cloves garlic, finely chopped

1 small onion, chopped (1/4 cup)

1/4 cup chopped imported
   prosciutto or fully cooked ham
   (about 2 ounces)

2 boneless, skinless chicken breasts
   (about 1/2 pound), cut into
   1-inch pieces

1/2 cup vodka or chicken broth

1/2 cup whipping (heavy) cream

1/2 cup sliced pitted imported
   Kalamata or large pitted ripe
   olives

1 tablespoon chopped fresh parsley

1/2 teaspoon pepper

1 package (16 ounces) mostaccioli
   or penne rigate pasta

1/4 cup freshly grated or shredded
   imported Parmesan cheese

PREP: 20 MIN; COOK: 40 MIN
6 main-course or 8 first-course servings

1. Heat butter and oil in 10-inch skillet over medium-high heat. Cook garlic and onion in butter mixture about 5 minutes, stirring occasionally, until onion is tender.

2. Stir in prosciutto and chicken. Cook about 5 minutes, stirring occasionally, until chicken is brown. Stir in vodka. Cook uncovered until liquid has evaporated.

3. Stir in whipping cream, olives, parsley and pepper. Heat to boiling; reduce heat. Simmer uncovered about 30 minutes, stirring frequently, until thickened.

4. While sauce is simmering, cook and drain pasta as directed on package. Add pasta to sauce; toss gently until pasta is evenly coated. Sprinkle with cheese.

1 Serving: Calories 530 (Calories from Fat 180); Fat 20g (Saturated 9g); Cholesterol 70mg; Sodium 330mg; Carbohydrate 62g (Dietary Fiber 3g); Protein 23g
% Daily Value: Vitamin A 10%; Vitamin C 2%; Calcium 10%; Iron 20%
Diet Exchanges: 4 Starch, 2 Lean Meat, 2 Fat

Parola di Antonio

This is a modern pasta recipe popular in northern Italy. Cooks intrigued by different ways of cooking short-cut pastas found vodka to be an innovative addition to their repertoire. Brandy or grappa *is sometimes substituted for the vodka.*

Mostaccioli with Vodka Sauce

SAVORY FUSILLI
Fusilli Saporiti

1/4 cup olive oil

1 tablespoon capers

3 cloves garlic, finely chopped

2 cans (28 ounces each) Italian-style pear-shaped (plum) tomatoes, drained and chopped

1 red jalapeño chili, seeded and chopped

1/2 cup sliced pitted imported Kalamata or large pitted ripe olives

1/2 cup sliced pimiento-stuffed olives

1 tablespoon chopped fresh or 1 teaspoon dried oregano leaves

1 tablespoon chopped fresh or 1 teaspoon dried basil leaves

1 package (16 ounces) fusilli or rotini pasta

Freshly ground pepper

PREP: 20 MIN; COOK: 35 MIN
6 main-course or 8 first-course servings

1. Heat oil in 10-inch skillet over medium-high heat. Cook capers and garlic in oil about 3 minutes, stirring frequently, until garlic is soft.

2. Stir in tomatoes and chili. Heat to boiling; reduce heat. Cover and simmer 20 minutes, stirring occasionally.

3. Stir in olives, oregano and basil. Cover and simmer about 10 minutes, stirring occasionally, until thickened.

4. While sauce is simmering, cook pasta as directed on package. Drain pasta; return to saucepan. Add sauce; toss gently until pasta is evenly coated. Serve with pepper.

1 Serving: Calories 410 (Calories from Fat 135); Fat 15g (Saturated 2g); Cholesterol 65mg; Sodium 820mg; Carbohydrate 62g (Dietary Fiber 5g); Protein 12g
% Daily Value: Vitamin A 24%; Vitamin C 42%; Calcium 12%; Iron 30%
Diet Exchanges: 3 Starch, 3 Vegetable, 2 Fat

ROTINI WITH FRESH HERBS
Rotini alle Erbe

1 pound spinach leaves*

1/2 cup water

2 tablespoons butter or margarine

2 cloves garlic, finely chopped

2 tablespoons chopped fresh
basil leaves

2 tablespoons chopped fresh
dill weed

2 tablespoons chopped fresh
mint leaves

2 tablespoons chopped fresh parsley

1 cup whipping (heavy) cream

1/2 teaspoon salt

1/2 teaspoon pepper

1 package (16 ounces) vegetable-
flavored or plain rotini pasta

1/2 cup freshly grated or shredded
imported Parmesan cheese

*1 package (10 ounces) frozen chopped
spinach can be substituted for the fresh
spinach. Cook as directed on package;
drain well.

PREP: 20 MIN; COOK: 30 MIN
6 main-course or 8 first-course servings

1. Heat spinach and water to boiling in 4-quart Dutch oven or 12-inch skillet. Cover and cook about 5 minutes or until wilted; drain well.

2. Melt butter in 10-inch skillet over medium-high heat. Cook garlic in butter about 3 minutes, stirring frequently, until soft. Stir in basil, dill weed, mint, parsley, spinach, whipping cream, salt and pepper. Heat to boiling; reduce heat. Cover and simmer 20 minutes, stirring frequently.

3. While spinach mixture is simmering, cook and drain pasta as directed on package. Add pasta and 1/4 cup of the cheese to spinach mixture; toss gently until pasta is evenly coated. Sprinkle with remaining 1/4 cup cheese.

1 Serving: Calories 475 (Calories from Fat 200); Fat 22g (Saturated 12g); Cholesterol 130mg; Sodium 450mg; Carbohydrate 57g (Dietary Fiber 4g); Protein 16g
% Daily Value: Vitamin A 60%; Vitamin C 14%; Calcium 22%; Iron 28%
Diet Exchanges: 4 Starch, 4 Fat

BOW-TIES WITH SALMON AND TARRAGON-MUSTARD SAUCE

Farfalle al Salmone e Dragoncello

1 package (16 ounces) farfalle pasta

1 tablespoon olive oil

1 medium onion, chopped
(1/2 cup)

1 tablespoon chopped fresh
tarragon leaves

1 tablespoon chopped fresh parsley

1/4 cup dry white wine or chicken
broth

1 cup whipping (heavy) cream or
half-and-half

2 teaspoons stone-ground mustard

2 packages (3 to 4 ounces each)
sliced salmon lox (smoked or
cured) cut into 1/2-inch-wide
strips

1/2 cup freshly grated or shredded
imported Parmesan cheese

PREP: 15 MIN; COOK: 15 MIN
6 main-course or 8 first-course servings

1. Cook and drain pasta as directed on package.

2. While pasta is cooking, heat oil in 10-inch skillet over medium heat. Cook onion, tarragon and parsley in oil about 5 minutes, stirring frequently, until onion is tender. Add wine. Cook uncovered about 4 minutes or until wine has evaporated. Stir in whipping cream and mustard. Heat to boiling; reduce heat. Simmer uncovered about 10 minutes or until sauce is thickened.

3. Add pasta, salmon and 1/4 cup of the cheese to sauce in skillet; toss gently until pasta is evenly coated. Sprinkle with remaining 1/4 cup cheese.

1 Serving: Calories 490 (Calories from Fat 180); Fat 20g (Saturated 10g); Cholesterol 60mg; Sodium 200mg; Carbohydrate 62g (Dietary Fiber 3g); Protein 18g
% Daily Value: Vitamin A 10%; Vitamin C 2%; Calcium 16%; Iron 18%
Diet Exchanges: 4 Starch, 1 Lean Meat, 3 Fat

Parola di Antonio

No longer just considered a classic from northern Italy, this recipe has become popular in fine restaurants. Originally, smoked lake trout from Alpine lakes was the main component, and the fish was entirely wrapped with fresh tarragon sprigs, then poached. More familiar to northern Italian regions, tarragon marries well with meats, but it is also congenial with rich, assertive ingredients such as salmon and mustard. The true flavor of tarragon develops when its leaves are chopped and cooked, and it offers a pleasant, piquant undertone, especially in a rich cream sauce.

Bow-Ties with Salmon and Tarragon-Mustard Sauce; Little Bread Rolls, page 174

BOW-TIE PASTA TIMBALE TOWER
Timballo di Farfalle

2 cups Classic Tomato Sauce*
   (page 140)

1 package (16 ounces) tricolor or
   regular farfalle pasta

1 tablespoon olive oil

1 cup diced fully cooked ham

1 cup thinly sliced mushrooms
   (3 ounces)

1/2 cup chopped red onion

1 medium carrot, thinly sliced
   (1/2 cup)

3 large eggs

1 cup chopped fresh basil leaves

1 cup shredded mozzarella cheese
   (4 ounces)

1/2 cup shredded provolone cheese
   (2 ounces)

3/4 cup freshly grated or shredded
   imported Parmesan cheese

1/2 cup frozen green peas, thawed

4 cherry tomatoes, cut in half

*2 cups tomato pasta sauce (from
28-ounce jar) can be substituted for
the Classic Tomato Sauce.

PREP: 20 MIN; COOK: 5 MIN; BAKE: 45 MIN
8 main-course or 10 first-course servings

1. Make Classic Tomato Sauce. While sauce is simmering, heat oven to 375°. Butter 2-quart round casserole or 4-quart microwavable measuring cup. Cook pasta as directed on package. Drain pasta, but do not rinse; set aside.

2. Heat oil in 10-inch skillet over medium heat. Cook ham, mushrooms, onion and carrot in oil about 8 minutes, stirring occasionally, until carrot is tender; drain.

3. Beat eggs slightly in large bowl with fork. Stir in mushroom mixture, basil, mozzarella cheese, provolone cheese, 1/2 cup of the Parmesan cheese and 1 cup of the sauce. Carefully stir in pasta and peas until pasta is evenly coated.

4. Spoon into casserole; cover with plastic wrap. Gently but firmly press pasta mixture into casserole until top is smooth; remove plastic wrap.

5. Cover and bake 45 minutes. Remove from oven; let stand covered 10 minutes. Meanwhile, heat remaining sauce until hot.

6. Uncover casserole; carefully turn upside down onto serving plate. Spoon sauce over top of pasta. Sprinkle with remaining 1/4 cup Parmesan cheese. Garnish with tomato halves.

1 Serving: Calories 470 (Calories from Fat 145); Fat 16g (Saturated 6g); Cholesterol 110mg; Sodium 910mg; Carbohydrate 61g (Dietary Fiber 4g); Protein 25g
% Daily Value: Vitamin A 26%; Vitamin C 12%; Calcium 32%; Iron 20%
Diet Exchanges: 3 Starch, 1 1/2 Medium-Fat Meat, 3 Vegetable, 1 Fat

Parola di Antonio

Regarded as a king of the pasta dishes, a timballo is a pasta cake that makes a towering statement at holiday tables throughout Italy. In times past, it was the highlight of Sunday family meals served with additional sauce.

Bow-Tie Pasta Timbale Tower

SARDINIAN RAVIOLI WITH AROMATIC TOMATO SAUCE
Ravioli Sardi al Sugo Aromatico

Homemade Pasta (page 92)

1 container (15 ounces) ricotta
cheese

1/2 cup freshly grated imported
Parmesan cheese

1 clove garlic, finely chopped

1/4 cup finely chopped fresh basil
leaves

1 tablespoon finely chopped fresh
parsley

3/4 teaspoon salt

1/4 teaspoon pepper

All-purpose flour

Aromatic Tomato Sauce (page 141)

4 quarts water

1 tablespoon salt

1/4 cup freshly grated or shredded
imported Parmesan cheese,
if desired

*For round ravioli, cut with 2-inch
tortelli cutter or round cookie cutter.*

PREP: 1 HR; STAND: 30 MIN; COOK: 6 MIN
8 main-course or 10 first-course servings

1. Make Homemade Pasta; divide dough in half. Roll one half into 28 x 12-inch rectangle on lightly floured surface. Cut into seven 12 x 4-inch rectangles. (Cover rectangles with plastic wrap until ready to use.) Repeat with remaining dough.

2. Mix ricotta cheese, 1/2 cup Parmesan cheese, the garlic, basil, parsley, 3/4 teaspoon salt and the pepper. Place ten 1-teaspoon mounds of cheese mixture about 1 1/2 inches apart in 2 rows on one rectangle. Moisten dough lightly around mounds with water; top with second rectangle. Press gently around mounds to seal. Cut between mounds to make 10 squares, using 2-inch ravioli cutter, pastry cutter or sharp knife.*

3. Place ravioli in single layer on lightly floured towels; sprinkle lightly with flour. Repeat with remaining rectangles and cheese mixture. Let stand uncovered at room temperature 30 minutes. (Cook immediately as directed in step 5, or cover and refrigerate up to 2 days in single layer on lightly floured towels. Or cover tightly and freeze up to 3 months; thaw covered in refrigerator before cooking.)

4. Meanwhile, make Aromatic Tomato Sauce; keep warm.

5. Heat water and 1 tablespoon salt to boiling in large kettle or stockpot; add ravioli. Boil uncovered about 6 minutes, stirring occasionally, until al dente (tender but firm). Begin testing for doneness when ravioli rise to surface of water. Drain ravioli. Top with sauce. Sprinkle with 1/4 cup Parmesan cheese.

1 Serving: Calories 210 (Calories from Fat 70); Fat 8g (Saturated 4g); Cholesterol 20mg; Sodium 850mg; Carbohydrate 26g (Dietary Fiber 2g); Protein 11g
% Daily Value: Vitamin A 30%; Vitamin C 26%; Calcium 26%; Iron 10%
Diet Exchanges: 1 Starch, 1/2 High-Fat Meat, 2 Vegetable, 1 Fat

Parola di Antonio

True to its original countryside taste, this delectable dish combines a mellow filling flavor with a pronounced Mediterranean tomato sauce flavor. For a more authentic variation, try using a round sawtooth-edged cookie cutter in place of a ravioli cutter and feta cheese in place of ricotta.

Cutting Ravioli

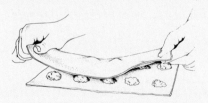

Place mounds of filling mixture about 1 1/2 inches apart in 2 rows on one rectangle of dough. Top with second rectangle of dough.

Press gently around mounds with fingers to seal.

Cut between mounds using pastry cutter or knife.

RAVIOLI WITH CLASSIC MEAT SAUCE
Ravioli alla Bolognese

Classic Meat Sauce (page 139)

Homemade Pasta (page 92) or
  Spinach Pasta (page 93)

1 cup chopped spinach

1 container (15 ounces) ricotta
  cheese

1/2 teaspoon freshly grated nutmeg

1/4 teaspoon salt

All-purpose flour

4 quarts water

1 tablespoon salt

Freshly grated imported Parmesan
  cheese, if desired

*For round ravioli, cut with 2-inch
tortelli cutter or round cookie cutter.*

PREP: 1 HR 20 MIN; STAND: 30 MIN; COOK: 6 MIN
6 main-course or 10 first-course servings

1. Make Classic Meat Sauce. While sauce is simmering, make Homemade Pasta; divide dough into half. Roll one half into 24 x 12-inch rectangle on lightly floured surface. Cut into six 12 x 4-inch rectangles. (Cover rectangles with plastic wrap until ready to use.) Repeat with remaining dough.

2. Mix spinach, ricotta cheese, nutmeg and 1/4 teaspoon salt. Place ten 1-teaspoon mounds of cheese mixture about 1 1/2 inches apart in 2 rows on one rectangle. Moisten dough lightly around mounds with water; top with second rectangle. Press gently around mounds to seal. Cut between mounds to make 10 squares, using 2-inch ravioli cutter, pastry cutter or sharp knife.*

3. Place ravioli in single layer on lightly floured towels; sprinkle lightly with flour. Repeat with remaining rectangles and cheese mixture. Let stand uncovered at room temperature 30 minutes. (Cook pasta immediately as directed below, or cover and refrigerate up to 2 days in single layer on lightly floured towels. Or cover tightly and freeze up to 3 months. Thaw covered in refrigerator before cooking.)

4. Heat water and 1 tablespoon salt to boiling in large kettle or stockpot; add ravioli. Boil uncovered about 6 minutes, stirring occasionally, until al dente (tender but firm). Begin testing for doneness when ravioli rise to surface of water. Drain ravioli. Top with sauce. Sprinkle with Parmesan cheese.

1 Serving: Calories 580 (Calories from Fat 250); Fat 28g (Saturated 11g); Cholesterol 75mg; Sodium 2850mg; Carbohydrate 56g (Dietary Fiber 6g); Protein 30g
% Daily Value: Vitamin A 66%; Vitamin C 50%; Calcium 34%; Iron 30%
Diet Exchanges: 3 Starch, 2 High-Fat Meat, 2 Vegetable, 2 Fat

Ravioli with Classic Meat Sauce

TORTELLINI WITH MUSHROOM AND BRANDY SAUCE
Tortellini alla Panna e Funghi

2 tablespoons butter or margarine

2 cloves garlic, finely chopped

1 small onion, finely chopped
(1/4 cup)

3 cups thinly sliced mushrooms
(8 ounces)

1/4 cup brandy or chicken broth

4 cups whipping (heavy) cream

1/2 teaspoon freshly grated nutmeg

1/2 teaspoon pepper

1 package (16 ounces) fresh or
dried cheese-filled tortellini

1/2 cup freshly grated or shredded
imported Parmesan cheese

Freshly ground pepper, if desired

PREP: 15 MIN; COOK: 35 MIN
6 main-course or 8 first-course servings

1. Melt butter in 10-inch skillet over medium-high heat. Cook garlic and onion in butter about 3 minutes, stirring frequently, onion is until tender. Stir in mushrooms. Cook 5 minutes.

2. Stir in brandy. Cook uncovered until liquid has evaporated. Stir in whipping cream, nutmeg and 1/2 teaspoon pepper. Heat to boiling; reduce heat. Simmer uncovered about 20 minutes, stirring frequently, until thickened.

3. While sauce is simmering, cook and drain tortellini as directed on package. Add tortellini to sauce; toss gently until tortellini is evenly coated. Sprinkle with cheese. Serve with pepper.

1 Serving: Calories 690 (Calories from Fat 540); Fat 60g (Saturated 37g); Cholesterol 290mg; Sodium 380mg; Carbohydrate 24g (Dietary Fiber 1g); Protein 15g
% Daily Value: Vitamin A 50%; Vitamin C 2%; Calcium 32%; Iron 10%
Diet Exchanges: 1 Starch, 1 Skim Milk, 11 Fat

CLASSIC MEAT SAUCE
Ragù Bolognese

2 tablespoons olive oil

2 tablespoons butter or margarine

2 medium carrots, finely chopped (1 cup)

1 medium onion, chopped (1/2 cup)

1/2 pound bulk Italian sausage

1/2 pound lean ground beef

3 cans (28 ounces each) Italian-style pear-shaped (plum) tomatoes, drained and chopped

1/2 cup dry red wine or beef broth

1 teaspoon salt

1 teaspoon dried oregano leaves

1/2 teaspoon pepper

PREP: 15 MIN; COOK: 1 HR
About 6 cups sauce

1. Heat oil and butter in 4-quart Dutch oven over medium-high heat until butter is melted. Cook carrots and onion in oil mixture about 8 minutes, stirring occasionally, until carrots and onion are tender.

2. Stir in sausage and beef. Reduce heat to medium. Cook, stirring occasionally, until sausage is no longer pink and beef is brown; drain.

3. Stir in remaining ingredients. Heat to boiling; reduce heat to low. Cover and simmer 45 minutes, stirring occasionally.

4. Use sauce immediately, or cover and refrigerate up to 48 hours or freeze up to 2 months.

1/2 Cup: Calories 170 (Calories from Fat 100); Fat 11g (Saturated 4g); Cholesterol 25mg; Sodium 640mg; Carbohydrate 11g (Dietary Fiber 2g); Protein 8g
% Daily Value: Vitamin A 26%; Vitamin C 24%; Calcium 6%; Iron 10%
Diet Exchanges: 1/2 Lean Meat, 2 Vegetable, 2 Fat

Parola di Antonio

Bologna is a noted food capital famous for its fresh filled tortellini and huge mortadella hams—the granddaddy of the meat we call Bologna ham. This is also the home of the classic Bolognese sauce, which has often been copied in America. This recipe is the authentic version of Bolognese sauce and may surprise you with its rich and subtle flavors.

CLASSIC TOMATO SAUCE
Sugo

1 tablespoon olive oil

4 cloves garlic, finely chopped

1 small onion, chopped (1/4 cup)

2 cans (28 ounces each) Italian-style
pear-shaped (plum) tomatoes,
drained

2 tablespoons chopped fresh or
2 teaspoons dried basil leaves

2 tablespoons chopped fresh or
2 teaspoons dried oregano leaves

1/2 teaspoon salt

1/2 teaspoon pepper

PREP: 10 MIN; COOK: 50 MIN
About 4 1/2 cups sauce

1. Heat oil in 3-quart saucepan over medium-high heat. Cook garlic and onion in oil about 5 minutes, stirring frequently, until onion is tender.

2. Place tomatoes in food processor or blender. Cover and process until smooth. Stir tomatoes and remaining ingredients into onion mixture. Heat to boiling; reduce heat. Simmer uncovered 45 minutes, stirring occasionally.

3. Use sauce immediately, or cover and refrigerate up to 48 hours or freeze up to 2 months.

1/2 Cup: Calories 50 (Calories from Fat 20); Fat 2g (Saturated 0g); Cholesterol 0mg;
Sodium 380mg; Carbohydrate 8g (Dietary Fiber 2g); Protein 2g
% Daily Value: Vitamin A 10%; Vitamin C 20%; Calcium 6%; Iron 6%
Diet Exchanges: 2 Vegetable

AROMATIC TOMATO SAUCE
Sugo Aromatico

1 tablespoon olive oil

2 cloves garlic, finely chopped

1 small onion, finely chopped
(1/4 cup)

1 small carrot, finely chopped

1 red jalapeño chili, seeded and
finely chopped

1 tablespoon chopped fresh or
1 teaspoon dried basil leaves

3 bay leaves

4 roma (plum) tomatoes, finely
chopped*

1 can (28 ounces) Italian-style pear-
shaped (plum) tomatoes, drained
and chopped

*4 canned Italian-style pear-shaped
(plum) tomatoes, drained and finely
chopped, can be used when fresh roma
tomatoes aren't available.*

PREP: 10 MIN; COOK: 25 MIN
About 3 cups sauce

1. Heat oil in 3-quart saucepan over medium-high heat. Cook garlic, onion, carrot and chili in oil about 3 minutes, stirring frequently, until onion is tender.

2. Stir in basil, bay leaves and fresh and canned tomatoes. Heat to boiling; reduce heat. Cover and simmer about 20 minutes, stirring occasionally, until sauce is thickened. Remove bay leaves.

1/2 Cup: Calories 65 (Calories from Fat 25); Fat 3g (Saturated 0g); Cholesterol 0mg; Sodium 200mg; Carbohydrate 10g (Dietary Fiber 2g); Protein 2g
%Daily Value: Vitamin A 30%; Vitamin C 34%; Calcium 4%; Iron 6%
Diet Exchanges: 2 Vegetable, 1/2 Fat

Parola di Antonio

In the past, bay leaves were considered a winter substitute for basil, especially in mountainous areas where the bay laurel tree favors the chilly weather. Leaving bay leaves intact allows their full aroma to be released while preventing possible mouth cuts from the sharp edges of broken leaves. Before serving the sauce, remember to remove the leaves to prevent any accidents.

FRESH TOMATO SAUCE
Salsa Al Pomodori Saltati

1 can (28 ounces) Italian-style pear-
   shaped (plum) tomatoes, drained

2 cloves garlic, finely chopped

1 tablespoon chopped fresh or
   1 teaspoon dried basil leaves

1 tablespoon chopped fresh parsley
   or 1 teaspoon parsley flakes

1 tablespoon grated imported
   Parmesan cheese

1 teaspoon olive oil

1/2 teaspoon salt

1/2 teaspoon pepper

6 medium tomatoes, diced
   (4 1/2 cups)

3/4 cup imported Kalamata, pitted
   or pitted ripe olives, cut in half

1 tablespoon capers, if desired

PREP: 5 MIN
4 cups sauce

1. Place all ingredients except diced tomatoes, olives and capers in food processor or blender. Cover and process until smooth.

2. Mix tomato mixture, diced tomatoes, olives and capers.

3. Use sauce immediately, or cover and refrigerate up to 48 hours or freeze up to 2 months.

1/2 Cup: Calories 60 (Calories from Fat 20); Fat 2g (Saturated 0g); Cholesterol 0mg; Sodium 420mg; Carbohydrate 10g (Dietary Fiber 2g); Protein 2g
% Daily Value: Vitamin A 12%; Vitamin C 26%; Calcium 4%; Iron 8%
Diet Exchanges: 2 Vegetable

Parola di Antonio

Although this tomato sauce is called "fresh," it starts with canned tomatoes. The canned tomatoes provide the liquid, and the addition of the fresh chopped tomatoes gives texture and a fresh flavor. Also, this sauce isn't cooked, so each ingredient maintains its own flavor characteristic rather than being blended together during cooking. I use grated instead of shredded Parmesan cheese so it dissolves in the sauce rather than remaining in small pieces.

Top to bottom: Fresh Tomato Sauce; Tomato-Cream Sauce, page 144; Aromatic Tomato Sauce, page 141

TOMATO-CREAM SAUCE
Salsa Rosa

1 tablespoon olive oil

1 clove garlic, finely chopped

1 medium onion, chopped (1/2 cup)

1 tablespoon chopped fresh parsley
  or 1 teaspoon parsley flakes

1 tablespoon chopped fresh or
  1 teaspoon dried basil leaves

1 can (28 ounces) Italian-style
  pear-shaped (plum) tomatoes,
  drained and chopped

1/2 cup whipping (heavy) cream

1/2 teaspoon ground nutmeg

1/4 teaspoon salt

1/8 teaspoon pepper

PREP: 15 MIN; COOK: 20 MIN
About 2 cups sauce

1. Heat oil in 12-inch skillet over medium-high heat. Cook garlic, onion, parsley, basil and tomatoes in oil 10 minutes, stirring occasionally.

2. Stir in remaining ingredients. Cook about 20 minutes, stirring occasionally, until sauce is thickened.

3. Use sauce immediately, or cover and refrigerate up to 24 hours. Freezing is not recommended because sauce will separate when reheated.

1/2 Cup: Calories 165 (Calories from Fat 115); Fat 13g (Saturated 6g); Cholesterol 35mg; Sodium 450mg; Carbohydrate 12g (Dietary Fiber 3g); Protein 3g
% Daily Value: Vitamin A 20%; Vitamin C 26%; Calcium 8%; Iron 6%
Diet Exchanges: 2 Vegetable, 2 1/2 Fat

HOMEMADE PIZZA SAUCE
Salsa Semplice per Pizze

2 cans (28 ounces each) Italian-style
   pear-shaped (plum) tomatoes,
   drained

1 tablespoon chopped fresh or
   1 teaspoon dried basil leaves

1 tablespoon chopped fresh or
   1 teaspoon dried oregano leaves

1 teaspoon grated Romano or
   imported Parmesan cheese

2 teaspoons olive oil

1/4 teaspoon salt

1/4 teaspoon pepper

4 cloves garlic

PREP: 5 MIN
About 3 cups sauce

1. Place all ingredients in food processor or blender. Cover and process until smooth.

2. Use sauce immediately, or cover and refrigerate up to 48 hours or freeze up to 2 months.

1/2 Cup: Calories 65 (Calories from Fat 20); Fat 2g (Saturated 0g); Cholesterol 0mg;
Sodium 480mg; Carbohydrate 12g (Dietary Fiber 3g); Protein 3g
% Daily Value: Vitamin A 16%; Vitamin C 30%; Calcium 8%; Iron 8%
Diet Exchanges: 2 Vegetable

WALNUT-BASIL SAUCE
Salsa di Noci

1 cup olive oil

1/2 cup coarsely chopped walnuts

1/2 cup chopped fresh basil leaves

1/2 cup chopped fresh parsley

1/4 cup grated Romano or
   imported Parmesan cheese

1 teaspoon salt

1 teaspoon pepper

2 cloves garlic

PREP: 10 MIN
About 1 1/2 cups sauce

Place all ingredients in blender or food processor. Cover and blend on medium speed about 3 minutes, stopping blender occasionally to scrape sides, until smooth.

1/4 Cup: Calories 405 (Calories from Fat 385); Fat 43g (Saturated 6g); Cholesterol 5mg;
Sodium 440mg; Carbohydrate 3g (Dietary Fiber 1g); Protein 3g
%Daily Value: Vitamin A 4%; Vitamin C 12%; Calcium 4%; Iron 4%
Diet Exchanges: 9 Fat

BASIL-GARLIC SAUCE
Pesto

1 cup chopped fresh basil leaves

1/2 cup freshly grated imported
  Parmesan cheese

1/2 cup pine nuts

1/2 cup chopped fresh parsley

1/2 cup olive oil

1 teaspoon salt

1/4 teaspoon pepper

3 cloves garlic

PREP: 10 MIN
About 1 1/2 cups sauce

1. Place all ingredients in food processor or blender. Cover and process until smooth.

2. Use sauce immediately, or cover and refrigerate up to 5 days or freeze up to 1 month.

1/4 Cup: Calories 280 (Calories from Fat 250); Fat 28g (Saturated 5g); Cholesterol 5mg;
Sodium 560mg; Carbohydrate 4g (Dietary Fiber 2g); Protein 5g
% Daily Value: Vitamin A 6%; Vitamin C 6%; Calcium 14%;Iron 6%
Diet Exchanges: 1 Vegetable, 5 1/2 Fat

Parola di Antonio

Originally from Genoa, pesto is now used throughout Italy and America. It's a highly versatile sauce made with basil that adds a fresh, pungent flavor to pasta, vegetables, bruschetta and salads. There are variations of pesto using combinations of other herbs, including parsley and mint, and other nuts, such as walnuts, in the place of pine nuts, but the classic recipe here is favored over all. When you find fresh basil, be sure to make extra batches of pesto. You can freeze it for later use (don't add the cheese until you thaw the pesto), so you can enjoy a taste of summer all year long.

Basil-Garlic Sauce

Fresh Mozzarella and Tomato Pizza, page 154

CHAPTER FOUR

Pizze Rustiche,
Breadse Panini

PIZZA, BREADS AND
SANDWICHES

HOMEMADE PIZZA DOUGH
Pasta per Pizze

One Crust

1 package regular active dry yeast

1/2 cup warm water (105° to 115°)

1 1/4 to 1 1/2 cups all-purpose
   flour

1 teaspoon olive or vegetable oil

1/2 teaspoon salt

1/2 teaspoon sugar

Two Crusts

2 packages regular active dry yeast

1 cup warm water (105° to 115°)

2 1/3 to 2 2/3 cups all-purpose
   flour

2 teaspoons olive or vegetable oil

1 teaspoon salt

1/2 teaspoon sugar

Three Crusts

2 packages regular active dry yeast

1 1/2 cups warm water
   (105° to 115°)

3 3/4 to 4 cups all-purpose flour

1 tablespoon olive or vegetable oil

1 teaspoon salt

1/2 teaspoon sugar

PREP: 20 MIN; RISE: 20 MIN; REFRIGERATE: 2 HR
One, two or three crusts (8 wedges per crust)

1. Dissolve yeast in warm water in large bowl. Stir in half of the flour, the oil, salt and sugar. Stir in enough of the remaining flour to make dough easy to handle.

2. Place dough on lightly floured surface. Knead about 10 minutes or until smooth and springy. Place dough in greased bowl, turning dough to grease all sides. Cover and let rise in warm place 20 minutes.

3. Gently push fist into dough to deflate. Cover and refrigerate at least 2 hours but no longer than 48 hours. (If dough should double in size during refrigeration, gently push fist into dough to deflate.)

1 Wedge: Calories 75 (Calories from Fat 10); Fat 1g (Saturated 0g); Cholesterol 0mg;
Sodium 150mg; Carbohydrate 15g (Dietary Fiber 1g); Protein 2g
%Daily Value: Vitamin A 0%; Vitamin C 0%; Calcium 0%; Iron 6%
Diet Exchanges: 1 Starch

CLASSIC PIZZA
Pizza Classica

Homemade Pizza Dough for One Crust* (page 150) or 1 pouch (6.5 ounces) pizza crust mix

1/2 cup Homemade Pizza Sauce (page 145) or purchased pizza sauce

1 pound bulk Italian sausage

1 small onion, chopped (1/2 cup)

1 cup shredded mozzarella cheese (4 ounces)

1/2 cup shredded provolone cheese (2 ounces)

1/4 cup chopped fresh basil leaves

1/2 cup chopped imported prosciutto or fully cooked smoked ham (about 4 ounces)

*1 container (10 ounces) refrigerated pizza dough can be substituted for the Homemade Pizza Dough. Shape dough into 12-inch circle instead of rectangle as directed on container. Bake about 18 minutes or until crust is golden brown.

PREP: 35 MIN; RISE: 20 MIN; REFRIGERATE: 2 HR; BAKE: 20 MIN
1 pizza (8 wedges)

1. Make Homemade Pizza Dough and Homemade Pizza Sauce.

2. Heat oven to 425°. Cook sausage and onion in 10-inch skillet over medium heat, stirring occasionally, until sausage is no longer pink; drain.

3. Press dough into 12-inch circle on ungreased cookie sheet, 12-inch pizza pan or pizza screen, using floured fingers. Press dough from center to edge so edge is slightly thicker than center.

4. Spread pizza sauce over dough to within 1/2 inch of edge. Mix cheeses; sprinkle over sauce. Spoon sausage mixture over cheeses. Sprinkle with basil and prosciutto.

5. Bake 15 to 20 minutes or until crust is golden brown and cheeses are melted and lightly browned.

1 Wedge: Calories 295 (Calories from Fat 155); Fat 17g (Saturated 7g); Cholesterol 50mg; Sodium 850mg; Carbohydrate 18g (Dietary Fiber 1g); Protein 18g
%Daily Value: Vitamin A 4%; Vitamin C 4%; Calcium 16%; Iron 10%
Diet Exchanges: 1 Starch, 2 High-Fat Meat

Parola di Antonio

For Italians, pizza is an extension of bread. Pizza in some form has always been present throughout most of Italian history, and every region has its favorite variations. In a bakery shop in the ruins of Pompeii, archaeologists found a bakery shop with evidence of a flatbread topped with garum—*a fish-and-spice paste—that was a form of pizza.*

CLASSIC FOUR-SEASONS PIZZA
Pizza Quattro Stagioni

Homemade Pizza Dough for One
Crust* (page 150) or 1 pouch
(6.5 ounces) pizza crust mix

1/2 cup Homemade Pizza Sauce
(page 145) or purchased pizza
sauce

1 cup shredded mozzarella cheese
(4 ounces)

1/3 cup shredded provolone cheese

1/3 cup chopped prosciutto or fully
cooked ham (about 3 ounces)

1/4 cup chopped fresh basil leaves

2 teaspoons capers

4 marinated artichoke hearts,
drained and cut into fourths

4 flat anchovy fillets in oil

3 roma (plum) tomatoes, peeled
and chopped

1 teaspoon olive oil

12 imported Kalamata olives, pitted

*1 container (10 ounces) refrigerated
pizza dough can be substituted for the
Homemade Pizza Dough. Shape dough
into 12-inch circle instead of rectangle
as directed on container. Bake about
10 minutes or until crust is golden

PREP: 30 MIN; RISE: 20 MIN; REFRIGERATE: 2 HR; BAKE: 10 MIN
1 pizza (8 wedges)

1. Make Homemade Pizza Dough and Homemade Pizza Sauce.

2. Move oven rack to lowest position. Heat oven to 500°. Press dough into 12-inch circle on ungreased cookie sheet, 12-inch pizza pan or pizza screen, using floured fingers. Press dough from center to edge so edge is slightly thicker than center.

3. Spread pizza sauce over dough to within 1/2 inch of edge. Mix cheeses; sprinkle over sauce. Arrange prosciutto, basil, capers, artichoke hearts, anchovy fillets and tomatoes on cheese. Drizzle with oil. Top with olives.

4. Bake 8 to 10 minutes or until crust is golden and cheeses are melted.

1 Wedge: Calories 185 (Calories from Fat 70); Fat 8g (Saturated 3g); Cholesterol 15mg; Sodium 600mg; Carbohydrate 20g (Dietary Fiber 2g); Protein 10g
%Daily Value: Vitamin A 6%; Vitamin C 8%; Calcium 16%; Iron 10%
Diet Exchanges: 1 Starch, 1 Medium-Fat Meat, 1 Vegetable

Parola di Antonio

The Classic Four-Seasons Pizza is an edible display of the year's seasons. Spring is represented by fresh basil and chunks of tomatoes. Summer brings out capers and the best anchovies. The golden colors of melted cheeses are for fall. And prosciutto is one of the more nourishing foods available in winter.

Classic Four-Seasons Pizza

FRESH MOZZARELLA AND TOMATO PIZZA
Pizza Margherita

Homemade Pizza Dough for One Crust* (page 150) or 1 pouch (6.5 ounces) pizza crust mix

4 ounces fresh mozzarella, well drained

2 roma (plum) tomatoes, thinly sliced

1/4 teaspoon salt

Fresh cracked pepper to taste

1/4 cup thin strips fresh basil leaves

1 tablespoon chopped fresh oregano leaves

1 tablespoon small capers, if desired

1 tablespoon extra-virgin olive oil

1 container (10 ounces) refrigerated pizza dough can be substituted for the Homemade Pizza Dough. Shape dough into 12-inch circle instead of rectangle as directed on container. Bake about 18 minutes or until crust is golden brown.

PREP: 35 MIN; RISE: 20 MIN; REFRIGERATE: 2 HR; BAKE: 20 MIN
1 pizza (8 wedges)

1. Make Homemade Pizza Dough. Cut mozzarella into 1/4-inch slices.

2. Move oven rack to lowest position. Heat oven to 425°. Press dough into 12-inch circle on cookie sheet, 12-inch pizza pan or pizza screen, using floured fingers. Press dough from center to edge so edge is slightly thicker than center.

3. Place cheese on dough to within 1/2 inch of edge. Arrange tomatoes on cheese. Sprinkle with salt, pepper, 2 tablespoons of the basil, the oregano and capers. Drizzle with oil.

4. Bake about 20 minutes or until crust is golden brown and cheese is melted. Sprinkle with remaining 2 tablespoons basil.

1 Wedge: Calories 130 (Calories from Fat 45); Fat 5g (Saturated 2g); Cholesterol 5mg; Sodium 300mg; Carbohydrate 16g (Dietary Fiber 1g); Protein 6g
%Daily Value: Vitamin A 2%; Vitamin C 2%; Calcium 10%; Iron 6%
Diet Exchanges: 1 Starch, 1 Fat

Mozzarella and Tomato Pizza (Pizza Margherita): Substitute 2 cups shredded mozzarella cheese (8 ounces) for the fresh mozzarella. Sprinkle 1 cup of the cheese over dough. Continue as directed—except sprinkle with remaining 1 cup cheese before drizzling with oil.

Parola di Antonio

Queen Margherita was served three different pizzas on an official visit to Naples, the pizza capital of the world. She selected the one that had a few simple, fresh ingredients—mozzarella, tomatoes and basil. Use only the freshest of fresh mozzarella or it will become dry and not as tasty after baking. If fresh isn't available, use shredded mozzarella that melts and creates those wonderful long suppli al telefono, *or strings. Buon Appetito!*

PIZZA WITH SPINACH, PROSCIUTTO AND GOAT CHEESE
Pizza al Prosciutto e Spinaci

Homemade Pizza Dough for One
Crust* (page 150) or 1 pouch
(6.5 ounces) pizza crust mix

2 cups spinach leaves (about 2 1/2
ounces)

1 teaspoon extra-virgin olive oil

3 flat anchovy fillets in oil, drained
and coarsely chopped

2 cloves garlic, finely chopped

2 ounces prosciutto or fully cooked
smoked ham, coarsely chopped
(about 1/4 cup)

1 cup crumbled goat cheese (about
5 1/2 ounces)

1 teaspoon chopped fresh chives

1 tablespoon chopped fresh basil
leaves

1/4 teaspoon fresh cracked pepper

*1 container (10 ounces) refrigerated
pizza dough can be substituted for the
Homemade Pizza Dough. Shape dough
into 12-inch circle instead of rectangle
as directed on container. Bake about 18
minutes or until crust is golden brown.*

PREP: 35 MIN; RISE: 20 MIN; REFRIGERATE: 2 HR; BAKE: 20 MIN
1 pizza (8 wedges)

1. Make Homemade Pizza Dough.

2. Move oven rack to lowest position. Heat oven to 425°.
   Press dough into 12-inch circle on ungreased cookie sheet,
   12-inch pizza pan or pizza screen, using floured fingers.
   Press dough from center to edge so edge is slightly thicker
   than center.

3. Arrange spinach on dough; drizzle with oil. Sprinkle with
   remaining ingredients.

4. Bake about 20 minutes or until crust is golden brown.

1 Wedge: Calories 175 (Calories from Fat 80); Fat 9g (Saturated 5g); Cholesterol 25mg;
Sodium 380mg; Carbohydrate 16g (Dietary Fiber 1g); Protein 7g
%Daily Value: Vitamin A 10%; Vitamin C 2%; Calcium 12%; Iron 8%
Diet Exchanges: 1 Starch, 1 High-Fat Meat

PIZZA WITH SMOKED SALMON AND ASPARAGUS
Pizza agli Asparagi e Salmone

Homemade Pizza Dough for Two
  Crusts* (page 150) or 2 pouches
  (6.5 ounces each) pizza crust mix

1 package (10 ounces) frozen
  asparagus cuts, thawed

1 package (3 ounces) sliced smoked
  salmon (lox), cut into 1/2-inch
  strips

1 cup crumbled Gorgonzola cheese
  (8 ounces)

1 tablespoon chopped fresh
  basil leaves

2 teaspoons chopped fresh
  tarragon leaves

3 cloves fresh garlic, finely chopped

2 teaspoons extra-virgin olive oil

*2 containers (10 ounces each) refriger-
ated pizza dough can be substituted for
the Homemade Pizza Dough. Shape
dough into 12-inch circles instead of
rectangles as directed on container.
Bake about 18 minutes or until crust
is deep golden brown.

PREP: 35 MIN; RISE: 20 MIN; REFRIGERATE: 2 HR; BAKE: 20 MIN
2 pizzas (8 wedges each)

1. Make Homemade Pizza Dough.

2. Move oven rack to lowest position. Heat oven to 425°.
   Divide dough in half. Press half of the dough into 12-inch
   circle on ungreased cookie sheet, 12-inch pizza pan or
   pizza screen, using floured fingers. Press dough from center to edge so edge is slightly thicker than center. Repeat
   with remaining dough.

3. Arrange half each of the asparagus, salmon and cheese on
   1 dough circle. Sprinkle with half each of the basil, tarragon and garlic. Drizzle with 1 teaspoon of the oil. Repeat
   with remaining dough and ingredients.

4. Bake about 20 minutes or until crust is deep golden
   brown and cheese is melted.

1 Wedge: Calories 115 (Calories from Fat 35); Fat 4g (Saturated 2g); Cholesterol 5mg;
Sodium 310mg; Carbohydrate 15g (Dietary Fiber 1g); Protein 6g
%Daily Value: Vitamin A 2%; Vitamin C 2%; Calcium 4%; Iron 6%
Diet Exchanges: 1 Starch, 1 Fat

Parola di Antonio

*I find this to be an impressive pizza with its delicate smoky salmon flavor
topped off with the piquant touch of cheese. Either sliced or flaked smoked
salmon can adorn this pizza—you can choose. I happen to prefer the bright
color and texture of lox, which is a cold-smoked salmon. It is smoked at a
lower temperature for a longer period of time and is available in thin slices.
Hot-smoked salmon is smoked at a higher temperature for a shorter period
of time and has a flaky texture.*

Pizza with Smoked Salmon and Asparagus

SEAFOOD PIZZA
Pizza Marinara

Homemade Pizza Dough for One Crust* (page 150) or 1 pouch (6.5 ounces) pizza crust mix

1 cup Homemade Pizza Sauce (page 145) or purchased pizza sauce

12 uncooked medium shrimp in shells

1/2 pound bay scallops or sea scallops

1 cup shredded mozzarella cheese (4 ounces)

1/2 cup shredded provolone cheese (2 ounces)

8 flat anchovy fillets in oil, drained

1/2 cup chopped fresh basil leaves

1/2 teaspoon pepper

4 cloves garlic, finely chopped

*1 container (10 ounces) refrigerated pizza dough can be substituted for the Homemade Pizza Dough. Shape dough into 12-inch circle instead of rectangle as directed on container. Bake about 10 minutes or until crust is golden.

PREP: 35 MIN; RISE: 20 MIN; REFRIGERATE: 2 HR; BAKE: 10 MIN
1 pizza (8 wedges)

1. Make Homemade Pizza Dough and Homemade Pizza Sauce.

2. Move oven rack to lowest position. Heat oven to 500°. Peel shrimp, leaving tails intact. Make a shallow cut lengthwise down back of each shrimp; wash out vein. If using sea scallops, cut in half.

3. Press dough into 12-inch circle on ungreased cookie sheet, 12-inch pizza pan or pizza screen, using floured fingers. Press dough from center to edge so edge is slightly thicker than center.

4. Spread pizza sauce over dough to within 1/2 inch of edge. Mix cheeses; sprinkle over sauce. Arrange shrimp, anchovy fillets and scallops on cheeses. Mix basil, pepper and garlic; sprinkle over seafood.

5. Bake about 10 minutes or until shrimp are pink and firm, scallops are white and cheeses are melted.

1 Wedge: Calories 195 (Calories from Fat 65); Fat 7g (Saturated 3g); Cholesterol 35mg; Sodium 600mg; Carbohydrate 19g (Dietary Fiber 1g); Protein 15g
%Daily Value: Vitamin A 8%; Vitamin C 6%; Calcium 20%; Iron 12%
Diet Exchanges: 1 Starch, 1 High-Fat Meat, 1 Vegetable

PIZZA FOLDOVER
Calzone

Homemade Pizza Dough for One Crust* (page 150) or 1 pouch (6.5 ounces) pizza crust mix

1/3 cup Homemade Pizza Sauce (page 145) or purchased pizza sauce

1/4 cup shredded mozzarella cheese

1/4 cup shredded provolone cheese

1/4 cup chopped imported prosciutto or fully cooked ham (about 2 ounces)

1/4 cup chopped pepperoni or Genoa salami (about 2 ounces)

2 tablespoons chopped fresh basil leaves

1 container (10 ounces) refrigerated pizza dough can be substituted for the Homemade Pizza Dough. Shape dough into 12-inch circle instead of rectangle as directed on container. Bake about 18 minutes or until crust is golden brown.

PREP: 30 MIN; RISE: 20 MIN; REFRIGERATE: 2 HR; BAKE: 25 MIN
2 servings

1. Make Homemade Pizza Dough and Homemade Pizza Sauce.

2. Heat oven to 375°. Grease cookie sheet. Press dough into 12-inch circle on cookie sheet, using floured fingers.

3. Mix cheeses; place on half of circle to within 1 inch of edge. Mix prosciutto and pepperoni; sprinkle over cheeses. Pour pizza sauce over prosciutto and pepperoni. Sprinkle with basil.

4. Lift and gently stretch other half of dough over filling; press edges of dough together with fingers or fork to seal. Cut slit in top.

5. Bake 20 to 25 minutes or until golden brown.

1 Serving: Calories 580 (Calories from Fat 225); Fat 25g (Saturated 10g); Cholesterol 50mg; Sodium 1780mg; Carbohydrate 66g (Dietary Fiber 4g); Protein 27g
%Daily Value: Vitamin A 10%; Vitamin C 8%; Calcium 24%; Iron 30%
Diet Exchanges: 4 Starch, 2 High-Fat Meat, 1 Vegetable, 1 Fat

Parola di Antonio

A calzone *is like a stuffed, folded pizza. A circle of pizza dough is folded in half over a succulent filling, then sealed around the edges. During baking, the filling plumps, stretching the dough somewhat until it resembles a "stuffed stocking," the literal translation of* calzone.

RUSTIC PIZZA PIE
Pizza Rustica

Homemade Pizza Dough for Two
Crusts (page 150) or 2 pouches
(6.5 ounces each) pizza crust mix

1 cup Homemade Pizza Sauce
(page 145) or purchased
pizza sauce

1/2 pound bulk Italian sausage

1 cup shredded mozzarella cheese
(4 ounces)

1/2 cup shredded provolone cheese
(2 ounces)

1/2 cup sliced mushrooms

1/2 cup chopped Genoa salami
(about 3 ounces)

1 medium onion, thinly sliced

1 cup chopped fresh basil leaves

1 tablespoon olive oil

1 egg, beaten

*2 containers (10 ounces each) refriger-
ated pizza dough can be substituted for
the Homemade Pizza Dough. Shape
dough into 13-inch circle instead of
rectangle as directed on container.*

PREP: 40 MIN; RISE: 20 MIN; REFRIGERATE: 2 HR; BAKE: 30 MIN
1 double-crust pizza (8 wedges)

1. Make Homemade Pizza Dough and Homemade Pizza
   Sauce.

2. Heat oven to 425°. Grease pie plate, 10 x 1 1/2 inches. Cook
   sausage in 10-inch skillet over medium heat, stirring
   occasionally, until no longer pink; drain.

3. Divide dough in half. Press or roll one half of dough into
   13-inch circle on lightly floured surface; place in pie plate.
   Sprinkle sausage over dough in pie plate. Mix cheeses;
   sprinkle over sausage. Top with pizza sauce, mushrooms,
   salami, onion and basil; drizzle with oil.

4. Press or roll remaining dough into 11-inch circle on lightly floured surface; place over filling. Pinch edges of dough
   together to seal; roll up edge of dough, forming a rim.
   Prick top of dough thoroughly with fork; brush with egg.

5. Bake about 30 minutes or until golden brown. Serve hot
   or cold.

1 Wedge: Calories 315 (Calories from Fat 160); Fat 18g (Saturated 7g); Cholesterol 60mg;
Sodium 910mg; Carbohydrate 23g (Dietary Fiber 2g); Protein 17g
%Daily Value: Vitamin A 12%; Vitamin C 14%; Calcium 20%; Iron 14%
Diet Exchanges: 2 Starch, 1 High-Fat Meat, 1 Vegetable, 1 1/2 Fat

Parola di Antonio

Rustic pizza pies, or focaccias, *come from rural southern Italy. They were
prepared for holidays throughout the year and reflect the religious laws of
the Catholic church.* Sfinciuni, *a Sicilian focaccia, is filled with seafood,
eggs and vegetables during Lent when meat is prohibited, but it can be filled
with meats the rest of the year.*

Rustic Pizza Pie

STUFFED ROLLED FOLDOVER
Stromboli Ripieno

Homemade Pizza Dough for Two
Crusts (page 150) or 2 pouches
(6.5 ounces each) pizza crust mix

1/2 cup Homemade Pizza Sauce
(page 145) or purchased pizza
sauce

1 cup shredded mozzarella cheese
(4 ounces)

2 ounces thinly sliced imported
prosciutto or fully cooked
smoked ham

24 large basil leaves

12 thin slices Genoa salami (about
1/4 pound)

1 cup shredded provolone cheese
(4 ounces)

2 containers (10 ounces each) refrigerated pizza dough can be substituted for the Homemade Pizza Dough. Shape dough into 12 x 8 inch rectangle.

PREP: 35 MIN; RISE: 20 MIN; REFRIGERATE: 2 HR; BAKE: 20 MIN
2 foldovers (6 slices each)

1. Make Homemade Pizza Dough and Homemade Pizza Sauce.

2. Heat oven to 400°. Grease cookie sheet.

3. Divide dough in half. Press half of dough into 12 x 8-inch rectangle on lightly floured surface, using floured fingers. Sprinkle 1/2 cup of the mozzarella cheese over rectangle to within 1 inch of long sides and 1/2 inch of short sides. Layer half each of the pizza sauce, prosciutto, basil and salami on cheese. Sprinkle with 1/2 cup of the provolone cheese.

4. Starting at a long side, fold edge to center. Carefully fold again so folded side meets other edge. Pinch edge of dough into folded edge to seal; pinch ends to seal. Place on cookie sheet. Repeat with remaining dough and ingredients.

5. Bake about 20 minutes or until golden brown. To serve, cut into 2-inch slices.

1 Slice: Calories 200 (Calories from Fat 80); Fat 9g (Saturated 4g); Cholesterol 25mg; Sodium 610mg; Carbohydrate 20g (Dietary Fiber 1g); Protein 11g
%Daily Value: Vitamin A 4%; Vitamin C 2%; Calcium 14%; Iron 8%
Diet Exchanges: 1 Starch, 1 High-Fat Meat, 1 Vegetable

Parola di Antonio

Popular on Italy's east coast, stromboli is a variation of the pizza foldover, calzone. Rather than folding the dough over the filling just once as for a calzone, the dough is folded over twice to form a compact roll. The result is chewier and denser than a simple foldover. Let the baked rolls stand a few minutes before slicing them so the filling will thicken slightly and not ooze out as much. Stromboli also works well as a buffet-table item because it is good when eaten hot or cool.

Stuffed Rolled Foldover

"SLIPPER" BREAD
Ciabatta Stirata

2 packages regular active dry yeast

1 1/2 cups very warm water
(115° to 120°)

3 to 3 1/4 cups bread flour

1 teaspoon salt

1/2 teaspoon sugar

1 tablespoon olive oil

PREP: 20 MIN; RISE: 1 HR 50 MIN; BAKE: 40 MIN
2 loaves (16 slices each)

1. Stir yeast in warm water in small bowl; let stand about 5 minutes, stirring occasionally, until yeast comes to top of water. Meanwhile, mix 3 cups of the flour, the salt and sugar in large bowl.

2. Stir yeast mixture into flour mixture, using wooden spoon, until flour is moistened. Stir in oil. Shape dough into a ball, using hands. (Dough should be soft and slightly sticky. If the dough is too wet, work into small amounts of flour until dough holds together.)

3. Place dough on lightly floured surface. Knead 10 to 12 minutes or until dough is smooth and springy. Place dough in greased and floured large bowl. Cover and let rise in warm place about 40 minutes or until double. (Dough is ready if indentation remains when touched.)

4. Gently push fist into dough to deflate. Place dough on lightly floured surface. Divide dough in half; shape each half into a ball. Cover and let rise on surface about 40 minutes or until double.

5. Grease and lightly flour 2 cookie sheets. Stretch 1 ball of dough into 18 x 6-inch rectangle by pulling edges away from each other. (If dough is sticky, dust lightly with flour while stretching.) Place on cookie sheet. Gently flatten dough with fingers until about 1 inch thick. Repeat with remaining dough. Cover and let rise about 30 minutes or until double. (Top will be uneven and bumpy.)

6. Heat oven to 375°. Dust loaves lightly with flour. Bake 35 to 40 minutes or until loaves are golden brown and sound hollow when tapped. (If necessary, cover and refrigerate 1 loaf while the other loaf bakes.) Remove from cookie sheets to wire racks; cool.

1 Slice: Calories 55 (Calories from Fat 10); Fat 1g (Saturated 0g); Cholesterol 0mg; Sodium 95mg; Carbohydrate 10g (Dietary Fiber 0g); Protein 1g
%Daily Value: Vitamin A 0%; Vitamin C 0%; Calcium 0%; Iron 4%
Diet Exchanges: 1/2 Starch

Parola di Antonio

The word ciabatta *means "slipper," and* stirata *means "pulled and pressed." This flour-dusted flatbread is shaped like an old slipper, hence its name. The dough should be quite soft and slightly sticky, but I find it is still easy to handle. To make a* grande *sandwich, I split the bread horizontally and spread it with pesto, mustard, mayonnaise or the Olive Marinade on page 178. Then I layer it with slices of cheeses, meats, roasted vegetables, greens—or whatever combination I have the urge to create. Cut it into slices and enjoy.*

A Tribute to Bread

Before the days of mass production, it was common practice for professional bakers to bake small loaves of bread daily and for Italian women to take the loaves home in cloth-covered baskets. The baking of bread had religious significance: the slits on top of the bread were a tribute to God for leavening the dough, the white dusting of flour a thanks for supplying bread in harsh, sometimes snowy winters and the cornmeal often found on the bottom a reminder of the summer's bountiful days.

RUSTIC OLIVE BREAD
Pane Alle Olive

2 packages regular active dry yeast

1 cup very warm water
(115° to 120°)

2 1/2 to 3 cups bread flour

1/2 cup whole wheat flour

1 tablespoon olive oil

1/2 teaspoon salt

1 cup imported Kalamata olives,
pitted and cut in half

PREP: 25 MIN; RISE: 1 HR; BAKE: 1 HR
1 loaf (16 slices)

1. Stir yeast in warm water in large bowl; let stand 10 minutes until yeast begins to bubble. Stir in 2 cups of the bread flour, the whole wheat flour, oil and salt until smooth. Stir in enough of the remaining bread flour to make dough easy to handle.

2. Place dough on lightly floured surface. Knead about 10 minutes or until smooth and springy. Add olives; knead about 2 minutes longer or until olives are evenly distributed.

3. Shape dough into a ball; place on floured surface. Dust top lightly with flour. Cover and let rise about 30 minutes or until double. (Dough is ready when indentation remains when touched.)

4. Grease cookie sheet; dust lightly with flour. Gently push fist into dough to deflate. Shape into round loaf. Place on cookie sheet. Let rise uncovered about 30 minutes or until double.

5. Heat oven to 375°. Bake about 1 hour or until deep golden brown. Remove from cookie sheet to wire rack; cool.

1 Slice: Calories 235 (Calories from Fat 45); Fat 5g (Saturated 1g); Cholesterol 0mg; Sodium 400mg; Carbohydrate 44g (Dietary Fiber 4g); Protein 7g
%Daily Value: Vitamin A 0%; Vitamin C 0%; Calcium 2%; Iron 20%
Diet Exchanges: 3 Starch

Parola di Antonio

During the fall harvesting of olives around the hill farmhouses, the scent of wood-burning ovens stacked with olive loaves would entice the field workers to finish their labor quickly and return home for a just reward.

Rustic Olive Bread

WHITE BREAD
Pane Bianco

4 packages regular active dry yeast

1 cup warm water (105° to 115°)

1 cup warm milk (105° to 115°)

5 1/2 to 6 cups bread flour or
  all-purpose flour

1 tablespoon salt

1 tablespoon butter or margarine,
  softened

1 teaspoon sugar

PREP: 35 MIN; RISE: 1 HR 15 MIN; BAKE: 55 MIN
1 loaf (16 slices)

1. Dissolve yeast in warm water in large bowl. Stir in milk, 4 cups of the flour, the salt, butter and sugar. Stir in enough of the remaining flour to make dough easy to handle. Place dough on lightly floured surface. Knead 5 minutes. Cover and let rest 20 minutes.

2. Knead dough on lightly floured surface about 10 minutes or until smooth and springy. Place dough in large greased bowl, turning dough to grease all sides. Cover and let rise in warm place about 45 minutes or until double. (Dough is ready if indentation remains when touched.)

3. Grease cookie sheet. Gently push fist into dough to deflate. Gently pat dough into 14 x 10-inch rectangle on lightly floured surface. Roll up tightly, beginning at 10-inch side. Pinch edge of dough into roll to seal well. Roll gently back and forth to taper ends. Place seam side down on cookie sheet. Cover and let rise in warm place about 30 minutes or until double.

4. Heat oven to 325°. Make 3 slashes, about 1/4 inch deep, across loaf; dust with flour. Bake about 55 minutes or until loaf is golden brown and sounds hollow when tapped. Remove from cookie sheet to wire rack; cool.

1 Slice: Calories 185 (Calories from Fat 20); Fat 2g (Saturated 1g); Cholesterol 5mg;
Sodium 460mg; Carbohydrate 38g (Dietary Fiber 2g); Protein 6g
%Daily Value: Vitamin A 0%; Vitamin C 0%; Calcium 2%; Iron 14%
Diet Exchanges: 2 1/2 Starch

ITALIAN FLATBREAD
Focaccia

1 package regular active dry yeast

1 cup warm water (105° to 115°)

1/4 cup olive or vegetable oil

2 teaspoons sugar

1/4 teaspoon salt

2 1/2 to 3 cups bread flour or
   all-purpose flour

Olive or vegetable oil

1 tablespoon coarse (kosher) salt,
   if desired

Red Bell Pepper and Onion Focaccia (Focaccia alla Cipolla e Peperoni Rossi): Omit coarse salt. Cook 2 medium red bell peppers, cut into 1/4-inch rings, and 1 medium onion, sliced, in 1 tablespoon olive oil in 10-inch skillet over medium heat, stirring occasionally, just until tender. Arrange on dough circles after brushing with oil.

Rosemary Focaccia (Focaccia al Rosmarino): Omit coarse salt. After brushing dough circles with oil, sprinkle each with 1 tablespoon chopped fresh rosemary leaves and 1 tablespoon grated or shredded imported Parmesan cheese.

PREP: 25 MIN; RISE: 1 HR 50 MIN; BAKE: 15 MIN
2 flatbreads (12 servings each)

1. Dissolve yeast in warm water in large bowl. Add 1/4 cup oil, the sugar, 1/4 teaspoon salt and 2 cups of the flour. Beat with electric mixer on medium speed 3 minutes, scraping bowl occasionally. Stir in enough of the remaining flour until dough is soft and leaves side of bowl.

2. Place dough on lightly floured surface. Knead 5 to 10 minutes or until dough is smooth and springy. Place dough in greased large bowl, turning dough to grease all sides. Cover and let rise in warm place 1 to 1 1/2 hours or until double. (Dough is ready when indentation remains when touched.)

3. Grease 2 cookies sheets. Gently push fist into dough to deflate. Divide in half. Press each half into 12-inch circle on cookie sheet, using oiled fingers. Cover and let rise in warm place 20 minutes.

4. Heat oven to 425°. Gently make depressions in dough at 1-inch intervals with fingers. Brush with oil; sprinkle with coarse salt. Bake 12 to 15 minutes or until golden brown.

1 Serving: Calories 80 (Calories from Fat 25); Fat 3g (Saturated 0g); Cholesterol 0mg;
Sodium 25mg; Carbohydrate 11g (Dietary Fiber 0g); Protein 2g
%Daily Value: Vitamin A 0%; Vitamin C 0%; Calcium 0%; Iron 4%
Diet Exchanges: 1 Starch

FLORENTINE ROSEMARY BREAD
Pan Di Ramerino Di Firenze

3 packages regular active dry yeast

1 1/2 cups warm water
    (105° to 115°)

3 to 3 1/2 cups bread flour or
    all-purpose flour

1 tablespoon sugar

1 teaspoon salt

1/4 cup olive oil

1 tablespoon golden raisins

1 tablespoon chopped fresh
    rosemary leaves

1 egg white, beaten

PREP: 35 MIN; RISE: 1 HR 30 MIN; BAKE: 40 MIN
6 loaves (2 servings each)

1. Dissolve yeast in warm water in large bowl. Stir in 2 cups of the flour, the sugar and salt. Stir in enough of the remaining flour to make dough easy to handle.

2. Place dough on lightly floured surface. Knead about 10 minutes or until smooth and springy. Place dough in large greased bowl; sprinkle with flour. Cover and let rise in warm place 50 to 60 minutes or until double. (Dough is ready if indentation remains when touched.)

3. Meanwhile, heat oil in 8-skillet over medium-high heat. Cook raisins and rosemary in oil 3 minutes, stirring constantly, until raisins just begin to brown; cool.

4. Grease 2 cookie sheets. Gently push fist into dough to deflate. Place dough on lightly floured surface. Knead in raisin mixture until evenly distributed. Divide dough into 6 equal parts. Shape each part into 3-inch round on cookie sheet. Cover and let rise in warm place 20 to 30 minutes or until double.

5. Heat oven to 325°. Cut an X about 1/4 inch deep in top of each round. Bake 30 minutes; brush with egg white. Bake about 10 minutes or until loaves are deep golden brown and sound hollow when tapped. (Refrigerate 3 loaves while other loaves bake if necessary.)

1 Serving: Calories 175 (Calories from Fat 45); Fat 5g (Saturated 1g); Cholesterol 0mg;
Sodium 200mg; Carbohydrate 29g (Dietary Fiber 1g); Protein 5g
%Daily Value: Vitamin A 0%; Vitamin C 0%; Calcium 0%; Iron 10%
Diet Exchanges: 2 Starch, 1/2 Fat

Florentine Rosemary Bread

SWEET BREAD WREATH
Corona Dolce

Homemade Pizza Dough for
   Three Crusts (page 150)

2 eggs, slightly beaten

1/4 cup sugar

1/2 teaspoon ground anise

1/2 teaspoon ground cinnamon

1/4 teaspoon ground nutmeg

PREP: 30 MIN; RISE: 1 HR 20 MIN; REFRIGERATE: 2 HR; BAKE: 30 MIN
1 wreath (16 slices)

1. Make Homemade Pizza Dough.

2. Heat oven to 350°. Grease cookie sheet. Divide dough into 3 equal parts. Roll each part into 26-inch rope on lightly floured surface. Braid ropes gently and loosely; pinch ends together. Shape braid into wreath on cookie sheet; pinch ends together. Cover and let rise in warm place about 1 hour or until double. (Dough is ready if indentation remains when touched.)

3. Brush eggs over dough. Mix remaining ingredients; sprinkle over dough. Bake 25 to 30 minutes or until golden brown. Remove from cookie sheet to wire rack; cool.

1 Serving: Calories 135 (Calories from Fat 20); Fat 2g (Saturated 0g); Cholesterol 25mg;
Sodium 160mg; Carbohydrate 26g (Dietary Fiber 1g); Protein 4g
%Daily Value: Vitamin A 0%; Vitamin C 0%; Calcium 0%; Iron 8%
Diet Exchanges: 1 1/2 Starch

Parola di Antonio

This beautiful, decorative bread wreath shows the versatility of pizza dough. Here it is sweetened, spiced and braided to form a wreath. You can also form the dough into other shapes—a heart, a braided loaf—whatever appeals to you.

HERBED BREADSTICKS
Grissini Speziati

Homemade Pizza Dough for Three
Crusts (page 150)

Herb Topping (below)

PREP: 20 MIN; RISE: 20 MIN; REFRIGERATE: 2 HR; BAKE: 10 MIN
24 breadsticks

1. Make Homemade Pizza Dough and Herb Topping.

2. Heat oven to 400°. Grease 2 cookie sheets. Press or roll dough into 24 x 12-inch rectangle on lightly floured surface. Sprinkle topping evenly over dough; gently press topping into dough.

3. Cut dough into 24 strips, each 12 x 1 inch. Place strips 1/2 inch apart on cookie sheets. Bake about 10 minutes or until golden brown. Remove from cookie sheets to wire racks; cool.

1 tablespoon freshly grated
    imported Parmesan cheese

1 tablespoon freshly grated
    Romano cheese

1 teaspoon dried oregano leaves

1 teaspoon dried basil leaves

1/2 teaspoon garlic salt

1/2 teaspoon pepper

Herb Topping
Mix all ingredients.

1 Breadstick: Calories 75 (Calories from Fat 10); Fat 1g (Saturated 0g); Cholesterol 0mg;
Sodium 125mg; Carbohydrate 15g (Dietary Fiber 1g); Protein 2g
%Daily Value: Vitamin A 0%; Vitamin C 0%; Calcium 0%; Iron 6%
Diet Exchanges: 1 Starch

Parola di Antonio

Grissini *are thin, crisp breadsticks believed to have been created by a Turinese baker in the late seventeenth century. I like to keep pizza dough in my refrigerator so I can bake up a quick batch of breadsticks at the spur of the moment. I prefer the herb breadsticks, but if I am serving them with a spicier dish, I'll sprinkle them with sesame seed or coarse salt before baking instead of sprinkling with herbs.*

LITTLE BREAD ROLLS
Panini

2 packages regular active dry yeast

1 cup warm water (105° to 115°)

2 1/2 to 3 cups bread flour or
all-purpose flour

2 teaspoons olive oil

1/2 teaspoon sugar

1/2 teaspoon salt

PREP: 20 MIN; RISE: 1 HR 30 MIN; BAKE: 45 MIN
6 rolls

1. Dissolve yeast in warm water in large bowl. Stir in 2 cups of the flour, the oil, sugar and salt. Stir in enough of the remaining flour to make dough easy to handle.

2. Place dough on lightly floured surface. Knead about 10 minutes until smooth and springy. Shape dough into ball; dust lightly with flour. Cover and let rise in warm place about 1 hour or until double. (Dough is ready if indentation remains when touched.)

3. Grease cookie sheet. Gently push fist into dough to deflate. Divide into 6 equal parts. Roll each part on lightly floured surface into 2 1/2-inch ball. Gently shape each ball into oval, about 3 x 1 1/2 inches, tapering ends slightly. Dust top and bottoms lightly with flour. Place on cookie sheet. Cover and let rise in warm place 30 minutes.

4. Heat oven to 350°. Bake about 45 minutes or until golden brown. Remove from cookie sheet to wire rack; cool.

1 Roll: Calories 220 (Calories from Fat 20); Fat 2g (Saturated 0g); Cholesterol 0mg;
Sodium 200mg; Carbohydrate 45g (Dietary Fiber 2g); Protein 7g
%Daily Value: Vitamin A 0%; Vitamin C 0%; Calcium 0%; Iron 16%
Diet Exchanges: 3 Starch

Parola di Antonio

Panini, *small breads or little bread rolls, are found in various shapes and sizes in Italy. In* caffe *bars you will find glass cases bursting with rows of these rolls filled with inventive and tasty combinations. Italians eat them while standing at counters when they can no longer spend hours relaxing over the midday meal.*

Left: Herbed Rolls, page 176; right: Little Bread Rolls

HERBED ROLLS
Michetta

2 packages regular active dry yeast

1 cup warm water (105° to 115°)

2 1/2 to 3 cups bread flour or
    all-purpose flour

2 teaspoons olive oil

1/2 teaspoon sugar

1/2 teaspoon salt

Herb Topping (page 173)

PREP: 20 MIN; RISE: 1 HR 45 MIN; BAKE: 40 MIN
6 rolls

1. Dissolve yeast in warm water in large bowl. Stir in 2 cups of the flour, the oil, sugar and salt. Stir in enough of the remaining flour to make dough easy to handle.

2. Place dough on lightly floured surface. Knead about 10 minutes or until smooth and springy. Shape dough into a ball; dust lightly with flour. Cover and let rise on surface about 1 hour or until double. (Dough is ready when indentation remains when touched.)

3. Grease large cookie sheet; lightly flour. Gently push fist into dough to deflate. Divide into 6 equal parts. Shape each part into a ball; flatten slightly. Place on cookie sheet. Let rise uncovered in warm place 30 minutes.

4. Make Herb Topping. Cut a circle, 1 inch in diameter and 1/4 inch deep, in top of each roll, using sharp, thin knife. Cut five evenly spaced lines, 1/4 inch deep, from circle halfway down side of roll. Sprinkle each roll with topping. Let rise uncovered in warm place 15 minutes.

5. Heat oven to 350°. Bake about 40 minutes or until golden brown. Remove from cookie sheet to wire rack; cool.

1 Roll: Calories 205 (Calories from Fat 25); Fat 3g (Saturated 1g); Cholesterol 0mg; Sodium 310mg; Carbohydrate 40g (Dietary Fiber 2g); Protein 7g
%Daily Value: Vitamin A 0%; Vitamin C 0%; Calcium 4%; Iron 16%
Diet Exchanges: 2 1/2 Starch, 1/2 Fat

Parola di Antonio

True michetta, the quintessential bread of Milan, have a crisp, crunchy crust, a flowerlike design on top and an interior that is almost hollow. This recipe doesn't create the hollow interior, but you can still enjoy the flowerlike design on top and the chewy, yeasty interior.

GRILLED PESTO-CHICKEN SANDWICH
Panini con Pollo e Pesto

3/4 cup Basil-Garlic Sauce (page 146), Walnut-Basil Sauce (page 145) or purchased basil pesto

4 boneless, skinless chicken breast halves (about 1 1/4 pounds)

1/2 teaspoon salt

4 crusty oval rolls or Little Bread Rolls (page 174), split

2 roma (plum) tomatoes, cut lengthwise into 1/4-inch slices

8 to 12 large fresh basil leaves

Broiled Pesto-Chicken Sandwich:
Marinate chicken as directed. Set oven control to broil. Brush broiler pan rack with olive or vegetable oil. Place chicken on rack in broiler pan. Broil with tops 4 to 6 inches from heat 15 to 20 minutes, turning once, until juice is no longer pink when centers of thickest pieces are cut.

PREP: 15 MIN; MARINATE: 1 HR; GRILL: 20 MIN
4 servings

1. Make Basil-Garlic Sauce; reserve 1/4 cup. Place chicken in shallow glass or plastic dish. Brush tops of chicken with half of the remaining sauce; turn chicken. Brush with other half of sauce; sprinkle with salt. Cover and refrigerate at least 1 hour but no longer than 24 hours.

2. Heat coals or gas grill as directed by manufacturer for direct heat. Grill chicken uncovered 4 to 6 inches from medium heat 15 to 20 minutes, turning once, until juice is no longer pink when centers of thickest pieces are cut.

3. Spread reserved Basil-Garlic Sauce over cut sides of rolls. Place chicken on bottom halves of rolls; top with tomatoes, basil and tops of rolls.

1 Serving: Calories 575 (Calories from Fat 340); Fat 38g (Saturated 6g); Cholesterol 65mg; Sodium 970mg; Carbohydrate 30g (Dietary Fiber 2g); Protein 30g
%Daily Value: Vitamin A 6%; Vitamin C 8%; Calcium 10%; Iron 18%
Diet Exchanges: 2 Starch, 3 Lean Meat, 6 Fat

ROASTED EGGPLANT AND RED PEPPER SANDWICH
Panini agli Ortaggi Arrosto

1/4 cup Olive Marinade (below)

1 small eggplant (about 3/4 pound), cut into 1/2-inch slices

1/2 teaspoon salt

2 large red bell peppers* (about 6 ounces each)

1 tablespoon olive oil

4 crusty oval rolls or Little Bread Rolls (page 174), split

1 jar (7 ounces) roasted sweet peppers can be substituted for the roasted fresh bell peppers. Omit peppers from step 3.

PREP: 1 HR; BAKE: 16 MIN
4 servings

1. Make Olive Marinade. Meanwhile, heat oven to 375°. Sprinkle eggplant with salt; let stand 10 minutes. Cut bell peppers lengthwise in half; remove seeds and membrane.

2. Place eggplant and peppers, skin sides down, in ungreased jelly roll pan, 15 1/2 x 10 1/2 x 1 inch, or on large cookie sheet. Brush vegetables with oil. Bake uncovered 8 minutes; turn. Bake about 8 minutes longer or until eggplant is tender and peppers have brown spots. Cool until easy to handle. Cut peppers lengthwise into 1/2-inch strips.

3. Gently toss eggplant and peppers with 1/4 cup olive marinade in large bowl; let stand 10 minutes. Fill rolls with eggplant mixture. Serve with remaining marinade.

1/2 cup imported Kalamata olives, pitted and coarsely chopped

1/2 cup imported green Greek olives, pitted and coarsely chopped

1 teaspoon small capers

1 clove garlic, coarsely chopped

1 teaspoon chopped fresh parsley

1 teaspoon chopped fresh savory leaves

1 teaspoon balsamic vinegar

1/2 cup extra-virgin olive oil

1 tablespoon freshly grated imported Parmesan cheese

Olive Marinade

Place all ingredients in food processor. Cover and process about 1 minute, using quick on-and-off motions, until coarsely chopped. Cover and refrigerate at least 1 hour to blend flavors but no longer than 1 week.

1 Serving: Calories 345 (Calories from Fat 170); Fat 19g (Saturated 4g); Cholesterol 5mg; Sodium 930mg; Carbohydrate 39g (Dietary Fiber 6g); Protein 11g
%Daily Value: Vitamin A 48%; Vitamin C 100%; Calcium 20%; Iron 14%
Diet Exchanges: 2 Starch, 2 Vegetable, 3 Fat

Roasted Eggplant and Red Pepper Sandwich

Chicken with Spicy Red and Yellow Pepper Sauce, page 208

CHAPTER FIVE

*Carne, Pollame
e Pesce*

SAVORY MEAT, CHICKEN AND
SEAFOOD MAIN COURSES

BEEF ROAST WITH PARMESAN AND CREAM
Manzo alla Panna

3-pound beef boneless rump roast

2 ounces imported Parmesan cheese, cut into 2 x 1/4 x 1/4-inch strips

2 tablespoons butter or margarine

2 tablespoons olive oil

1/2 teaspoon salt

1/2 teaspoon pepper

1/2 cup dry red wine or beef broth

1 cup whipping (heavy) cream

1/2 cup freshly grated imported Parmesan cheese

PREP: 15 MIN; COOK: 2 HR; STAND: 20 MIN
10 servings

1. Make small, deep cuts in all sides of beef with sharp knife. Insert 1 cheese strip completely in each cut.

2. Heat butter and oil in 4-quart Dutch oven over medium-high heat until butter is melted. Cook beef in butter mixture, turning occasionally, until brown on all sides. Sprinkle beef with salt and pepper. Add wine. Cook uncovered until about 5 minutes or until liquid has evaporated.

3. Pour whipping cream over beef; reduce heat. Cover and simmer about 2 hours or until beef is tender.

4. Place beef on warm platter; cover loosely with tent of aluminum foil to keep warm. Skim fat from juices in Dutch oven. Stir grated cheese into juices. Heat to boiling over medium heat, stirring constantly and scraping particles from bottom of pan. Cut beef into thin slices. Serve with cream sauce.

1 Serving: Calories 295 (Calories from Fat 170); Fat 19g (Saturated 10g); Cholesterol 105mg; Sodium 420mg; Carbohydrate 1g (Dietary Fiber 0g); Protein 30g
%Daily Value: Vitamin A 8%; Vitamin C 0%; Calcium 16%; Iron 14%
Diet Exchanges: 4 Lean Meat, 1 1/2 Fat

Parola di Antonio

Italians always allow their roasts to warm up to room temperature before cooking, a custom with which Americans may be uncomfortable due to concern about possible health hazards. One way to keep the roast tender without letting it warm to room temperature is to cut deep slits on all sides of the meat and insert bacon into the slits. The fat helps baste the meat as it cooks. I also find that inserting cheese into the meat not only adds additional fat for moistness but also adds a wonderful, subtle flavor to the meat.

GRILLED STEAK, FLORENTINE STYLE
Bistecca alla Fiorentina

1/4 cup chopped fresh parsley

1/4 cup olive oil

4 cloves garlic, cut into pieces

4 beef T-bone steaks, about 1 inch thick (about 8 ounces each)

1 teaspoon salt

1/2 teaspoon freshly ground pepper

Broiled Steak, Florentine Style:
Set oven control to broil. Brush broiler pan rack with olive or vegetable oil. Cut outer edge of fat on beef steaks diagonally at 1-inch intervals to prevent curling (do not cut into beef). Place beef on rack in broiler pan. Broil with tops 3 to 4 inches from heat 5 minutes for medium-rare or 7 minutes for medium. Turn; generously brush with oil mixture. Broil 5 to 8 minutes longer until desired doneness.

PREP: 5 MIN; GRILL: 14 MIN
4 servings

1. Brush grill rack with olive or vegetable oil. Heat coals or gas grill as directed by manufacturer for direct heat.

2. Place parsley, oil and garlic in food processor or blender. Cover and process until smooth.

3. Cut outer edge of fat on beef steaks diagonally at 1-inch intervals to prevent curling (do not cut into beef).

4. Cover and grill beef 3 to 4 inches from medium heat 5 minutes for medium-rare or 7 minutes for medium, brushing frequently with oil mixture. Turn; brush generously with oil mixture. Grill 5 to 7 minutes longer until desired doneness. Sprinkle with salt and pepper. Discard any remaining oil mixture.

1 Serving: Calories 330 (Calories from Fat 205); Fat 23g (Saturated 5g); Cholesterol 80mg; Sodium 660mg; Carbohydrate 1g (Dietary Fiber 0g); Protein 30g
%Daily Value: Vitamin A 2%; Vitamin C 4%; Calcium 2%; Iron 16%
Diet Exchanges: 4 Medium-Fat Meat, 1 Fat

Parola di Antonio

A true Bistecca alla Fiorentina *can be enjoyed only in Florence because it requires a special* Chianina *breed of beef found near Florence. However, we are privileged to have great beef available to us, so we can enjoy an almost authentic* fiorentina *T-bone steak. The steaks should consist of only the fillet and the strip, so if the steaks have a "tail" piece on the narrow end, be sure to trim it off. When handling the steaks, use tongs or a spatula instead of a fork, so you won't pierce the beef during cooking, allowing the juices to cook out.*

BEEF STEW, BOLOGNA STYLE
Manzo Stracotto Alla Bolognese

1 1/2 pounds beef boneless sirloin steak, about 1 inch thick

1 tablespoon olive oil

4 ounces sliced imported pancetta or lean bacon, cut into 1/2-inch pieces

1 medium onion, chopped (1/2 cup)

1 medium green bell pepper, chopped (1 cup)

2 cloves garlic, finely chopped

1 tablespoon chopped fresh parsley

1 cup sweet red wine or beef broth

1 tablespoon balsamic vinegar

1/4 teaspoon salt

1/4 teaspoon pepper

2 medium potatoes, cut into 1-inch pieces

1 medium carrot, thinly sliced (1/2 cup)

2 fresh or dried bay leaves

PREP: 15 MIN; COOK: 1 HR 10 MIN
6 servings

1. Remove fat from beef. Cut beef into 1-inch cubes.

2. Heat oil in nonstick 4-quart Dutch oven over medium heat. Cook pancetta, onion, bell pepper, garlic and parsley in oil about 10 minutes, stirring occasionally, until pancetta is brown.

3. Stir in beef and remaining ingredients. Heat to boiling; reduce heat. Cover and simmer about 1 hour, stirring occasionally, until beef is tender. Remove bay leaves.

1 Serving: Calories 220 (Calories from Fat 65); Fat 7g (Saturated 2g); Cholesterol 60mg; Sodium 390mg; Carbohydrate 15g (Dietary Fiber 2g); Protein 25g
%Daily Value: Vitamin A 16%; Vitamin C 22%; Calcium 2%; Iron 16%
Diet Exchanges: 1/2 Starch, 3 Lean Meat, 1 Vegetable

Parola di Antonio

This recipe comes straight from the culinary capital of Italy, Bologna. A good Lambrusco wine is the best choice, both for cooking and for drinking during the dinner. The potatoes can be peeled or unpeeled, whichever way you like them best.

Beef Stew, Bologna Style

GRILLED BEEF SHORT RIBS WITH SAVORY LEMON SAUCE

Costolette Di Manzo Braciato in Salsa Gremolata

2 pounds beef country-style
   short ribs

Savory Lemon Marinade (below)

1/2 cup dry white wine or chicken
   broth

1/2 cup crumbled dry ricotta or
   feta cheese

PREP: 10 MIN; MARINATE: 8 HR; COOK: 20 MIN
4 servings

1. Place beef in shallow glass or plastic dish. Make Savory Lemon Marinade; pour over beef. Turn beef to coat both sides. Cover dish and refrigerate at least 8 hours but no longer than 24 hours, turning beef occasionally.

2. Brush grill rack with olive or vegetable oil. Heat coals or gas grill as directed by manufacturer for direct heat. Remove beef from marinade; remove 1/4 cup marinade and reserve remaining marinade. Cover and grill beef 2 to 4 inches from medium-high heat about 16 minutes, turning and brushing occasionally with the 1/4 cup marinade during first 10 minutes grilling. Continue grilling, turning occasionally, until beef is brown on outside and light pink when cut near bone.

3. Heat remaining marinade to boiling; boil 1 minute. Stir in wine. Pour marinade over beef. Sprinkle with cheese.

1/2 cup olive oil

1 tablespoon finely shredded
   lemon peel

1/4 cup fresh lemon juice

1/4 cup chopped fresh parsley

1/2 teaspoon coarsely ground black
   pepper

1/2 teaspoon salt

4 cloves garlic, finely chopped

Savory Lemon Marinade

Mix all ingredients.

1 Serving: Calories 395 (Calories from Fat 295); Fat 33g (Saturated 9g); Cholesterol 60mg; Sodium 280mg; Carbohydrate 4g (Dietary Fiber 0g); Protein 20g
%Daily Value: Vitamin A 4%; Vitamin C 6%; Calcium 10%; Iron 10%
Diet Exchanges: 3 High-Fat Meat, 2 Fat

GRILLED MEAT AND VEGETABLE KABOBS
Spiedini Fantasia

1/4 cup Basil-Garlic Sauce (page 146) or purchased basil pesto

1 pound lamb boneless shoulder

3/4 pound beef or veal tenderloin

1/2 cup dry white wine or chicken broth

3 tablespoons fresh lemon juice

8 ounces medium mushrooms, stems removed

1 medium red bell pepper, cut into 1-inch pieces

1 medium green bell pepper, cut into 1-inch pieces

1 medium yellow bell pepper, cut into 1-inch pieces

16 fresh sage leaves

2 leeks, cut into 1-inch pieces

8 cherry tomatoes

Broiled Meat and Vegetable Kabobs: Set oven control to broil. Brush broiler pan rack with olive or vegetable oil. Broil with tops about 3 inches from heat 5 minutes. Turn kabobs; brush with marinade. Broil 10 minutes longer turning kabobs once and brush with marinade until meat is desired doneness. Discard any remaining marinade.

PREP: 25 MIN; MARINATE: 1 HR; GRILL: 16 MIN
4 servings

1. Make Basil-Garlic Sauce. Remove fat from lamb. Cut lamb and beef into 1-inch cubes. Place meat in glass or plastic bowl. Mix sauce, wine and lemon juice; pour over meat. Cover and refrigerate at least 1 hour but no longer than 24 hours.

2. Remove meat from marinade; reserve marinade. Thread meat, mushrooms, bell peppers, sage leaves and leeks alternately on each of eight 9-inch metal skewers, leaving space between each piece. Add tomato to end of each skewer.

3. Brush grill rack with olive or vegetable oil. Heat coals or gas grill as directed by manufacturer for direct heat. Cover and grill kabobs 3 to 4 inches from medium heat 8 minutes. Turn; brush generously with marinade. Grill 8 minutes longer until meat is desired doneness. Discard any remaining marinade.

1 Serving: Calories 360 (Calories from Fat 170); Fat 19g (Saturated 5g); Cholesterol 95mg; Sodium 260mg; Carbohydrate 15g (Dietary Fiber 4g); Protein 36g
%Daily Value: Vitamin A 28%; Vitamin C 100%; Calcium 10%; Iron 28%
Diet Exchanges: 4 Medium-Fat Meat, 3 Vegetable

GRILLED MEATBALLS KABOBS
Polpette allo Spiedo

1 pound ground beef, pork and veal
   mixture (meat loaf mixture)

1 tablespoon chopped fresh parsley

1 tablespoon chopped fresh or
   1 teaspoon dried basil leaves

1 teaspoon salt

1/4 teaspoon pepper

1 small onion, finely chopped
   (1/4 cup)

2 cloves garlic, finely chopped

1 egg

2 large green bell peppers, cut into
   1-inch squares

PREP: 25 MIN; GRILL: 10 MIN
4 servings

1. Brush grill rack with olive or vegetable oil. Heat coals or gas grill as directed by manufacturer for direct heat.

2. Mix all ingredients except bell peppers. Shape mixture into 1-inch balls. Thread meatballs and bell pepper squares alternately on each of four 12-inch metal skewers, leaving space between each piece.

3. Cover and grill kabobs about 4 inches from medium heat about 10 minutes, turning frequently, until meatballs are no longer pink in center.

1 Serving: Calories 240 (Calories from Fat 125); Fat 14g (Saturated 5g); Cholesterol 125mg; Sodium 660mg; Carbohydrate 7g (Dietary Fiber 2g); Protein 23g
% Daily Value: Vitamin A 6%; Vitamin C 62%; Calcium 2%; Iron 10%
Diet Exchanges: 3 Medium-Fat Meat, 1 Vegetable

Broiled Meatball Kabobs: Set oven control to broil. Brush broiler pan rack with olive or vegetable oil. Broil with tops about 3 inches from heat 5 minutes; turn kabobs. Broil 4 to 5 minutes longer or until meatballs are no longer pink in center.

Parola di Antonio

The green bell pepper is slightly more flavorful than the other colored peppers, but use any color you like. Be sure to leave some space between each meatball and pepper square so the meatballs cook evenly. Serve these smoky-tasting meatballs and peppers alongside mounds of creamy Three-Mushroom Risotto (page 54) for a flavorful outdoor treat.

Grilled Meatballs Kabobs

CHILLED VEAL WITH TUNA SAUCE
Vitello Tonnato ai Capperi

2- to 3-pound veal boneless sirloin
   roast

1/2 teaspoon pepper

1/2 pound sliced bacon

1 tablespoon olive oil

3 tablespoons olive oil

3 tablespoons fresh lemon juice

1 tablespoon capers

1 can (6 ounces) tuna in oil, drained

4 flat anchovy fillets

1 hard-cooked egg yolk

Lemon wedges, if desired

Chopped fresh parsley or parsley
   sprigs, if desired

PREP: 25 MIN; ROAST: 1 HR; STAND: 15 MIN; CHILL: 12 HR
6 servings

1. Heat oven to 325°. Sprinkle veal with pepper. Wrap bacon slices around veal. Insert meat thermometer so tip is in center of thickest part of veal and does not rest in fat. Drizzle 1 tablespoon oil over bottom of shallow roasting pan. Place veal in pan.

2. Roast uncovered 35 to 60 minutes or until thermometer reads 155°. Remove from oven; cover loosely with tent of aluminum foil and let stand 15 to 20 minutes or until temperature rises to 160° (medium). Remove bacon and discard. Cut veal into thin slices; arrange on serving platter, overlapping slightly.

3. Place 3 tablespoons oil, the lemon juice, capers, tuna, anchovy fillets and egg yolk in food processor or blender. Cover and process until light and foamy. Pour sauce over veal.

4. Cover and refrigerate at least 12 hours but no longer than 24 hours. Serve cold. Garnish with lemon wedges and parsley.

1 Serving: Calories 325 (Calories from Fat 170); Fat 19g (Saturated 5g); Cholesterol 160mg; Sodium 420mg; Carbohydrate 0g (Dietary Fiber 0g); Protein 39g
%Daily Value: Vitamin A 2%; Vitamin C 0%; Calcium 4%; Iron 10%
Diet Exchanges: 5 1/2 Lean Meat, 1/2 Fat

Parola di Antonio

This luxurious cold-veal platter from northern Italy consists of thinly sliced roasted veal that is covered with a creamy tuna sauce that has a hint of lemon. This is the ideal dish for entertaining because it can be waiting in the refrigerator for your guests' arrival. I find this is also a good way to camouflage that leftover cooked turkey after the holidays. Or to plan ahead, roast a small turkey breast just for making this delicious cold entrée to adorn your holiday buffet table.

BRAISED VEAL ROAST
Vitello in Padella

1/4 cup finely chopped imported prosciutto or fully cooked ham (about 2 ounces)

2 tablespoons chopped fresh or 1 teaspoon dried sage leaves

2 cloves garlic, finely chopped

2- to 3-pound veal boneless sirloin roast

3 tablespoons butter or margarine

1 small onion, thinly sliced

1/2 teaspoon salt

1/2 teaspoon pepper

1 cup Chianti wine, dry red wine or beef broth

1 cup whipping (heavy) cream

PREP: 15 MIN; COOK: 1 HR 25 MIN
6 servings

1. Mix prosciutto, sage and garlic. Make about 30 deep cuts in all sides of veal with sharp knife. Place 1/2 teaspoon prosciutto mixture in each cut.

2. Melt butter in 4-quart Dutch oven over medium heat. Cook onion in butter about 5 minutes, stirring occasionally, until tender. Cook veal in onion mixture about 15 minutes, turning occasionally, until brown on all sides. Sprinkle with salt and pepper. Add wine; cook uncovered about 5 minutes or until liquid is reduced to about 1/3 cup.

3. Pour whipping cream over veal. Heat to boiling; reduce heat to low. Cover and simmer about 1 hour, spooning pan juices over veal occasionally, until veal is tender.

4. Place veal on warm platter; cover loosely with tent of aluminum foil to keep warm. Skim fat from juices in Dutch oven. Heat to boiling over medium heat, stirring constantly and scraping particles from bottom of pan. Cut veal into thin slices. Serve with cream sauce.

1 Serving: Calories 360 (Calories from Fat 225); Fat 25g (Saturated 14g); Cholesterol 180mg; Sodium 520mg; Carbohydrate 3g (Dietary Fiber 0g); Protein 30g
%Daily Value: Vitamin A 14%; Vitamin C 0%; Calcium 6%; Iron 8%
Diet Exchanges: 4 Lean Meat, 1 Fat

"JUMP-IN-THE-MOUTH" VEAL
Saltimbocca alla Romana

8 veal top round or round steaks,
    1/4 inch thick (about 1 1/2
    pounds)

1/2 cup all-purpose flour

8 thin slices imported prosciutto
    or fully cooked ham

8 thin slices (1 ounce each)
    mozzarella cheese

8 fresh sage leaves

1/4 cup butter or margarine

1/2 cup dry white wine or chicken
    broth

1/2 teaspoon salt

1/4 teaspoon pepper

PREP: 15 MIN; COOK: 10 MIN
4 servings

1. Lightly pound each veal steak with meat mallet to tenderize and to flatten slightly. Coat veal with flour; shake off excess. Layer 1 slice each of prosciutto and cheese and 1 sage leaf on each veal slice. Roll up veal; tie with butcher string or secure with toothpicks.

2. Melt butter in 10-inch skillet over medium heat. Cook veal rolls in butter about 5 minutes, turning occasionally, until brown. Add wine; sprinkle rolls with salt and pepper. Cover and cook over medium-high heat about 5 minutes or until veal is no longer pink in center.

1 Serving: Calories 550 (Calories from Fat 240); Fat 30g (Saturated 17g); Cholesterol 190mg; Sodium 1190mg; Carbohydrate 15g (Dietary Fiber 1g); Protein 50g
%Daily Value: Vitamin A 8%; Vitamin C 0%; Calcium 22%; Iron 6%
Diet Exchanges: 1 Starch, 7 Lean Meat, 2 Fat

Parola di Antonio

The translation of this dish's name, "jump in the mouth," is a whimsical description of how the combination of flavors springs to life when you bite into saltimbocca. *Italians prefer veal to beef, especially milk-fed veal, and* saltimbocca *is delicious with either* vitello, *milk-fed veal, or* vitellone, *grass-fed veal.* Vitellone *is the less tender of the two, so it needs to be pounded very thin to ensure that it will become tender in the short cooking time.*

"Jump-in-the-Mouth" Veal; Garlic and Romaine Salad, page 262

PORK ROAST WITH ROSEMARY
Arista Arrosto al Rosmarino

2 tablespoons chopped fresh or
   2 teaspoons dried rosemary
   leaves, crumbled

4 cloves garlic, finely chopped

3- to 3 1/2-pound pork loin center
   roast (bone-in)

1 teaspoon salt

1/2 teaspoon pepper

1 tablespoon butter or margarine

1 small onion, chopped (1/4 cup)

2 tablespoons olive oil

PREP: 15 MIN; ROAST: 1 HR 15 MIN; STAND: 20 MIN
8 servings

1. Heat oven to 325°. Mix rosemary and garlic. Make 8 to 10 deep cuts about 2 inches apart in all sides of pork with sharp knife. Place small amount of rosemary mixture in each cut. Sprinkle pork with salt and pepper.

2. Melt butter in shallow roasting pan in oven; sprinkle with onion. Place pork in pan; drizzle with oil. Insert meat thermometer so tip is in center of thickest part of pork and does not rest in fat. Roast uncovered about 1 hour 15 minutes or until thermometer reads 155°. Remove from oven; cover with tent of aluminum foil and let stand 15 to 20 minutes or until temperature rises to 160° (medium)

1 Serving: Calories 225 (Calories from Fat 115); Fat 13g (Saturated 4g); Cholesterol 75mg; Sodium 350mg; Carbohydrate 1g (Dietary Fiber 0g); Protein 26g
%Daily Value: Vitamin A 0%; Vitamin C 0%; Calcium 0%; Iron 4%
Diet Exchanges: 4 Lean Meat

Parola di Antonio

If you love rosemary, as I do, add a bed of fresh rosemary sprigs on top of the onions before placing the pork in the pan. The piney aroma of the rosemary will permeate the air.

PEPPERED PORK CHOPS
Costolette di Maiale al Pepe

1 tablespoon whole black peppercorns, coarsely crushed

6 pork loin chops, 3/4 inch thick
(about 2 pounds)

2 tablespoons butter or margarine

2 tablespoons olive oil

4 cloves garlic, cut in half

1 cup sliced mushrooms (3 ounces)

1/2 teaspoon salt

1/2 cup dry Marsala wine, dry red
wine or beef broth

PREP: 10 MIN; COOK: 25 MIN
6 servings

1. Sprinkle half of the crushed peppercorns over one side of pork chops; gently press into pork. Turn pork; repeat with remaining peppercorns.

2. Heat butter and oil in 12-inch skillet over medium-high heat until butter is melted. Cook garlic in butter mixture, stirring frequently, until golden. Cook pork in butter mixture about 5 minutes or until brown; turn pork.

3. Add mushrooms, salt and wine; reduce heat. Cover and simmer about 15 minutes or until pork is slightly pink when cut near bone.

1 Serving: Calories 260 (Calories from Fat 155); Fat 17g (Saturated 6g); Cholesterol 75mg; Sodium 280mg; Carbohydrate 2g (Dietary Fiber 0g); Protein 24g
%Daily Value: Vitamin A 2%; Vitamin C 0%; Calcium 0%; Iron 6%
Diet Exchanges: 3 1/2 Medium-Fat Meat

PORK TENDERLOIN WITH PROSCIUTTO
Lonza di Maiale al Prosciutto

1 1/2 pounds pork tenderloin

2 tablespoons olive oil

1/4 cup chopped imported
   prosciutto or fully cooked ham
   (about 2 ounces)

2 tablespoons chopped fresh
   sage leaves

2 tablespoons chopped fresh parsley

2 tablespoons chopped sun-dried
   tomatoes in oil

1 small onion, chopped (1/4 cup)

1/2 cup dry white wine or
   chicken broth

1/2 cup whipping (heavy) cream
   or half-and-half

1/2 teaspoon pepper

1/4 teaspoon salt

PREP: 10 MIN; COOK: 35 MIN
6 servings

1. Cut pork diagonally across grain into 1/2-inch slices. Heat oil in 12-inch skillet over medium-high heat. Cook prosciutto, sage, parsley, tomatoes and onion in oil about 5 minutes, stirring frequently, until onion is tender.

2. Add pork to skillet. Cook about 10 minutes, turning pork occasionally, until pork is light brown. Stir in remaining ingredients. Heat to boiling; reduce heat. Simmer uncovered about 20 minutes, stirring occasionally, until pork is no longer pink in center and sauce is thickened.

1 Serving: Calories 255 (Calories from Fat 145); Fat 16g (Saturated 6g); Cholesterol 90mg; Sodium 290mg; Carbohydrate 3g (Dietary Fiber 1g); Protein 26g
%Daily Value: Vitamin A 6%; Vitamin C 4%; Calcium 2%; Iron 8%
Diet Exchanges: 4 Lean Meat, 1 Fat

Parola di Antonio

Italian prosciutto, slowly cured and aged, is usually sweet tasting and is an ideal accompaniment to appetizers and other meat dishes. In this recipe, it marries well with the subtle yet zealous flavor of sun-dried tomatoes. Italian cooks enjoy simple, natural flavors such as these, and you can too!

Pork Tenderloin with Prosciutto

NEW-STYLE PORK CHOPS
Maiale Nuovo Stile

6 pork loin or rib chops, about
  1 inch thick (about 2 pounds)

1 cup dry Marsala wine, dry red
  wine or beef broth

1 tablespoon balsamic vinegar

1 tablespoon fresh lemon juice

1 teaspoon honey

2 tablespoons olive oil

1 tablespoon chopped fresh
  thyme leaves

1 tablespoon chopped fresh parsley

1/2 teaspoon salt

1/2 teaspoon pepper

1 cup imported Kalamata olives,
  pitted

1 medium red onion, chopped

2 cloves garlic, finely chopped

PREP: 10 MIN; MARINATE: 8 HR; COOK: 45 MIN
6 servings

1. Place pork in shallow glass or plastic dish. Mix wine, vinegar, lemon juice and honey; pour over pork. Turn pork to coat both sides. Cover and refrigerate at least 8 hours but no longer than 24 hours, turning occasionally.

2. Heat oil in 12-inch skillet over medium-high heat. Cook remaining ingredients in oil about 5 minutes, stirring frequently, until onion is tender.

3. Remove pork from marinade; reserve marinade. Add pork to skillet. Cook about 10 minutes, turning pork once, until pork is brown. Add reserved marinade. Heat to boiling; reduce heat. Cover and simmer about 20 minutes or until pork is slightly pink when cut near bone. Serve pork with pan sauce.

1 Serving: Calories 230 (Calories from Fat 115); Fat 13g (Saturated 3g); Cholesterol 65mg; Sodium 430mg; Carbohydrate 6g (Dietary Fiber 1g); Protein 23g
%Daily Value: Vitamin A 0%; Vitamin C 2%; Calcium 2%; Iron 10%
Diet Exchanges: 3 Medium-Fat Meat, 1 Vegetable

Parola di Antonio

A departure from regular run-of-the-mill pork chops, this recipe offers a surprising twist of flavor with the tangy sour taste of vinegar and wine with the sweet hint of honey. A longer marinating time is in order for a flavorful, tender rendition. As always, fresh herbs are a top priority.

New-Style Pork Chops

BEANS WITH SAUSAGE
Salsiccia e Fagioli

2 cups Classic Tomato Sauce*
   (page 140)

1 tablespoon olive oil

1 medium red onion, chopped

1 tablespoon chopped fresh parsley

1 tablespoon chopped fresh
   basil leaves

1 pound bulk Italian sausage,
   crumbled

2 tablespoons dry red wine,
   if desired

1 can (19 ounces) fava beans
   or cannellini beans, drained

*2 cups tomato pasta sauce (from
28-ounce jar) can be substituted for
the Classic Tomato Sauce.

PREP: 4 MIN; COOK: 40 MIN
6 servings

1. Make Classic Tomato Sauce.

2. While sauce is simmering, heat oil in 10-inch skillet over medium-high heat. Cook onion, parsley and basil in oil about 5 minutes, stirring occasionally, until onion is tender. Stir in sausage. Cook about 10 minutes, stirring frequently, until sausage is no longer pink; drain.

3. Stir in sauce and remaining ingredients. Heat to boiling; reduce heat. Simmer uncovered 20 minutes, stirring occasionally, to blend the flavors.

1 Serving: Calories 320 (Calories from Fat 170); Fat 19g (Saturated 6g); Cholesterol 45mg; Sodium 850mg; Carbohydrate 26g (Dietary Fiber 7g); Protein 18g
%Daily Value: Vitamin A 8%; Vitamin C 30%; Calcium 4%; Iron 14%
Diet Exchanges: 2 Starch, 2 Medium-Fat Meat

Parola di Antonio

Clearly a southern Italian recipe, this dish is versatile as an entrée or as a topping for polenta. Traditionally, it was served in the wintertime and prepared in thick clay casseroles placed in the fireplace amidst glowing coals. Fava beans are in season during winter months in southern Italy, and the slow cooking brings out their full flavor. Other large beans, such as cannellini and butter beans, work as well. A robust red wine such as Chianti or Burgundy is recommended to complement the flavors.

GRILLED LAMB CHOPS WITH MINT

Costolette d'Agnello alla Menta

8 lamb loin or rib chops, 1 inch thick (about 2 pounds)

1/4 cup chopped fresh mint leaves

1/2 cup red wine vinegar

1/4 cup olive oil

1 tablespoon sugar

1/2 teaspoon salt

1/4 teaspoon pepper

Broiled Lamb Chops with Mint:
Marinate lamb as directed. Set oven control to broil. Place lamb on rack in broiler pan. Broil with tops 3 to 4 inches from heat 5 minutes for medium-rare (145°) or 7 minutes for medium (160°). Turn; brush generously with marinade. Broil 4 minutes longer until desired doneness. Discard any remaining marinade.

PREP: 10 MIN; MARINATE: 1 HR; GRILL: 11 MIN
4 servings

1. Cut outer edge of fat on lamb chops diagonally at 1-inch intervals to prevent curling (do not cut into lamb). Place lamb in rectangular baking dish, 11 x 7 x 1 1/2 inches.

2. Place 1/4 cup of the mint and the remaining ingredients in food processor or blender. Cover and process until smooth; pour over lamb. Cover and refrigerate at least 1 hour but no longer than 8 hours.

3. Brush grill rack with olive or vegetable oil. Heat coals or gas grill as directed by manufacturer for direct heat. Remove lamb from marinade; reserve marinade. Cover and grill lamb 3 to 4 inches from medium heat 5 minutes for medium-rare (145°) or 7 minutes for medium (160°). Turn; brush generously with marinade. Grill 4 minutes longer until desired doneness. Discard any remaining marinade.

1 Serving: Calories 250 (Calories from Fat 135); Fat 15g (Saturated 4g); Cholesterol 80mg; Sodium 360mg; Carbohydrate 3g (Dietary Fiber 0g); Protein 26g
%Daily Value: Vitamin A 2%; Vitamin C 4%; Calcium 0%; Iron 12%
Diet Exchanges: 4 Lean Meat, 1/2 Fat

LAMB WITH SWEET PEPPERS AND GARLIC SAUCE
Agnello All'Aglio e Peperoni Dolci

2 pounds lamb boneless shoulder

2 tablespoons olive oil

1/4 cup chopped fresh parsley

1/4 cup chopped fresh mint leaves

4 anchovy fillets in oil, finely
    chopped

4 cloves garlic, finely chopped

2 medium green onions, thinly sliced
    (2 tablespoons)

1 medium yellow bell pepper,
    cut into 1-inch squares

1 medium red bell pepper,
    cut into 1-inch squares

1 teaspoon salt

1/2 teaspoon pepper

1 cup dry white wine or
    chicken broth

3 tablespoons all-purpose flour

PREP: 15 MIN; COOK: 20 MIN; BAKE: 45 MIN
4 servings

1. Heat oven to 375°. Remove fat from lamb. Cut lamb into 1-inch pieces.

2. Heat oil in ovenproof 4-quart Dutch oven over medium-high heat. Cook parsley, mint, anchovies, garlic and onions in oil about 5 minutes, stirring frequently, until onions are tender.

3. Stir in lamb. Cook about 10 minutes, stirring occasionally, until lamb is brown. Stir in bell peppers. Sprinkle with salt and pepper.

4. Shake wine and flour in tightly covered container until smooth; stir into lamb mixture. Heat to boiling. Cover and bake about 45 minutes or until lamb is tender.

1 Serving: Calories 310 (Calories from Fat 145); Fat 16g (Saturated 5g); Cholesterol 105mg; Sodium 950mg; Carbohydrate 9g (Dietary Fiber 2g); Protein 35g
%Daily Value: Vitamin A 22%; Vitamin C 78%; Calcium 4%; Iron 22%
Diet Exchanges: 4 1/2 Lean Meat, 2 Vegetable

Parola di Antonio

This hearty lamb stew works best when baked in a clay casserole, so the wine flavor and moisture will be completely infused into the meat. So if you have a clay casserole or pot, go ahead and use it. An aromatic dry white wine such as Vernaccia or Malvasia will suit this dish well, and also makes an excellent accompaniment for the dinner.

Lamb with Sweet Peppers and Garlic Sauce

VENISON WITH ROSEMARY SAUCE
Cervo al Rosmarino

8 venison chops or steaks,
   1/2 inch thick

1/2 teaspoon salt

1/2 teaspoon pepper

1/4 cup butter or margarine

1 tablespoon chopped fresh or
   1 teaspoon dried rosemary
   leaves, crumbled

2 cloves garlic, cut in half

1/4 cup Chianti wine, dry red wine
   or beef broth

1/4 cup whipping (heavy) cream

**Pork Chops with Rosemary Sauce
(Costolette di Maiale al
Rosmarino):** Substitute 4 pork loin
chops, 3/4 inch thick (about 1 1/2
pounds), for the venison chops.
After adding the wine and whipping
cream, increase cook time to about
15 minutes or until pork is slightly
pink when cut near bone.

PREP: 15 MIN; COOK: 25 MIN
4 servings

1. Remove fat from venison. Sprinkle venison with salt and pepper.

2. Melt butter in 12-inch skillet over medium heat. Cook rosemary and garlic in butter, stirring occasionally, until garlic is golden. Cook venison in butter mixture about 10 minutes, turning once, until venison is brown.

3. Add wine and whipping cream. Heat to boiling; reduce heat to low. Cover and cook about 10 minutes or until venison is tender.

1 Serving: Calories 420 (Calories from Fat 200); Fat 22g (Saturated 12g); Cholesterol 245mg; Sodium 470mg; Carbohydrate 1g (Dietary Fiber 0g); Protein 54g
%Daily Value: Vitamin A 12%; Vitamin C 0%; Calcium 2%; Iron 44%
Diet Exchanges: 7 1/2 Lean Meat

ROASTED CHICKEN WITH LEMON AND HERBS
Pollo Arrosto al Limone ed Erbette

4 cloves garlic, finely chopped

1 tablespoon chopped fresh flat-leaf
   or curly parsley

1 tablespoon chopped fresh
   sage leaves

1 tablespoon chopped fresh chives

3- to 3 1/2-pound whole
   broiler-fryer chicken

1 lemon, cut in half

2 tablespoons olive oil

1/2 teaspoon salt

1/4 teaspoon pepper

PREP: 15 MIN; ROAST: 1 HR 30 MIN
6 servings

1. Heat oven to 375°. Mix garlic, parsley, sage and chives.

2. Fold wings of chicken across back with tips touching. Make several 1-inch-deep cuts in chicken. Insert about 1/2 teaspoon herb mixture in each cut until all herb mixture is used. Rub lemon halves over skin of the chicken. Squeeze remaining juice from lemon halves; set aside.

3. Tie or skewer drumsticks to tail. Place chicken, breast side up, on rack in shallow roasting pan. Drizzle oil over chicken; sprinkle with salt and pepper. Insert meat thermometer so tip is in thickest part of inside thigh muscle and does not touch bone.

4. Roast uncovered 1 to 1 1/2 hours, brushing occasionally with remaining lemon juice, until thermometer reads 180° and juice of chicken is no longer pink when center of thigh is cut. Remove from oven; let stand about 15 minutes for easiest carving.

1 Serving: Calories 255 (Calories from Fat 145); Fat 16g (Saturated 4g); Cholesterol 85mg; Sodium 280mg; Carbohydrate 1g (Dietary Fiber 0g); Protein 27g
%Daily Value: Vitamin A 4%; Vitamin C 0%; Calcium 2%; Iron 6%
Diet Exchanges: 4 Lean Meat, 1 Fat

Parola di Antonio

Many Italians grew up accustomed to this simple yet rewarding recipe. Reserved for Sundays, it was (and still is) an opportunity to brighten the family table and have a "shared" course besides the traditional daily pasta fix. An excellent accompaniment is roasted potatoes and red onions. To make, cut several baking potatoes into 1 1/2-inch pieces and cut a couple of onions into wedges; tuck the potatoes and onions around the chicken in the roasting pan about 30 minutes after the chicken has started roasting. Sprinkle them with salt and pepper and some chopped fresh parsley for a little added flavor.

ROASTED CHICKEN WITH WALNUT-BASIL SAUCE
Pollo allo Spiedo con Pesto

3/4 cup Walnut-Basil Sauce
(page 145)

3- to 3 1/2-pound whole
broiler-fryer chicken

2 tablespoons olive oil

1/2 cup chopped red onion

1 medium stalk celery, chopped
(1/2 cup)

2 tablespoons chopped pitted
imported Kalamata olives

PREP: 15 MIN; ROAST: 1 HR 30 MIN
6 servings

1. Heat oven to 375°. Make Walnut-Basil Sauce.

2. Starting at the back opening of the chicken and using fingers, carefully separate skin from meat on the chicken breast and thighs, being careful not to tear skin. Spread about 1/4 cup of the sauce between the skin and meat of the chicken. (A couple of whole basil leaves can be placed under the skin if desired).

3. Heat oil in 10-inch skillet over medium heat. Cook onion, celery and olives in oil about 5 minutes, stirring occasionally, until celery is tender.

4. Fold wings of chicken across back with tips touching. Spoon onion mixture into cavity of chicken. Tie or skewer drumsticks to tail. Place chicken, breast side up, on rack in shallow roasting pan. Insert meat thermometer so tip is in thickest part of inside thigh muscle and does not touch bone.

5. Brush chicken with about half of the remaining sauce. Roast uncovered 1 to 1 1/2 hours, brushing occasionally with remaining sauce, until thermometer reads 180° and juice of chicken is no longer pick when center of thigh is cut. Remove from oven; let stand about 15 minutes for easiest carving.

1 Serving: Calories 375 (Calories from Fat 260); Fat 29g (Saturated 6g); Cholesterol 85mg; Sodium 170mg; Carbohydrate 2g (Dietary Fiber 1g); Protein 27g
%Daily Value: Vitamin A 4%; Vitamin C 2%; Calcium 4%; Iron 8%
Diet Exchanges: 4 Medium-Fat Meat, 2 Fat

Roasted Chicken with Walnut-Basil Sauce

CHICKEN WITH SPICY RED AND YELLOW PEPPER SAUCE
Pollo alla Peperonata

3- to 3 1/2-pound cut-up
   broiler-fryer chicken

1/2 cup all-purpose flour

1/4 cup chopped fresh parsley

1 tablespoon chopped anchovy
   fillets in oil

1 teaspoon crushed red pepper

2 cloves garlic, finely chopped

2 tablespoons olive oil

1 large red bell pepper, cut into
   1-inch pieces

1 large yellow bell pepper, cut into
   1-inch pieces

1 tablespoon chopped fresh or
   1 teaspoon dried basil leaves

1/2 cup dry white wine or chicken
   broth

1 teaspoon salt

PREP: 15 MIN; COOK: 10 MIN; BAKE: 1 HR
6 servings

1. Heat oven to 375°. Coat chicken with flour; shake off excess flour.

2. Mix parsley, anchovies, red pepper and garlic. Heat oil in 12-inch skillet over medium-high heat. Cook parsley mixture in oil 5 minutes, stirring frequently. Add chicken. Cook about 10 minutes, turning once, until chicken is lightly browned on all sides.

3. Place chicken, skin sides down, in ungreased rectangular pan, 13 x 9 x 2 inches. Arrange bell peppers around chicken. Sprinkle basil over chicken and bell peppers.

4. Add wine to skillet. Heat to boiling, stirring constantly to loosen particles on bottom of skillet; pour over chicken and peppers. Sprinkle with salt.

5. Bake uncovered 30 minutes. Turn chicken. Bake about 30 minutes longer or until juice of chicken is no longer pink when centers of thickest pieces are cut.

1 Serving: Calories 320 (Calories from Fat 155); Fat 17g (Saturated 4g); Cholesterol 85mg; Sodium 570mg; Carbohydrate 12g (Dietary Fiber 1g); Protein 29g
%Daily Value: Vitamin A 22%; Vitamin C 94%; Calcium 4%; Iron 12%
Diet Exchanges: 4 Medium-Fat Meat, 2 Vegetable, 1 Fat

Parola di Antonio

Swing to the Deep South—of Italy, that is—with this flavorful dish. The intense heat from the crushed red pepper in the soffritto—*a mixture of onion, garlic and other vegetables and herbs that are quickly sautéed in oil or butter—penetrates into the chicken, along with the pleasant underlying flavor of the sweet basil and peppers. This recipe is a flashback to the peasant countryside inns of southern Italy, served at your own table.*

HUNTER'S CHICKEN
Pollo alla Cacciatora

1/2 cup all-purpose flour

1 teaspoon salt

1/2 teaspoon pepper

3- to 3 1/2-pound cut-up
broiler-fryer chicken

1/4 cup olive oil

1 medium onion, sliced

1 cup dry white wine or chicken
broth

2 cups sliced mushrooms
(about 5 ounces)

1 cup imported Kalamata olives,
pitted, or pitted large ripe olives

1 cup canned Italian-style pear-
shaped tomatoes, drained and
chopped

1/2 cup chicken broth

PREP: 20 MIN; COOK: 45 MIN
6 servings

1. Mix flour, salt and pepper. Coat chicken with flour mixture; shake off excess flour mixture.

2. Heat oil in 12-inch skillet or 4-quart Dutch oven over medium-high heat. Cook onion in oil about 5 minutes, stirring occasionally, until tender. Add chicken. Cook about 15 minutes, turning occasionally, until brown on all sides. Stir in wine. Cook uncovered until liquid has evaporated.

3. Stir in remaining ingredients. Heat to boiling; reduce heat. Cover and simmer about 20 minutes or until juice of chicken is no longer pink when centers of thickest pieces are cut.

1 Serving: Calories 380 (Calories from Fat 225); Fat 25g (Saturated 5g); Cholesterol 85mg; Sodium 910mg; Carbohydrate 12g (Dietary Fiber 2g); Protein 29g
%Daily Value: Vitamin A 8%; Vitamin C 6%; Calcium 6%; Iron 16%
Diet Exchanges: 1 Starch, 4 Medium-Fat Meat

Parola di Antonio

Cacciatora *means "hunter style" in Italian. One Italian legend holds that this dish was created by a hunter's wife when the unlucky hunter returned home with only a few mushrooms and olives. Others attribute this recipe to hunters who used basic ingredients—olive oil, tomatoes, mushrooms and wine—to flavor their catch. Whether using wild rabbit or other game, or chicken or veal from the market, a cacciatora combines meats and basic ingredients into a memorable dish.*

CHICKEN BAKED WITH ARTICHOKES AND POTATOES
Pollo con Carciofi e Patate

2 tablespoons olive oil

1/2 pound chicken livers, chopped

1 medium onion, chopped (1/2 cup)

2 cloves garlic, finely chopped

2 tablespoons chopped fresh or
  1 teaspoon dried sage leaves,
  crumbled

1 tablespoon chopped fresh parsley

1 tablespoon capers

1 can (14 ounces) artichoke hearts,
  drained and cut into fourths

3- to 3 1/2-pound cut-up broiler-
  fryer chicken

1 1/2 pounds new potatoes (10 to
  12), cut into 1-inch pieces

1/2 cup dry white wine or chicken
  broth

2 tablespoons fresh lemon juice

1 teaspoon salt

1 teaspoon freshly ground pepper

PREP: 15 MIN; COOK: 20 MIN; BAKE: 1 HR
6 servings

1. Heat oven to 425°.

2. Heat oil in 10-inch skillet over medium-high heat. Cook livers, onion, garlic, sage, parsley and capers in oil about 8 minutes, stirring frequently, until livers are no longer red. Spread liver mixture in ungreased rectangular pan, 13 x 9 x 2 inches.

3. Spread artichokes over liver mixture. Place chicken, skin sides down, and potatoes on artichokes. Mix wine and lemon juice; pour over chicken and potatoes. Sprinkle with salt and pepper.

4. Bake uncovered 30 minutes. Turn chicken and potatoes. Bake about 30 minutes longer or until chicken is brown on outside and juice of chicken is no longer pink when centers of the thickest pieces are cut.

1 Serving: Calories 400 (Calories from Fat 160); Fat 18g (Saturated 5g); Cholesterol 230mg; Sodium 720mg; Carbohydrate 27g (Dietary Fiber 6g); Protein 36g
%Daily Value: Vitamin A 100%; Vitamin C 18%; Calcium 6%; Iron 28%
Diet Exchanges: 1 Starch, 4 Medium-Fat Meat, 2 Vegetable, 1 Fat

Parola di Antonio

This down-to-earth, simple recipe is as easy to make as it is to enjoy. The blend of flavors and ingredients makes it a natural for a hearty dinner. For a variation from central Italy, use a couple of bay leaves for the sage and chopped fresh rosemary for the parsley. Or give it a little zest by stirring a couple tablespoons of honey and a dash or two of ground saffron into the liver mixture before spreading it in the pan.

Chicken Baked with Artichokes and Potatoes

CHICKEN IN OLIVE-WINE SAUCE
Pollo alle Olive Marengo

2 slices bacon, cut into 1-inch pieces

1 medium onion, chopped (1/2 cup)

2 cloves garlic, finely chopped

1 tablespoon chopped fresh or
   1 teaspoon dried rosemary
   leaves, crumbled

4 boneless, skinless chicken breast
   halves (about 1 1/4 pounds)

1/2 cup pimiento-stuffed olives

1/2 cup dry red wine or chicken
   broth

1 cup seasoned croutons

1 tablespoon chopped fresh parsley

PREP: 10 MIN; COOK: 25 MIN
4 servings

1. Cook bacon, onion, garlic and rosemary in 10-inch skillet over medium-high heat about 8 minutes, stirring occasionally, until bacon is crisp. Remove bacon with slotted spoon; set aside.

2. Add chicken to skillet. Cook about 5 minutes, turning frequently, until chicken is brown. Add olives, wine and bacon. Cover and cook about 12 minutes or until juice of chicken is no longer pink when centers of thickest pieces are cut.

3. Place chicken on serving platter. Sprinkle with croutons and parsley.

1 Serving: Calories 270 (Calories from Fat 80); Fat 9g (Saturated 2g); Cholesterol 90mg; Sodium 620mg; Carbohydrate 9g (Dietary Fiber 1g); Protein 34g
%Daily Value: Vitamin A 2%; Vitamin C 2%; Calcium 4%; Iron 10%
Diet Exchanges: 4 Very Lean Meat, 2 Vegetable, 1 1/2 Fat

CHICKEN WITH RED WINE SAUCE
Pollo al Marsala

4 boneless, skinless chicken breast
halves (about 1 1/4 pounds)

1/3 cup all-purpose flour

1/4 teaspoon salt

1/4 teaspoon pepper

2 tablespoons olive oil

2 cloves garlic, finely chopped

1 cup sliced mushrooms (3 ounces)

1/4 cup chopped fresh parsley or
1 tablespoon parsley flakes

1/2 cup dry Marsala wine or
chicken broth

PREP: 20 MIN; COOK: 23 MIN
4 servings

1. Flatten each chicken breast half to 1/4-inch thickness between sheets of plastic wrap or waxed paper. Mix flour, salt and pepper. Coat chicken with flour mixture; shake off excess flour.

2. Heat oil in 10-inch skillet over medium-high heat. Cook garlic, mushrooms and parsley in oil 5 minutes, stirring frequently.

3. Add chicken to skillet. Cook uncovered about 8 minutes, turning once, until chicken is brown. Add wine. Cook uncovered 8 to 10 minutes or until chicken is no longer pink in center.

1 Serving: Calories 290 (Calories from Fat 100); Fat 11g (Saturated 2g); Cholesterol 85mg; Sodium 230mg; Carbohydrate 11g (Dietary Fiber 1g); Protein 33g
%Daily Value: Vitamin A 2%; Vitamin C 4%; Calcium 2%; Iron 10%
Diet Exchanges: 1/2 Starch, 4 Lean Meat, 1 Vegetable

CHICKEN BREASTS WITH TARRAGON-MUSTARD SAUCE

Petti di Pollo al Dragoncello e Senape

6 boneless, skinless chicken breast
   halves (about 1 3/4 pounds)

1/3 cup all-purpose flour

2 tablespoons olive oil

8 medium green onions, sliced
   (1/2 cup)

2 tablespoons chopped fresh or
   1 1/2 teaspoons dried tarragon
   leaves

1/2 cup dry white wine or chicken
   broth

1 1/2 cups whipping (heavy) cream

2 teaspoons stone-ground mustard

1 teaspoon finely chopped seeded
   red jalapeño chili or 1/4 teaspoon ground red pepper
   (cayenne)

1/2 teaspoon salt

1/2 teaspoon pepper

PREP: 15 MIN; COOK: 40 MIN
6 servings

1. Flatten each chicken breast half to 1/4-inch thickness between sheets of plastic wrap or waxed paper. Coat chicken with flour; shake off excess flour.

2. Heat oil in 12-inch skillet over medium heat. Cook onions and tarragon in oil about 3 minutes, stirring occasionally, until onions are tender. Cook 3 pieces chicken in onion mixture about 5 minutes, turning occasionally, until chicken is lightly browned. Remove chicken from skillet; cover loosely with aluminum foil tent to keep warm. Repeat with remaining chicken.

3. Add wine to skillet. Cook uncovered, stirring constantly to loosen particles on bottom of skillet, until liquid has evaporated.

4. Stir whipping cream, mustard, chili, salt and pepper into skillet. Heat to boiling; reduce heat. Simmer uncovered about 5 minutes, stirring occasionally, until slightly thickened.

5. Return chicken to skillet. Cover and cook over medium-low heat 10 to 15 minutes, spooning sauce over chicken occasionally, until chicken is no longer pink in center.

1 Serving: Calories 400 (Calories from Fat 245); Fat 27g (Saturated 13g); Cholesterol 145mg; Sodium 310mg; Carbohydrate 7g (Dietary Fiber 0g); Protein 31g
%Daily Value: Vitamin A 14%; Vitamin C 2%; Calcium 6%; Iron 8%
Diet Exchanges: 1/2 Starch, 4 Lean Meat, 3 Fat

Parola di Antonio

Hailing from the Alpine region of Italy, this recipe marries the richness of cream with the light, almost exotic flavor of the spices. Well known by Venetian merchants who were expert spice traders for centuries, mustard and other spices were introduced to Europe from the Middle East and Far East.

Chicken Breasts with Tarragon-Mustard Sauce;
Warm Tomato and Olive Salad, page 270

CHICKEN BREASTS IN LEMON-CAPER SAUCE
Piccata di Pollo

4 boneless, skinless chicken breast halves (about 1 1/4 pounds)

1/3 cup all-purpose flour

1/4 cup butter or margarine

2 cloves garlic, finely chopped

1 cup dry white wine or chicken broth

2 tablespoons fresh lemon juice

1/4 teaspoon pepper

1 tablespoon capers

PREP: 15 MIN; COOK: 16 MIN
4 servings

1. Flatten each chicken breast half to 1/4-inch thickness between sheets of plastic wrap or waxed paper. Coat chicken with flour; shake off excess flour.

2. Melt butter in 12-inch skillet over medium-high heat. Cook chicken and garlic in butter about 6 minutes, turning once, until chicken is brown.

3. Add wine and lemon juice; reduce heat to medium. Sprinkle chicken with pepper. Cook 8 to 10 minutes, turning once, until chicken is no longer pink in center. Sprinkle with capers.

Veal in Lemon-Caper Sauce (Vitello in Salsa oi Capperi): Substitute 1 1/2 pounds veal for scallopini, (about 1/4 inch thick) for the chicken. Decrease wine to 1/2 cup. Make as directed above—except after adding wine and lemon juice, heat just until hot (do not cook 8 to 10 minutes). Sprinkle with capers.

1 Serving: Calories 340 (Calories from Fat 145); Fat 16g (Saturated 8g); Cholesterol 115mg; Sodium 220mg; Carbohydrate 8g (Dietary Fiber 0g); Protein 32g
%Daily Value: Vitamin A 10%; Vitamin C 2%; Calcium 2%; Iron 10%
Diet Exchanges: 1/2 Starch, 4 Lean Meat, 2 Fat

Parola di Antonio

The term piccata *is a variant on* piccante, *or "sharp" and "tangy." This light, zesty dish from northern Italy combines tangy lemon juice with the briny flavor of capers. Since Roman times, capers have been a basic ingredient in Italy's favorite sauces. Beautiful caper bushes grow throughout the Mediterranean countries. The caper buds are picked before they flower, pickled in a brine made with sea salt and aged for several months.*

CHICKEN, MILAN STYLE
Pollo alla Milanese

6 boneless, skinless chicken breast
halves (about 1 3/4 pounds)

1/2 teaspoon salt

1/4 teaspoon pepper

2 eggs, beaten

1 tablespoon fresh lemon juice

1/3 cup all-purpose flour

1 cup Italian-style dry bread crumbs

1/2 cup butter or margarine

1 lemon, cut into wedges

Chopped fresh parsley or parsley
sprigs, if desired

PREP: 20 MIN; COOK: 15 MIN
6 servings

1. Flatten each chicken breast half to 1/4-inch thickness between sheets of plastic wrap or waxed paper. Sprinkle with salt and pepper. Mix eggs and lemon juice. Coat chicken with flour; shake off excess flour. Dip chicken into egg mixture, then coat with bread crumbs; shake off excess crumbs.

2. Melt butter in 12-inch skillet over medium heat. Cook chicken in butter 10 to 15 minutes, turning once, until chicken is golden brown on outside and no longer pink in center.

3. Place chicken on warm platter; pour any remaining butter from skillet over chicken. Garnish with lemon wedges and parsley.

Veal, Milan Style (Vitello alla Mila): Substitute 6 veal cutlets, about 1/2 inch thick, for the chicken. Make as directed—except do not flatten; cook in butter about 8 minutes, turning once, until veal is light golden brown.

1 Serving: Calories 390 (Calories from Fat 200); Fat 22g (Saturated 11g); Cholesterol 190mg; Sodium 530mg; Carbohydrate 16g (Dietary Fiber 1g); Protein 33g
%Daily Value: Vitamin A 14%; Vitamin C 0%; Calcium 6%; Iron 12%
Diet Exchanges: 1 Starch, 4 Lean Meat, 2 Fat

CHICKEN WITH SAVORY SAUCE
Tranci di Pollo All'Agro

2 tablespoons olive oil

4 medium green onions, sliced
(1/4 cup)

2 tablespoons chopped fresh
rosemary leaves

2 tablespoons chopped fresh parsley

2 teaspoons chopped fresh thyme
leaves

2 cloves garlic, finely chopped

1 red jalapeño chili, seeded and
finely chopped

6 boneless, skinless chicken thighs
or 4 chicken breast halves
(about 1 1/4 pounds)

1 cup sliced shiitake or regular
white mushrooms (3 ounces)

1 cup dry white wine or
chicken broth

1 tablespoon balsamic vinegar

1 tablespoon currants

1/2 teaspoon salt

PREP: 15 MIN; COOK: 1 HR
4 servings

1. Heat oil in 12-inch skillet over medium heat. Cook onions, rosemary, parsley, thyme, garlic and chili in oil 5 minutes, stirring frequently.

2. Add chicken to skillet. Cook about 15 minutes, turning occasionally, until chicken is brown. Add mushrooms, 1/2 cup of the wine and the vinegar. Heat to boiling; reduce heat. Simmer uncovered about 5 minutes or until about half of the liquid has evaporated.

3. Pour remaining 1/2 cup wine over chicken; sprinkle with currants and salt. Cover and simmer about 20 minutes or until juice of chicken is no longer pink when centers of thickest pieces are cut. Uncover and cook 5 minutes longer to crisp chicken.

1 Serving: Calories 260 (Calories from Fat 90); Fat 10g (Saturated 2g); Cholesterol 85mg; Sodium 380mg; Carbohydrate 6g (Dietary Fiber 1g); Protein 32g
%Daily Value: Vitamin A 12%; Vitamin C 22%; Calcium 4%; Iron 12%
Diet Exchanges: 4 Lean Meat, 1 Vegetable

Parola di Antonio

This interesting recipe is also known as pollo ubriaco *("drunken chicken"); sometimes two full cups of wine (one white and one red) are added. In this case, the vinegar offers the contrast of flavor in place of red wine, and the currants bring an interesting sweet effect to the peppery undertone.*
Dip slices of toasted rustic bread in the juices for a delicious treat.

Chicken with Savory Sauce;
Tomato and Potato Salad with Herbs, page 271

BREADED CHICKEN CUTLETS WITH RED ONION
Pollo al Burro e Cipolla

6 boneless, skinless chicken breast
halves (about 1 3/4 pounds)

2 eggs

1 tablespoon fresh lemon juice

1 teaspoon pepper

1 1/2 cups Italian-style dry bread
crumbs

2 tablespoons olive oil

2 tablespoons butter or margarine

1 small red onion, sliced

1 tablespoon chopped fresh parsley

1 lemon, cut into wedges

**Breaded Turkey Cutlets with
Red Onion (Cotolette di Tacchino
Impanate alla Cipolla Zossa):**
Substitute 6 slices (about 3 ounces
each) uncooked turkey breast for
the chicken. Make as directed—
except flatten slices to 1/4 inch
if necessary.

PREP: 20 MIN; COOK: 25 MIN
6 servings

1. Flatten each chicken breast half to 1/4-inch thickness between sheets of plastic wrap or waxed paper. Beat eggs slightly with fork; stir in lemon juice and pepper. Dip chicken into egg mixture, then coat with bread crumbs; shake off excess crumbs.

2. Heat oil and butter in 12-inch skillet over medium-high heat. Cook onion and parsley in oil mixture about 4 minutes, stirring occasionally, until onion is tender. Remove onion with slotted spoon; set aside.

3. Add 3 pieces chicken to skillet. Cook about 5 minutes, turning once, until brown. Remove chicken from skillet to platter; cover loosely with aluminum foil tent to keep warm. Repeat with remaining chicken.

4. Return chicken to skillet; top with onion. Cover and cook about 8 minutes or until chicken is no longer pink in center. Sprinkle with additional parsley if desired. Serve with lemon wedges.

1 Serving: Calories 320 (Calories from Fat 115); Fat 13g (Saturated 4g); Cholesterol 140mg; Sodium 300mg; Carbohydrate 18g (Dietary Fiber 1g); Protein 34g
%Daily Value: Vitamin A 4%; Vitamin C 0%; Calcium 8%; Iron 14%
Diet Exchanges: 1 Starch, 4 Lean Meat, 1 Vegetable

Parola di Antonio

Here is a simple chicken recipe to cure boredom and satisfy a hungry soul. The rich golden brown coating combines with the tartness of the lemon and the mild flavor of red onion. For a lighter rendition of this recipe, omit the egg yolks and beat the egg whites with 2 tablespoons fat-free (skim) milk.

ROASTED STUFFED SEA BASS
Persico Ripieno

1 cup seasoned croutons

1 cup sliced mushrooms (3 ounces)

1/2 cup dry white wine, vegetable
broth or chicken broth

1 tablespoon chopped fresh parsley

1 tablespoon chopped fresh
basil leaves

1/2 teaspoon salt

1/2 teaspoon pepper

1 clove garlic, finely chopped

1 egg

1 pan-dressed sea bass or whitefish
(about 2 1/2 pounds)

1/4 cup olive oil

PREP: 15 MIN; BAKE: 1 HR
4 servings

1. Heat oven to 350°. Mix all ingredients except sea bass and oil. Make 3 diagonal cuts on each side of fish. Place 1 tablespoon stuffing mixture in each cut. Fill cavity of fish with remaining stuffing mixture. Close opening with skewers; lace with string.

2. Place fish in shallow roasting pan; drizzle with oil. Bake uncovered 50 to 60 minutes or until fish flakes easily with fork. Remove string and skewers.

1 Serving: Calories 450 (Calories from Fat 200); Fat 22g (Saturated 5g); Cholesterol 180mg; Sodium 510mg; Carbohydrate 7g (Dietary Fiber 1g); Protein 52g
%Daily Value: Vitamin A 10%; Vitamin C 4%; Calcium 8%; Iron 20%
Diet Exchanges: 7 Lean Meat, 1 Vegetable, 1 Fat

Parola di Antonio

Italians have an ingenious and easy way, inherited from the ancient Romans, of roasting fish. They coat a gutted fish—without scaling or skinning it— with a thick layer of salt to form an unbroken crust, then bake the fish in the oven. After baking, the salt and skin form a hard shell that breaks off easily, leaving succulent, moist fish that, surprisingly, isn't the least bit salty.

ROASTED LOIN OF MARLIN
Trancio di Pesce al Forno

1/4 cup olive oil

2 1/2 pounds marlin, tuna, salmon
or swordfish loin

1 medium lemon

8 medium green onions, chopped
(1/2 cup)

1/2 cup chopped fresh parsley

1 tablespoon chopped fresh tarragon leaves

3/4 teaspoon salt

1/4 teaspoon pepper

2 cloves garlic, finely chopped

1/2 cup white wine or
chicken broth

1 medium lemon, thinly sliced

**Pan-Roasted Marlin Steaks
(Tranci di Pesce Arrosto):**
Substitute 6 marlin, tuna, salmon
or swordfish steaks, about 3/4 inch
thick, for the loin. Cover and bake
10 minutes. Uncover; spoon pan
juices over fish. Cover and bake
about 10 minutes longer or until
center of fish flakes easily with fork.

PREP: 15 MIN; BAKE: 1 HR
6 servings

1. Heat oven to 375°. Drizzle oil in rectangular pan,
    13 x 9 x 2 inches, or shallow roasting pan. Make 12 to 14
    small cuts, about 1 inch deep, on top and sides of marlin
    loin with sharp knife. Cut lemon in half; rub all sides of
    fish with lemon halves, gently squeezing to release juice.
    Place fish in pan.

2. Mix onions, parsley, tarragon, salt, pepper and garlic. Fill
    each cut in fish with about 1 teaspoon of the herb
    mixture. Pour wine over fish; sprinkle with any remain-
    ing herb mixture. Arrange lemon slices, overlapping
    slightly, on fish.

3. Cover and bake 40 minutes. Uncover; spoon pan juices
    over fish. Cover and bake about 20 minutes longer or
    until center of fish flakes easily with fork. To serve, use a
    sharp knife to cut into serving pieces.

1 Serving: Calories 180 (Calories from Fat 45); Fat 5g (Saturated 1g); Cholesterol 90mg;
Sodium 440mg; Carbohydrate 1g (Dietary Fiber 0g); Protein 33g
%Daily Value: Vitamin A 4%; Vitamin C 4%; Calcium 4%; Iron 4%
Diet Exchanges: 5 Very Lean Meat

Parola di Antonio

*This recipe hails from the northern Italian Riviera, and it was once reserved for
official banquets and other important events. Sailors would actually wrap the fish
with tarragon and other herbs for a few days to let the flavors soak in. The loin is
the fillet from larger fish before it is cut into steaks. Be sure to order the loin from
your favorite fish market a day or two ahead before all the fish is cut into steaks.
The skin can be left on or removed before cooking. A key to success is to keep the
fish covered during cooking to help keep it moist.*

Roasted Loin of Marlin

GOLDEN FRIED TROUT
Trote Fritte

4 pan-dressed rainbow trout
(about 3/4 pound each)

1/2 cup dry white wine or
chicken broth

3 tablespoons fresh lemon juice

1 egg

1 cup all-purpose flour

1 cup Italian-style dry bread crumbs

Vegetable oil

1 lemon, sliced or cut into wedges

Parsley sprigs or chopped fresh
parsley, if desired

PREP: 20 MIN; COOK: 12 MIN
4 servings

1. Butterfly each trout by cutting lengthwise almost in half, leaving skin along back intact. Open fish to lie flat.

2. Beat wine, lemon juice and egg until blended. Coat fish with flour, then dip into egg mixture. Press bread crumbs on open cut side of each fish.

3. Heat oil (2 inches) in 4-quart Dutch oven to 375°. Fry 2 fish at a time 3 minutes; turn. Fry 2 to 3 minutes longer or until golden brown. Drain on paper towels. Serve with lemon and parsley.

1 Serving: Calories 655 (Calories from Fat 215); Fat 24g (Saturated 6g); Cholesterol 250mg; Sodium 400mg; Carbohydrate 36g (Dietary Fiber 1g); Protein 71g
%Daily Value: Vitamin A 10%; Vitamin C 4%; Calcium 10%; Iron 26%
Diet Exchanges: 2 Starch, 9 Lean Meat

Parola di Antonio

In Italian cuisine, fish are often butterflied before cooking. To butterfly a fish, cut it lengthwise almost in half, leaving the skin along the back connected. The fish will lie flat when opened. Breading is placed only on the meat side. The skin is then easily removed after cooking, without taking off the crunchy, golden brown breading.

GRILLED SALMON WITH MINT MARINADE
Salmone Marinato alla Menta

4 small salmon, tuna or swordfish
  steaks, 3/4 inch thick
    (about 1 1/2 pounds)

1/2 cup chopped fresh mint leaves

1/4 cup olive oil

3 tablespoons fresh lemon juice

1/2 teaspoon salt

1/2 teaspoon pepper

1 clove garlic, finely chopped

1 dried bay leaf

**Broiled Salmon with Mint
Marinade:** Marinate salmon as
directed. Set oven control to broil.
Place fish on rack in broiler pan.
Broil with tops about 4 inches from
heat about 5 minutes, brushing
frequently with marinade, until light
brown. Turn carefully; generously
brush with marinade. Broil 4 to 6
minutes longer until fish flakes
easily with fork.

PREP: 15 MIN; MARINATE: 1 HR; GRILL: 15 MIN
4 servings

1. Place salmon steaks in ungreased rectangular baking dish,
   11 x 7 x 1 1/2 inches. Beat remaining ingredients except
   bay leaf with wire whisk until blended; add bay leaf. Pour
   over fish. Cover and refrigerate at least 1 hour but no
   longer than 24 hours, turning fish occasionally.

2. Brush grill rack with olive or vegetable oil. Heat coals or
   gas grill as directed by manufacturer for direct heat.
   Remove fish from marinade; reserve marinade. Grill fish
   uncovered about 4 inches from medium-high heat 5 minutes, brushing frequently with marinade. Turn carefully;
   brush generously with marinade. Grill 5 to 10 minutes
   longer until fish flakes easily with fork.

3. Heat remaining marinade to rolling boil; remove bay leaf.
   Serve marinade with fish.

1 Serving: Calories 325 (Calories from Fat 200); Fat 22g (Saturated 4g); Cholesterol 95mg;
Sodium 380mg; Carbohydrate 1g (Dietary Fiber 0g); Protein 31g
%Daily Value: Vitamin A 6%; Vitamin C 4%; Calcium 2%; Iron 6%
Diet Exchanges: 4 Lean Meat, 2 Fat

Parola di Antonio

*Grilling is a popular and delicious method of preparing fish. Here are a few
hints to keep grilled fish moist and flavorful. For starters, I keep the grill rack
clean and brush it with olive oil to help prevent the fish from sticking. To
ensure even cooking and seal in moisture, keep the heat as even as possible
throughout the grilling time. I always turn the fish with long-handled
barbecue tongs or a turner instead of a fork, which will pierce the fish
and allow the juices to cook out.*

GRILLED SWORDFISH STEAKS
Pesce Spada alla Griglia

1/2 cup olive oil

2 tablespoons capers

Juice from 1/2 medium lemon

1 tablespoon chopped fresh parsley

1/2 teaspoon pepper

2 flat anchovy fillets in oil

2 cloves garlic

4 swordfish, tuna or salmon steaks, about 1 inch thick (about 2 pounds)

Broiled Swordfish Steaks: Marinate swordfish as directed. Set oven control to broil. Place fish on rack in broiler pan. Broil with tops about 4 inches from heat about 6 minutes, brushing frequently with marinade, until light brown. Turn carefully; generously brush with marinade. Broil 4 to 6 minutes longer, until fish flakes easily with fork.

PREP: 15 MIN; MARINATE: 1 HR; GRILL: 15 MIN
4 servings

1. Place all ingredients except swordfish steaks in food processor or blender. Cover and process until smooth.

2. Place fish in ungreased rectangular baking dish, 11 x 7 x 1 1/2 inches. Pour marinade over fish. Cover and refrigerate at least 1 hour but no longer than 24 hours, turning fish occasionally.

3. Brush grill rack with olive or vegetable oil. Heat coals or gas grill as directed by manufacturer for direct heat. Remove fish from marinade; reserve marinade. Grill fish uncovered about 4 inches from medium-high heat 5 minutes, brushing frequently with marinade. Turn carefully; brush generously with marinade. Grill 5 to 10 minutes longer until fish flakes easily with fork.

1 Serving: Calories 385 (Calories from Fat 240); Fat 27g (Saturated 5g); Cholesterol 105mg; Sodium 260mg; Carbohydrate 1g (Dietary Fiber 0g); Protein 35g
%Daily Value: Vitamin A 4%; Vitamin C 4%; Calcium 2%; Iron 6%
Diet Exchanges: 5 Lean Meat, 2 Fat

Parola di Antonio

Nothing beats the aroma of herbs. Soak your favorite fresh herbs—one kind or a bundle of several of your favorites—in water for about 30 minutes. Drain them and sprinkle them over the hot coals. Rosemary is a favorite I use—the aroma is splendido! *You may want to give soaked and drained garlic cloves a try, but be ready for your neighbors to come over when they smell the aroma.*

SAVORY FRESH TUNA

Tranci di tonno Fresco Saporiti

1/2 cup Basil-Garlic Sauce
  (page 146) or Walnut-Basil
  Sauce (page 145) or purchased
  basil pesto

1 tablespoon olive oil

2 medium green onions, chopped
  (2 tablespoons)

1 1/2 pounds yellowfin tuna or
  salmon fillets, about 3/4 inch
  thick

1/2 medium lemon

PREP: 15 MIN; COOK: 15 MIN
4 servings

1. Make Basil-Garlic Sauce. Heat oil in 10-inch nonstick skillet over medium heat. Cook onions in oil about 3 minutes, stirring occasionally, until tender.

2. Add sauce and tuna fillets to skillet. Squeeze juice from lemon half over fish. Heat to boiling; reduce heat to low. Cover and cook about 10 minutes or until fish flakes easily with fork.

1 Serving: Calories 350 (Calories from Fat 215); Fat g 24(Saturated 4g); Cholesterol 85mg; Sodium 240mg; Carbohydrate 3g (Dietary Fiber 1g); Protein 32g
%Daily Value: Vitamin A 4%; Vitamin C 2%; Calcium 14%; Iron 8%
Diet Exchanges: 4 Lean Meat, 1 Vegetable, 2 Fat

FILLET OF BASS, PARMA STYLE
Sogliole alla Parmigiana

1 1/2 pounds sea bass, sole or
pike fillets

1/4 cup all-purpose flour

2 tablespoons butter or margarine

2 medium green onions, thinly sliced
(2 tablespoons)

1 cup dry white wine or chicken
broth

2 tablespoons fresh lemon juice

1/2 teaspoon salt

1/4 teaspoon pepper

1/4 cup freshly grated or shredded
imported Parmesan cheese

PREP: 10 MIN; COOK: 10 MIN; BAKE: 15 MIN
4 servings

1. Heat oven to 375°. Coat sea bass fillets with flour; shake off excess flour. Melt butter in 12-inch ovenproof skillet over medium-low heat. Cook onions in butter about 5 minutes, stirring occasionally, until tender.

2. Add fish to skillet. Cook uncovered about 5 minutes or until light brown; turn fish carefully. Pour wine and lemon juice over fish. Sprinkle with salt, pepper and cheese.

3. Bake uncovered about 15 minutes or until cheese is melted and fish flakes easily with fork.

1 Serving: Calories 310 (Calories from Fat 145); Fat 14g (Saturated 7g); Cholesterol 95mg; Sodium 670mg; Carbohydrate 8g (Dietary Fiber 0g); Protein 34g
%Daily Value: Vitamin A 10%; Vitamin C 4%; Calcium 14%; Iron 12%
Diet Exchanges: 1/2 Starch, 5 Lean Meat, 1 1/2 Fat

Fillet of Bass, Parma Style; Piquant Salad, page 263

SEAFOOD STEW
Stufato Di Pesce

2 tablespoons olive oil

12 medium green onions, chopped (3/4 cup)

1/4 cup chopped sun-dried tomatoes in oil

1/4 cup chopped fresh basil leaves

4 cloves garlic, finely chopped

1 can (28 ounces) Italian-style pear-shaped (plum) tomatoes, undrained

1 bottle (8 ounces) clam juice

1 tablespoon anchovy paste

1 teaspoon crushed red pepper

2 dried bay leaves

1 pound monkfish, sea bass or cod steaks or fillets, cut into 1-inch pieces

1 pound tuna, salmon or swordfish steaks, cut into 1-inch pieces

12 uncooked peeled deveined large shrimp (about 1/2 pound), thawed if frozen

1 can (10 ounces) chopped clams, undrained, or 2 cans (6 1/2 ounces each) minced clams, undrained

PREP: 15 MIN; COOK: 45 MIN
6 servings

1. Heat oil in 4-quart Dutch oven over medium-high heat. Cook onions, sun-dried tomatoes, basil and garlic in oil about 5 minutes, stirring occasionally, until onions are tender.

2. Meanwhile, place canned tomatoes with liquid in food processor. Cover and process until almost smooth. Stir tomatoes, clam juice, anchovy paste, red pepper and bay leaves into Dutch oven. Heat to boiling; reduce heat. Cover and simmer 30 minutes.

3. Stir in remaining ingredients. Heat to boiling; reduce heat. Cover and simmer about 10 minutes or until fish flakes easily with fork and shrimp are pink and firm. Remove bay leaves.

1 Serving: Calories 305 (Calories from Fat 100); Fat 11g (Saturated 2g); Cholesterol 140mg; Sodium 590mg; Carbohydrate 11g (Dietary Fiber 2g); Protein 43g
%Daily Value: Vitamin A 20%; Vitamin C 32%; Calcium 14%; Iron 86%
Diet Exchanges: 6 Very Lean Meat, 2 Vegetable, 1 Fat

Parola di Antonio

Despite its humble Mediterranean origins, this easy recipe will impress you with its simplicity and flavor. Most ingredients are easily accessible in supermarkets, and with the help of the seafood department, you can plan ahead to prepare this stew upon the arrival of the freshest fish.

Seafood Stew

GRILLED SEAFOOD KABOBS
Spiedini di Pesce Misto

Lemon-Herb Marinade (right)

4 ounces salmon or tuna steak,
    cut into 1-inch cubes

4 ounces monkfish or cod steak,
    cut into 1-inch cubes

4 ounces rockfish or haddock steak,
    cut into 1-inch cubes

24 uncooked medium shrimp in
    shells, thawed if frozen

8 large mushroom caps

1 large red bell pepper, cut into
    1 1/2-inch pieces

4 medium green onions, cut into
    1-inch pieces

8 fresh bay leaves

Broiled Seafood Kabobs: Marinate kabobs as directed. Set oven control to broil. Place kabobs on rack in broiler pan. Broil with tops about 4 inches from heat 4 minutes, brushing occasionally with marinade. Turn kabobs; generously brush with marinade. Broil about 4 minutes longer, until fish flakes easily with fork. Remove bay leaves.

PREP: 30 MIN; MARINATE: 1 HR; GRILL: 10 MIN
4 servings

1. Make Lemon-Herb Marinade. Thread fish, shrimp, mushrooms, bell pepper, onions and bay leaves alternately on each of four 12-inch metal skewers, leaving space between each piece. Place kabobs in ungreased rectangular baking dish, 13 x 9 x 2 inches. Pour marinade over kabobs. Cover and refrigerate at least 1 hour but no longer than 24 hours.

2. Brush grill rack with olive or vegetable oil. Heat coals or gas grill as directed by manufacturer for direct heat. Remove kabobs from marinade; reserve marinade. Grill kabobs uncovered about 4 inches from medium-high heat about 5 minutes, brushing occasionally with marinade. Turn carefully; brush generously with marinade. Grill 5 minutes longer until fish flakes easily with fork. Remove bay leaves.

3. Heat remaining marinade to rolling boil. Serve marinade with kabobs.

1/2 cup olive oil

1 tablespoon chopped fresh basil
   leaves

1 tablespoon chopped fresh parsley

3 tablespoons fresh lemon juice

1 tablespoon capers

1 teaspoon freshly ground pepper

1/2 teaspoon salt

1 medium green onion, chopped
   (1 tablespoon)

Lemon-Herb Marinade

Place all ingredients in food processor or blender. Cover and
process until smooth.

1 Serving: Calories 315 (Calories from Fat 190); Fat 21g (Saturated 3g); Cholesterol 110mg;
Sodium 380mg; Carbohydrate 8g (Dietary Fiber 2g); Protein 25g
%Daily Value: Vitamin A 8%; Vitamin C 40%; Calcium 4%; Iron 14%
Diet Exchanges: 3 Lean Meat, 1 Vegetable, 3 Fat

BAKED JUMBO SHRIMP
Gamberoni al Forno

16 uncooked jumbo shrimp in shells
(about 1 1/2 pounds)

1/2 cup olive oil

2 tablespoons chopped fresh parsley

2 medium green onions, thinly sliced
(2 tablespoons)

2 cloves garlic, finely chopped

1 cup dry white wine or chicken
broth

1/2 medium lemon

1/2 teaspoon salt

1/2 teaspoon pepper

PREP: 20 MIN; BAKE 20 MIN
4 servings

1. Heat oven to 375°. Peel shrimp. (If shrimp are frozen, do not thaw; peel in cold water.) Make a shallow cut lengthwise down back of each shrimp; wash out vein.

2. Pour oil into rectangular baking dish, 13 x 9 x 2 inches. Place shrimp in oil; sprinkle with parsley, onions and garlic. Pour wine over shrimp. Squeeze juice from lemon over shrimp; sprinkle with salt and pepper. Bake uncovered about 20 minutes or until shrimp are pink and firm.

1 Serving: Calories 240 (Calories from Fat 170); Fat 19g (Saturated 3g); Cholesterol 80mg; Sodium 400mg; Carbohydrate 2g (Dietary Fiber 0g); Protein 9g
%Daily Value: Vitamin A 4%; Vitamin C 4%; Calcium 2%; Iron 10%
Diet Exchanges: 1 Lean Meat, 4 Fat

Grilled Shrimp Kabobs with Fresh Herbs, page 236

GRILLED SHRIMP KABOBS WITH FRESH HERBS
Spiedini di Gamberi alle Erbe

Rosemary-Lemon Marinade (right)

24 fresh large basil leaves

24 uncooked peeled deveined large
    shrimp (about 1 1/2 pounds),
    with tails left on

12 small pattypan squash, cut in half

24 cherry tomatoes

24 large cloves garlic

**Broiled Shrimp Kabobs with Fresh
Herbs:** Set oven control to broil.
Spray rack of broiler pan with cook-
ing spray, or brush with olive oil.
Place kabobs on rack in broiler pan.
Broil with tops about 4 inches from
heat about 12 minutes, turning and
brushing 2 or 3 times with mari-
nade, until shrimp are pink and firm.
Discard any remaining marinade.

PREP: 20 MIN; MARINATE: 20 MIN; GRILL: 12 MIN
6 servings

1. Make Rosemary-Lemon Marinade. Wrap basil leaf around
   each shrimp.

2. For each kabob, thread shrimp, squash half, tomato and
   garlic clove alternately on stem of rosemary sprig, leaving
   space between each piece. (Start threading at stem end,
   pulling it through to leaves at top.) Place kabobs in
   ungreased rectangular baking dish, 13 x 9 x 2 inches. Pour
   marinade over kabobs. Cover and refrigerate at least 20
   minutes but no longer than 2 hours.

3. Brush grill rack with olive or vegetable oil. Heat coals or
   gas grill as directed by manufacturer for direct heat.
   Remove kabobs from marinade; reserve marinade. Cover
   and grill kabobs 5 to 6 inches from medium heat about 12
   minutes, turning and brushing with marinade 2 or 3
   times, until shrimp are pink and firm. Discard any
   remaining marinade.

12 six-inch-long sprigs rosemary

1/4 cup fresh lemon juice

3 tablespoons olive oil

1 tablespoon dry white wine or
   lemon juice

1/2 teaspoon salt

1/2 teaspoon pepper

Rosemary-Lemon Marinade

Strip leaves from rosemary sprigs, leaving 1 inch of leaves at top intact; set sprigs aside for kabobs. Measure 1 tablespoon rosemary leaves; chop. (Store remaining leaves for other uses.) Mix chopped rosemary leaves and remaining ingredients.

1 Serving: Calories 105 (Calories from Fat 45); Fat 5g (Saturated 1g); Cholesterol 55mg; Sodium 200mg; Carbohydrate 9g (Dietary Fiber 2g); Protein 8g
%Daily Value: Vitamin A 8%; Vitamin C 18%; Calcium 4%; Iron 8%
Diet Exchanges: 1 Lean Meat, 2 Vegetable

Parola di Antonio

This recipe evokes the image of fragrant fields of wild rosemary waving from atop the craggy coastlines of Mediterranean islands. Use thick rosemary sprigs for the kabob "skewers" so they won't break when you assemble the kabobs. I like to trim the ends of the rosemary stems to a point so it's easier to slip the shrimp and vegetables onto the stem. Also, if you are finding that inserting the stem into the vegetables is difficult, poke an opening in the vegetable with a toothpick. One-inch slices of zucchini or yellow summer squash are equally as tasty as pattypan. Marinating the fully assembled kabobs allows the rosemary flavor to penetrate into the shrimp and vegetables.

SPICY BREADED SHRIMP
Gamberi Piccantissimi

1 1/2 pounds uncooked medium
   shrimp in shells

2 eggs

3 tablespoons fresh lemon juice

3 tablespoons amaretto or
   1/2 teaspoon almond extract

2 cloves garlic, finely chopped

Vegetable oil

3/4 cup all-purpose flour

1 teaspoon salt

1 teaspoon ground red pepper
   (cayenne)

1 teaspoon ground cinnamon

PREP: 20 MIN; MARINATE: 10 MIN; COOK: 20 MIN
6 servings

1. Peel shrimp, leaving tails on. (If shrimp are frozen, do not thaw; peel in cold water.) Make a shallow cut lengthwise down back of each shrimp; wash out vein. Rinse shrimp; pat dry.

2. Beat eggs slightly with fork in large bowl. Stir in lemon juice, amaretto and garlic. Add shrimp; toss until shrimp are evenly coated. Cover and refrigerate 10 minutes.

3. Heat oil (2 to 3 inches) in 4-quart Dutch oven to 325°. Mix flour, salt, red pepper and cinnamon. Remove shrimp from bowl one at a time, and coat with flour mixture.

4. Fry 5 or 6 shrimp at a time about 2 minutes or until golden brown. Remove with slotted spoon. Drain on paper towels.

1 Serving: Calories 205 (Calories from Fat 100); Fat 11g (Saturated 2g); Cholesterol 160mg;
Sodium 430mg; Carbohydrate 13g (Dietary Fiber 1g); Protein 14g
%Daily Value: Vitamin A 4%; Vitamin C 0%; Calcium 2%; Iron 14%
Diet Exchanges: 1 Starch, 2 Lean Meat, 1/2 Fat

Parola di Antonio

The Italian version of peel-and-eat shrimp was fairly common in the Venetian lagoon, where spices from Asia reigned. Whole large shrimp, with heads and shells intact, were breaded and fried. Then the shrimp were cut open and the succulent sweet meat was removed and eaten with the spicy golden brown coating. With some variations, it still prevails as a classic appetizer from the Adriatic coast. Not removing the shells also prevents the meat from drying and toughening while it is being fried. This recipe calls for removing the shells, but you may want to try it with the shells on. Just be sure to warn everyone before eating, so they don't bite into the shells!

Spicy Breaded Shrimp

SAVORY SHRIMP AND SCALLOPS
Gamberi e Vongole Saporiti

1 pound sea or bay scallops

2 tablespoons olive oil

1 clove garlic, finely chopped

2 medium green onions, chopped
(2 tablespoons)

1 medium green bell pepper, diced
(1 cup)

1 tablespoon chopped fresh parsley
or 1 teaspoon parsley flakes

1 pound uncooked peeled deveined
medium shrimp, thawed if frozen

1/2 cup dry white wine or chicken
broth

1 tablespoon fresh lemon juice

1/4 to 1/2 teaspoon crushed
red pepper

PREP: 25 MIN; COOK: 10 MIN
6 servings

1. If using sea scallops, cut in half. Heat oil in 10-inch skillet over medium heat. Cook garlic, onions, bell pepper and parsley in oil about 5 minutes, stirring occasionally, until bell pepper is crisp-tender.

2. Stir in scallops and remaining ingredients. Cook 4 to 5 minutes, stirring frequently, until shrimp are pink and firm and scallops are white.

1 Serving: Calories 150 (Calories from Fat 55); Fat 6g (Saturated 1g); Cholesterol 120mg; Sodium 230mg; Carbohydrate 3g (Dietary Fiber 1g); Protein 20g
%Daily Value: Vitamin A 6%; Vitamin C 18%; Calcium 6%; Iron 18%
Diet Exchanges: 3 Lean Meat, 1 Fat

Parola di Antonio

Scallops are available in two sizes. Sea scallops are the larger of the two, about 2 inches in diameter. Bay scallops are about 1/2 inch in diameter. Both sea and bay scallops are creamy white, sweet and mild flavored. Sea scallops may be tinted light orange or pink, and bay scallops may be tinted light tan or pink. You can use whichever is available, but you may want to cut the sea scallops in half.

LOBSTER WITH SPARKLING WINE SAUCE
Aragosta allo Spumante

1 gallon water

1 tablespoon salt

4 large lobster tails (about 1 pound each), thawed if frozen

2 tablespoons butter or margarine

6 roma (plum) tomatoes, peeled and chopped

2 medium green onions, sliced (2 tablespoons)

1 cup Asti Spumante, dry white wine or vegetable broth

2 tablespoons fresh lemon juice

PREP: 25 MIN; COOK: 25 MIN; COOL: 10 MIN
4 servings

1. Heat water and salt to boiling in large kettle or stockpot. Add lobster tails. Cover and heat to boiling; reduce heat. Simmer covered 12 minutes; drain. Cool about 10 minutes or until cool enough to handle. Crack shells; remove meat with sharp knife. Cut meat into 1-inch pieces.

2. Melt butter in 12-inch skillet over medium-high heat. Cook tomatoes and onions in butter, stirring frequently, until onions are tender.

3. Stir in lobster, wine and lemon juice. Cook uncovered over medium heat about 5 minutes, stirring occasionally, until most of the liquid has evaporated.

1 Serving: Calories 310 (Calories from Fat 65); Fat 7g (Saturated 4g); Cholesterol 180mg; Sodium 1500mg; Carbohydrate 8g (Dietary Fiber 1g); Protein 48g
%Daily Value: Vitamin A 14%; Vitamin C 14%; Calcium 14%; Iron 8%
Diet Exchanges: 7 Very Lean Meat, 1 Vegetable, 1 Fat

Savory Zucchini, page 257

CHAPTER SIX

Verdure e Insalata Fresca

FRESH GARDEN VEGETABLES AND SALADS

Olive Oils

Think of Italy and what comes to mind? The picture of gnarled olive trees from which come the wonderful olives and oils that are symbolic of Mediterranean life.

Olive oil ranges in flavor from delicate to rich and fruity and in color from pale yellow to cloudy deep green. A green tinge may indicate that the olives were green and barely ripe but not always; it can also indicate that the oil has a wonderful, intensely fruity taste and freshness.

Yellow oils usually mean the olives were picked late in the season when they were black and ripe. This could indicate a sweeter, rounder oil. Always be sure to smell and taste olive oil before using it to be sure it is fresh.

TASTING OLIVE OIL

Determining which type of olive oil to buy is based on personal preference and how the oil will be used.

To taste olive oils, pour a small amount into a clean wineglass. Swirl the glass just as you would when tasting wine, and smell the aroma. Does it have a good, clean oil aroma? Then take a tiny sip of the oil, sucking in air through your teeth, again like you would when tasting wine. Do you like the flavor and consistency of the oil in your mouth?

Try the oil on food—a slice of cooked potato, some pasta, a piece of bread, a leaf of crisp lettuce. Does the oil enhance the flavor of the food, or is it overpowering? Then you decide which olive oils you would like to keep in your pantry.

SELECTING OLIVE OIL

Olive oils are categorized by their acidity level and the process used to make them.

Extra-Virgin Olive Oil must be made from mechanical extraction of olives by the cold-press method, which uses no heat or chemicals. This oil has an acidity level of less than 1 percent and must have a perfect taste. Extra-virgin olive oil has a more intense, fruity flavor and aroma than other grades of oil. It is recognized by its green-gold or bright green color. Extra-virgin olive oil is excellent in salad dressings for fresh, crisp greens or as an accompaniment to raw or cooked vegetables.

Virgin Olive Oil is extracted from olives that may be less ripe and more blemished than those used for extra-virgin oil. It has a low acidity level of 3.3 percent and is moderately priced. This oil has slightly less flavor and color than extra-virgin olive oil. Virgin olive oil is excellent for skillet-frying because it doesn't smoke or change flavor due to heat, as extra-virgin oil does. It is also good as a condiment for cooked vegetables and meats.

Olive Oil, previously called "pure olive oil" or "100 percent pure olive oil," is the most widely available oil. This oil is extracted from leftover olive pulp after the pressing of extra-virgin oils. Heat and chemical solvents are used to aid extraction. Olive oil has an acidity level than the other oils, but it must have less than 5 percent. This oil is mild in flavor and golden in color and is a good choice for cooking and skillet-frying. It doesn't smoke easily or change flavor due to heat. Choose this oil when just a hint of olive oil flavor is desired.

Light or Extra-Light Oil refers to the flavor and color of this oil. It has the same number of calories and same amount of fat as all olive oil. These light oils have been highly filtered, resulting in a light-colored oil that tastes like vegetable oil. This olive oil can be used for high-temperature frying and in baking.

STORING OLIVE OIL

Proper storage is important to prolong the shelf life of oil and help prevent rancidity. Olive oil should be stored tightly covered in a dark, cool location—not near the stove—for up to one year. It is best not to refrigerate it if at all possible; moisture can collect on the lid and drip into the oil, which could cause it to become rancid more quickly. Refrigeration also causes olive oil to become cloudy and thick; although when brought to room temperature, it becomes clear and pourable. Be sure to keep several types of olive oil on hand to complement whatever dish you are preparing.

Extra-Virgin Olive Oil

Virgin Olive Oil

Olive Oil

Light Olive Oil

ASPARAGUS WITH PARMESAN
Asparagi alla Parmigiana

1 1/2 pounds asparagus

1 tablespoon olive oil

1 tablespoon butter or margarine

1 medium green onion, chopped
  (1 tablespoon)

1 clove garlic, finely chopped

1/2 teaspoon salt

1/4 teaspoon freshly ground pepper

1/4 cup freshly grated or shredded
  imported Parmesan cheese

PREP: 5 MIN; COOK: 4 MIN; BAKE: 10 MIN
4 servings

1. Break off tough bottom ends of asparagus. Heat 1 inch salted water (1/2 teaspoon to 1 cup water) to boiling in 3-quart saucepan. Add asparagus. Heat to boiling; reduce heat. Simmer uncovered 4 minutes; drain.

2. Meanwhile, heat oven to 375°. Place oil, butter, onion and garlic in ungreased square pan, 8 x 8 x 2 inches. Heat uncovered in oven 5 minutes.

3. Spread asparagus in pan. Sprinkle with salt, pepper and cheese. Bake uncovered about 10 minutes or until cheese is melted.

1 Serving: Calories 100 (Calories from Fat 65); Fat 7g (Saturated 3g); Cholesterol 10mg; Sodium 430mg; Carbohydrate 5g (Dietary Fiber 1g); Protein 5g
% Daily Value: Vitamin A 8%; Vitamin C 16%; Calcium 10%; Iron 4%
Diet Exchanges: 1 Vegetable, 1 1/2 Fat

Parola di Antonio

Lots of chefs have experimented with creative asparagus recipes. The best, however, are the traditional ones. Here is a classic from Parma, Parmesan's very hometown. Treat yourself by buying a piece of imported Parmesan cheese; it is best when freshly grated or shredded.

Although finding wild asparagus in Italy is still possible, both white and green cultivated asparagus are popular. Green asparagus is the most popular, and Italians prefer pencil-thin spears. In spring, asparagus is at its best when it is young, crisp and tender.

Asparagus with Parmesan

CAULIFLOWER AU GRATIN
Cavolfiore Gratinato

1 medium head cauliflower
   (2 pounds)

1 medium red onion, cut into
   8 wedges

1 tablespoon fresh lemon juice

1 tablespoon olive oil

2 large cloves garlic, finely chopped

1 tablespoon chopped fresh parsley

1/2 teaspoon coarsely ground
   pepper

2 tablespoons freshly grated or
   shredded imported Parmesan
   cheese

2 tablespoons freshly grated or
   shredded Asiago cheese

1/4 cup shredded provolone cheese

PREP: 10 MIN; COOK: 6 MIN; BAKE: 20 MIN
5 servings

1. Separate cauliflower into flowerets. Heat 1 inch water salted water (1/2 teaspoon salt to 1 cup water) to boiling in 3-quart saucepan. Add cauliflower, onion and lemon juice. Cover and heat to boiling; reduce heat. Simmer about 6 minutes or until cauliflower is just tender; drain.

2. Heat oven to 425°. Add oil to ungreased square pan, 9 x 9 x 2 inches; stir in garlic and parsley. Heat uncovered in oven 5 minutes.

3. Spread cauliflower and onion in pan; sprinkle with pepper and cheeses. Bake uncovered about 20 minutes or until cheese is melted and forms a golden brown crust.

1 Serving: Calories 100 (Calories from Fat 55); Fat 6g (Saturated 2g); Cholesterol 10mg;
Sodium 160mg; Carbohydrate 9g (Dietary Fiber 3g); Protein 6g
% Daily Value: Vitamin A 2%; Vitamin C 46%; Calcium 12%; Iron 4%
Diet Exchanges: 2 Vegetable, 1 Fat

Parola di Antonio

Unbeknownst to many, cauliflower often appears in company with anchovies in classic Neapolitan cuisine. This is a simple rendition without the anchovies, but it packs a lot of flavor. Adding lemon or vinegar to boiled vegetables was thought to diminish the pungency of a strong flavor and to improve tenderness. Of course, freshly grated cheese will do wonders.

STEWED GARBANZO BEANS WITH ONIONS
Fagioli in Umido con Cipolle

1 pound dried garbanzo beans
  (2 1/3 cups)

3 tablespoons butter or margarine

8 slices bacon, cut into 1/2-inch
  pieces

6 pearl onions, peeled and cut
  in half

2 cups chicken broth

1/2 teaspoon chopped fresh dill
  weed

1/2 teaspoon chopped fresh parsley

1/2 teaspoon pepper

PREP: 15 MIN; STAND: 1 HR; COOK: 2 1/2 HR
6 servings

1. Cover beans with water in 3-quart saucepan; heat to boiling. Boil uncovered 2 minutes; remove from heat. Cover and let stand 1 hour; drain.

2. Melt butter in 10-inch skillet over medium heat. Cook bacon and onions in butter, stirring frequently, until bacon is crisp. Stir in beans and remaining ingredients. Heat to boiling; reduce heat. Cover and simmer 2 to 2 1/2 hours or until beans are tender.

1 Serving: Calories 325 (Calories from Fat 125); Fat 14g (Saturated 6g); Cholesterol 20mg; Sodium 440mg; Carbohydrate 44g (Dietary Fiber 12g); Protein 18g
% Daily Value: Vitamin A 4%; Vitamin C 2%; Calcium 8%; Iron 26%
Diet Exchanges: 2 Starch, 1 Very Lean Meat, 3 Vegetable, 1 1/2 Fat

BRUSSELS SPROUTS WITH PROSCIUTTO
Cavolini di Bruxelles al Prosciutto

1 pound Brussels sprouts

2 tablespoons butter or margarine

1/2 teaspoon chicken bouillon granules

1 small onion, thinly sliced

1/4 cup chopped imported prosciutto (about 2 ounces)

2 tablespoons freshly grated or shredded imported Parmesan cheese

PREP: 15 MIN; COOK: 20 MIN
4 servings

1. Heat 1 inch salted water (1/2 teaspoon salt to 1 cup water) to boiling in 3-quart saucepan. Add Brussels sprouts. Heat to boiling; reduce heat. Cover and simmer about 10 minutes or until tender; drain.

2. Melt butter and bouillon granules in 10-inch skillet over medium-high heat. Cook onion in butter about 5 minutes, stirring occasionally, until tender. Stir in Brussels sprouts and prosciutto; reduce heat to low. Cover and cook about 2 minutes or until hot. Sprinkle with cheese.

1 Serving: Calories 125 (Calories from Fat 70); Fat 8g (Saturated 4g); Cholesterol 20mg; Sodium 380mg; Carbohydrate 11g (Dietary Fiber 5g); Protein 7g
% Daily Value: Vitamin A 10%; Vitamin C 42%; Calcium 8%; Iron 6%
Diet Exchanges: 2 Vegetable, 1 1/2 Fat

FRESH PEAS AND PROSCIUTTO

Piselli al Prosciutto per Contorno

1/4 cup olive oil

1/3 pound imported prosciutto, chopped (1/3 cup)

1 small onion, chopped (1/4 cup)

2 pounds green peas, shelled*

1/2 cup chicken broth

1 tablespoon sugar

1 tablespoon chopped fresh parsley

1/4 teaspoon salt

2 1/2 cups frozen green peas can be substituted for the fresh green peas. Cover and cook 3 to 5 minutes or until peas are hot.

PREP: 25 MIN; COOK: 15 MIN
4 servings

1. Heat oil in 10-inch skillet over medium-high heat. Cook prosciutto and onion in oil, stirring frequently, until onion is tender.

2. Reduce heat to medium. Stir in remaining ingredients. Cover and cook about 10 minutes or until peas are tender.

1 Serving: Calories 210 (Calories from Fat 135); Fat 15g (Saturated 2g); Cholesterol 5mg; Sodium 520mg; Carbohydrate 16g (Dietary Fiber 5g); Protein 8g
% Daily Value: Vitamin A 6%; Vitamin C 8%; Calcium 2%; Iron 8%
Diet Exchanges: 3 Vegetable, 3 Fat

POTATOES WITH ARTICHOKE HEARTS AND OLIVES
Carciofi Rustici

1 pound small red potatoes
(about 8), cut in half

1/3 cup olive oil

1 small onion, thinly sliced

2 packages (9 ounces each) frozen
artichoke hearts, thawed, or
2 cans (14 ounces each) artichoke
hearts, drained

1/4 cup sliced pitted imported
Greek green olives

2 tablespoons fresh lemon juice

1 tablespoon capers

1/2 teaspoon salt

1/8 teaspoon pepper

1/4 cup freshly grated or shredded
imported Parmesan cheese,
if desired

PREP: 15 MIN; COOK: 25 MIN
4 servings

1. Heat 1 inch salted water (1/2 teaspoon salt to 1 cup water) to boiling in 3-quart saucepan. Add potatoes. Heat to boiling; reduce heat. Cover and simmer about 10 minutes or until tender; drain.

2. Heat oil in 12-inch skillet over medium-high heat. Cook onion in oil about 5 minutes, stirring frequently, until tender. Reduce heat to medium. Stir in potatoes and remaining ingredients except cheese. Cook uncovered about 5 minutes, stirring frequently, until hot. Sprinkle with cheese.

1 Serving: Calories 270 (Calories from Fat 135); Fat 15g (Saturated 2g); Cholesterol 0mg; Sodium 930mg; Carbohydrate 36g (Dietary Fiber 9g); Protein 7g
% Daily Value: Vitamin A 2%; Vitamin C 22%; Calcium 8%; Iron 16%
Diet Exchanges: 2 Starch, 1 Vegetable, 2 Fat

MASHED POTATOES WITH PARMESAN AND OLIVE OIL
Patate della Duchessa Vergine

6 medium baking potatoes
(about 2 pounds)

4 cloves garlic, peeled

1/2 cup extra-virgin olive oil

1/2 cup freshly grated imported
Parmesan cheese

1 tablespoon fresh chopped parsley

1 teaspoon chopped fresh chives

PREP: 10 MIN; COOK: 25 MIN
4 servings

1. Peel potatoes; cut into large pieces. Heat 1 inch salted water (1/2 teaspoon salt to 1 cup water) to boiling in 3-quart saucepan. Add potatoes and garlic. Cover and heat to boiling; reduce heat. Boil 20 to 25 minutes or until potatoes are tender; drain. Shake pan with potatoes gently over low heat to dry.

2. Mash potatoes and garlic in medium bowl until no lumps remain. Add remaining ingredients; beat vigorously until potatoes are light and fluffy.

1 Serving: Calories 435 (Calories from Fat 280); Fat 31g (Saturated 6g); Cholesterol 10mg; Sodium 240mg; Carbohydrate 33g (Dietary Fiber 2g); Protein 8g
% Daily Value: Vitamin A 2%; Vitamin C 18%; Calcium 18%; Iron 4%
Diet Exchanges: 2 Starch, 6 Fat

Parola di Antonio

Here is a potato recipe that will turn a humble farmer's meal into a royal feast. Legend tells us that, while poor farmers could use only water and salt in their mashed potatoes, a young duchess in Parma loved this dish with extra-virgin olive oil and Parmesan; hence the nickname Patate della Duchessa Vergine.

PAN-ROASTED POTATOES
Patate Al Forno

6 medium baking potatoes
(about 2 pounds)

1 medium red onion, coarsely
chopped

2 tablespoons chopped fresh
rosemary leaves

4 cloves garlic, finely chopped

1/2 teaspoon salt

1/2 teaspoon pepper

1/4 cup olive oil

1/4 cup freshly grated or shredded
imported Parmesan cheese

PREP: 10 MIN; BAKE: 50 MIN
4 servings

1. Heat oven to 375°. Peel potatoes if desired; cut into 1 1/2-inch pieces. Toss potatoes, onion, rosemary, garlic, salt and pepper in rectangular pan, 13 x 9 x 2 inches. Drizzle with oil.

2. Bake uncovered 40 minutes, stirring occasionally. Sprinkle with cheese; toss until potatoes are evenly coated. Bake about 10 minutes longer or until potatoes are tender and golden brown.

1 Serving: Calories 350 (Calories from Fat 145); Fat 16g (Saturated 3g); Cholesterol 5mg; Sodium 430mg; Carbohydrate 49g (Dietary Fiber 5g); Protein 7g
% Daily Value: Vitamin A 0%; Vitamin C 22%; Calcium 12%; Iron 14%
Diet Exchanges: 3 Starch, 1 Vegetable, 2 Fat

Pan-Roasted Potatoes

SPINACH MILAN-STYLE
Spinaci alla Milanese

2 pounds spinach

2 tablespoons butter or margarine

2 cloves garlic, finely chopped

1/4 cup pine nuts

1/2 teaspoon freshly grated nutmeg

1/2 teaspoon salt

1/4 teaspoon pepper

2 tablespoons water

PREP: 10 MIN; COOK: 10 MIN
4 servings

1. Wash spinach thoroughly; drain. Remove stems and any yellow leaves.

2. Melt butter in 4-quart Dutch oven over medium heat. Cook garlic in butter about 5 minutes, stirring frequently, until just golden. Stir in pine nuts, nutmeg, salt and pepper.

3. Reduce heat to low. Gradually add spinach; sprinkle with water. Cover and cook about 5 minutes or until spinach is wilted.

1 Serving: Calories 145 (Calories from Fat 110); Fat 12g (Saturated 4g); Cholesterol 15mg; Sodium 470mg; Carbohydrate 8g (Dietary Fiber 5g); Protein 6g
% Daily Value: Vitamin A 100%; Vitamin C 38%; Calcium 16%; Iron 26%
Diet Exchanges: 2 Vegetable, 2 Fat

SAVORY ZUCCHINI
Zucchine Saporite

2 medium green zucchini (1 pound)

2 medium yellow summer squash (1 pound)

1/4 teaspoon salt

2 tablespoons olive oil

2 anchovy fillets in oil, finely chopped

1 tablespoon chopped fresh parsley

1 tablespoon chopped fresh mint leaves

2 cloves garlic, finely chopped

1/4 teaspoon pepper

PREP: 15 MIN; COOK: 15 MIN
4 servings

1. Cut zucchini and summer squash into 1/2-inch cubes. Sprinkle with salt. Let stand 10 minutes; pat dry with paper towels.

2. Heat oil in 12-inch skillet over medium heat. Stir in anchovies, parsley, mint and garlic. Cook 4 minutes, stirring frequently. Stir in zucchini, summer squash and pepper. Cover and cook about 8 minutes, stirring frequently, until zucchini is tender.

1 Serving: Calories 85 (Calories from Fat 65); Fat 7g (Saturated 1g); Cholesterol 0mg; Sodium 220mg; Carbohydrate 4g (Dietary Fiber 1g); Protein 2g
% Daily Value: Vitamin A 4%; Vitamin C 8%; Calcium 2%; Iron 2%
Diet Exchanges: 1 Vegetable, 1 Fat

Parola di Antonio

To salt or not to salt, that is the question. In general, Italians buy their groceries daily, and the local produce is always fresh and in season. If squash is genuinely fresh, small and firm, skip the salting.

FRESH BASIL AND SPINACH SALAD
Insalata al Basilico

5 ounces French or baby whole green beans or 1 1/4 cups 1-inch pieces regular green beans*

Balsamic Vinaigrette (below)

5 ounces spinach, torn into bite-size pieces (3 cups)

5 ounces fresh basil leaves, torn into bite-size pieces (3 cups)

2 hard-cooked eggs, coarsely chopped

3 tablespoons extra-virgin olive oil

1 teaspoon balsamic vinegar

1 teaspoon fresh lemon juice

1/2 teaspoon salt

1/2 teaspoon freshly ground pepper

1 1/4 cups frozen cut green beans can be substituted for the fresh green beans. Cook beans as directed on package; drain and cool to room temperature.

PREP: 20 MIN; COOK: 8 MIN; COOL: 30 MIN
4 servings

1. Heat 1 inch salted water (1/2 teaspoon salt to 1 cup water) to boiling in 2-quart saucepan. Add beans. Heat to boiling; reduce heat. Cover and simmer about 7 minutes or until beans are just tender; drain. Cool to room temperature, about 30 minutes.

2. Make Balsamic Vinaigrette. Place beans, spinach and basil in large glass or plastic bowl. Add vinaigrette; toss until evenly coated. Add eggs; toss gently.

Balsamic Vinaigrette

Shake all ingredients in tightly covered container.

1 Serving: Calories 145 (Calories from Fat 115); Fat 13g (Saturated 2g); Cholesterol 105mg; Sodium 350mg; Carbohydrate 5g (Dietary Fiber 3g); Protein 5g
% Daily Value: Vitamin A 40%; Vitamin C 24%; Calcium 10%; Iron 14%
Diet Exchanges: 1/2 Medium-Fat Meat, 1 Vegetable, 2 Fat

Parola di Antonio

A refreshing treat from Genoa in the Italian Riviera, this salad was an ideal snack for fishermen out at sea. Light to carry and easy to assemble, it was occasionally topped with cured anchovies for added protein. Both basil and spinach grow naturally, along with wild caper bushes and wildflowers, in the valleys of the Riviera's craggy coastline. I like to use the small, thin whole green beans known as French or baby green beans because they are so tender. If they aren't available, regular fresh green beans, cut into pieces, will also work.

Fresh Basil and Spinach Salad

MIXED SALAD GREENS, WILTED AND TOSSED
Insalata Cotta e Cruda

1/4 cup olive oil

8 medium green onions, chopped
  (1/2 cup)

2 tablespoons chopped fresh basil
  leaves

4 cloves garlic, finely chopped

8 cups organic mixed spring,
  baby or field salad greens

2 teaspoons fresh lemon juice

1 teaspoon honey

1/2 teaspoon salt

1/4 cup dry white wine or chicken
  broth

PREP: 10 MIN; COOK: 10 MIN; CHILL: 30 MIN
4 servings

1. Heat oil in 10-inch skillet over medium heat. Cook onions, basil, garlic and 2 cups of the salad greens in oil about 5 minutes, stirring occasionally, until greens are wilted.

2. Mix lemon juice, honey, salt and wine; stir into salad greens. Cook about 3 minutes, stirring frequently, until greens are evenly coated with wine mixture.

3. Place remaining greens in large bowl; add wilted greens mixture. Toss until well mixed. Cover and refrigerate at least 30 minutes but no longer than 1 hour before serving.

1 Serving: Calories 145 (Calories from Fat 120); Fat 14g (Saturated 2g); Cholesterol 0mg;
Sodium 310mg; Carbohydrate 6g (Dietary Fiber 2g); Protein 2g
% Daily Value: Vitamin A 10%; Vitamin C 22%; Calcium 4%; Iron 6%
Diet Exchanges: 1 Vegetable, 2 1/2 Fat

Parola di Antonio

Winter or summer, this salad will please everyone. It is interesting to observe the difference in flavor when the salad greens are cooked; they turn mellower and soft textured. In contrast, fresh mixed greens preserve a bit of pungent wild taste. The greens in this salad become vibrant with the freshness of basil and lemon.

Mixed Salad Greens, Wilted and Tossed

GARLIC AND ROMAINE SALAD
Insalata di Romanella ed Aglio

Lemon Vinaigrette (below)

1 large bunch romaine, torn into bite-size pieces (10 cups)

1 small red onion, sliced and separated into rings

1 jar (6 ounces) marinated artichoke hearts, undrained

1 cup imported Kalamata olives, pitted, or jumbo ripe olives

1/2 cup seasoned croutons

1/3 cup freshly shredded imported Parmesan cheese

PREP: 20 MIN
8 servings

1. Make Lemon Vinaigrette. Place romaine, onion, artichoke hearts and olives in large glass or plastic bowl. Add vinaigrette; toss gently until evenly coated.

2. Sprinkle with croutons and cheese. Serve immediately.

1/4 cup fresh lemon juice

2 tablespoons extra-virgin olive oil

1/4 teaspoon salt

1/4 teaspoon pepper

2 cloves garlic, finely chopped

Lemon Vinaigrette
Shake all ingredients in tightly covered container.

1 Serving: Calories 100 (Calories from Fat 65); Fat 7g (Saturated 2g); Cholesterol 5mg; Sodium 400mg; Carbohydrate 8g (Dietary Fiber 3g); Protein 4g
% Daily Value: Vitamin A 14%; Vitamin C 26%; Calcium 10%; Iron 8%
Diet Exchanges: 2 Vegetable, 1 Fat

PIQUANT SALAD
Insalata Piccante

8 ounces green beans

1 head radicchio

2 medium bulbs fennel, cut into
fourths

1 head Boston lettuce, torn into
bite-size pieces

1 jar (6 ounces) marinated artichoke
hearts, drained

Three-Herb Dressing (below)

PREP: 25 MIN; COOK: 10 MIN; COOL: 30 MIN
4 servings

1. Heat 1 inch salted water (1/2 teaspoon salt to 1 cup water) to boiling in 2-quart saucepan. Add beans. Heat to boiling; reduce heat. Cover and simmer about 7 minutes or until beans are just tender; drain. Cool to room temperature, about 30 minutes.

2. Arrange radicchio leaves around edge of large platter. Mix beans, fennel, Boston lettuce and artichoke hearts; place in center of radicchio-lined platter. Make Three-Herb Dressing; drizzle over salad.

1/2 cup extra-virgin olive oil

2 tablespoons fresh lemon juice

1 tablespoon capers

1/2 teaspoon chopped fresh or
1/8 teaspoon dried mint leaves

1/2 teaspoon chopped fresh or
1/8 teaspoon dried oregano
leaves

1/2 teaspoon chopped fresh or
1/8 teaspoon rubbed sage leaves

1/2 teaspoon salt

1/4 teaspoon pepper

1 clove garlic, finely chopped

Three-Herb Dressing

Shake all ingredients in tightly covered container.

1 Serving: Calories 315 (Calories from Fat 260); Fat 29g (Saturated 4g); Cholesterol 0mg;
Sodium 560mg; Carbohydrate 18g (Dietary Fiber 8g); Protein 4g
% Daily Value: Vitamin A 6%; Vitamin C 20%; Calcium 10%; Iron 12%
Diet Exchanges: 4 Vegetable, 5 Fat

ROASTED BEETS AND ONION SALAD
Insalata di Rape e Cipolle

1 1/2 pounds small beets (1 1/2 to
    2 inches in diameter)

2 medium red onions, cut into
    fourths

1/2 teaspoon salt

1/4 teaspoon coarsely ground
    pepper

2 tablespoons extra-virgin olive oil

2 tablespoons chopped fresh
    basil leaves

1 tablespoon balsamic vinegar

PREP: 10 MIN; BAKE: 40 MIN
6 servings

1. Heat oven to 425°. Cut off all but 2 inches of beet tops. Wash beets; leave whole with root ends attached.

2. Place beets and onions in ungreased rectangular pan, 13 x 9 x 2 inches. Sprinkle with salt and pepper. Drizzle with oil.

3. Bake uncovered about 40 minutes or until beets are tender. Let beets and onions cool until easy to handle. Peel beets and cut off root ends; cut beets into 1/2-inch slices. Separate onions into pieces.

4. Toss beets, onions, basil and vinegar. Serve at room temperature, or if desired, cover and refrigerate at least 1 hour but no longer than 48 hours.

1 Serving: Calories 90 (Calories from Fat 45); Fat 5g (Saturated 1g); Cholesterol 0mg; Sodium 250mg; Carbohydrate 11g (Dietary Fiber 2g); Protein 2g
% Daily Value: Vitamin A 0%; Vitamin C 4%; Calcium 2%; Iron 4%
Diet Exchanges: 2 Vegetable, 1 Fat

Parola di Antonio

A secret kept for too long, fresh beets have been recently rediscovered by Americans and are on their way to stardom. Most supermarkets now carry them fresh; if given a choice, pick the smaller, young beets. The flavor of fresh beets, especially when paired with basil and red onion, will make you forget all about the canned ones. For an additional treat, sauté the fresh beet greens with some chopped garlic in olive oil until the leaves are wilted and coated with oil. Serve a spoonful of the wilted beet greens alongside this beet and onion salad. This salad is quite common in southern Italy, specifically in the regions of Puglia and Calabria.

Roasted Beets and Onion Salad

NEAPOLITAN SALAD
Insalata di Rinforzo alla Napoletana

1 small head cauliflower
   (1 1/2 pounds)

8 ounces imported Kalamata olives,
   drained and pitted, or pitted
   large ripe olives

2 tablespoons capers

6 flat anchovy fillets in oil

4 hard-cooked eggs, cut into fourths

1/4 cup extra-virgin olive oil

1 tablespoon red wine vinegar

1/2 teaspoon salt

1/4 teaspoon pepper

PREP: 15 MIN; COOK: 10 MIN; COOL: 30 MIN
4 servings

1. Separate cauliflower into flowerets. Heat 1 inch salted water (1/2 teaspoon salt to 1 cup water) to boiling in 3-quart saucepan. Add cauliflower. Cover and heat to boiling; reduce heat. Simmer about 6 minutes or until cauliflower is just tender; drain. Let stand at room temperature about 30 minutes or until cool.

2. Place cauliflower in center of large plate. Arrange olives, capers, anchovy fillets and eggs around cauliflower. Mix remaining ingredients; pour over top.

1 Serving: Calories 290 (Calories from Fat 235); Fat 26g (Saturated 4g); Cholesterol 215mg; Sodium 1200mg; Carbohydrate 8g (Dietary Fiber 4g); Protein 10g
% Daily Value: Vitamin A 10%; Vitamin C 26%; Calcium 10%; Iron 18%
Diet Exchanges: 1 Medium-Fat Meat, 2 Vegetable, 4 Fat

WARM TRICOLOR BELL PEPPER SALAD
Peperonata ai Tre Colori

1/2 cup olive oil

2 cloves garlic, finely chopped

1 medium red onion, chopped

2 medium red bell peppers, cut into 1/2-inch strips

2 medium green bell peppers, cut into 1/2-inch strips

2 medium yellow bell peppers, cut into 1/2-inch strips

6 roma (plum) tomatoes, peeled if desired and chopped*

1/2 teaspoon salt

1/4 teaspoon pepper

6 canned Italian-style pear-shaped (plum) tomatoes can be substituted for the fresh tomatoes.

PREP: 25 MIN; COOK: 20 MIN
4 servings

1. Heat oil in 12-inch skillet over medium-high heat. Cook garlic and onion in oil, stirring frequently, until onion is tender. Reduce heat to medium-low. Stir in bell peppers. Cover and cook about 10 minutes or until bell peppers are tender. Remove peppers with slotted spoon; set aside.

2. Stir tomatoes, salt and pepper into skillet. Cook uncovered about 5 minutes, stirring gently and frequently, until hot.

3. Remove skin from peppers if desired. Arrange peppers in star shape on large plate. Spoon tomatoes in center of peppers; pour liquid from skillet over top. Serve hot or at room temperature.

1 Serving: Calories 320 (Calories from Fat 250); Fat 28g (Saturated 4g); Cholesterol 0mg; Sodium 310mg; Carbohydrate 18g (Dietary Fiber 4g); Protein 3g
% Daily Value: Vitamin A 44%; Vitamin C 100%; Calcium 2%; Iron 8%
Diet Exchanges: 4 Vegetable, 5 Fat

Parola di Antonio

Peperonata *is the most popular pepper salad in Italy. The colorful red, green and yellow peppers are easier to digest if they are skinned or soaked in milk before being cooked. If you choose not to remove the skins after cooking, however, your salad will be just as delicious. This makes a nice salad for a picnic or to take for a potluck meal because it can be served warm, so you don't have to worry about keeping it hot or cold.*

GRILLED RADICCHIO SALAD
Radicchio alla Griglia

2 large heads radicchio (about 10 ounces each)

3 large tomatoes, cut into 1/2-inch slices

1/4 cup extra-virgin olive oil

1 tablespoon chopped fresh or 1 teaspoon dried basil leaves

1 teaspoon chopped fresh or 1/4 teaspoon dried dill weed

1 teaspoon fresh lemon juice

1/4 teaspoon salt

1/4 teaspoon pepper

PREP: 15 MIN; GRILL: 10 MIN
6 servings

1. Remove outer leaves from radicchio and discard. Cut radicchio into 1/2-inch slices. Place radicchio and tomatoes in large bowl.

2. Mix remaining ingredients; pour evenly over radicchio and tomatoes. Gently toss until vegetables are evenly coated with herb mixture.

3. Heat coals or gas grill as directed by manufacturer for direct heat. Remove vegetables from herb mixture; reserve herb mixture. Place vegetables in grill basket.

4. Grill vegetables about 4 inches from medium-high heat 5 minutes. Turn basket over; drizzle reserved herb mixture over vegetables. Grill about 5 minutes longer or until radicchio is crisp-tender and tomatoes are warm. Serve immediately.

1 Serving: Calories 100 (Calories from Fat 80); Fat 9g (Saturated 1g); Cholesterol 0mg; Sodium 110mg; Carbohydrate 5g (Dietary Fiber 1g); Protein 1g
% Daily Value: Vitamin A 6%; Vitamin C 30%; Calcium 0%; Iron 2%
Diet Exchanges: 1 Vegetable, 1 1/2 Fat

Parola di Antonio

Radicchio, originally from the countryside of Venice, is now common fare in most restaurants, Italian or not. Italians are quite fond of strong radicchio flavors, and several types with varying degrees of bitterness are available there. Surprisingly, grilling radicchio helps to diminish some of the bitterness, and it adds a pleasant smoky flavor.

Grilled Radicchio Salad

WARM TOMATO AND OLIVE SALAD
Olive e Pomodori Saltati

1 jar (10 ounces) imported
  Kalamata olives, drained and
  pitted*

1 jar (10 ounces) imported Greek
  green olives, drained and pitted

2 tablespoons olive oil

2 tablespoons chopped fresh parsley

2 cloves garlic, finely chopped

8 small tomatoes, cut into fourths

1/2 teaspoon salt

1/4 teaspoon pepper

*1 can (5 3/4 ounces) pitted ripe olives
can be substituted for the Kalamata
olives.*

PREP: 20 MIN; STAND: 30 MIN; COOK: 5 MIN
6 servings

1. Cover olives with cold water. Let stand 30 minutes; drain and pat dry.

2. Heat oil in 10-inch nonstick skillet over medium-high heat. Cook parsley and garlic in oil, stirring frequently, until garlic is soft.

3. Reduce heat to medium. Stir in olives. Cook uncovered 3 minutes, stirring frequently. Stir in tomatoes, salt and pepper. Cook about 2 minutes, stirring gently, until tomatoes are warm.

1 Serving: Calories 165 (Calories from Fat 135); Fat 15g (Saturated 2g); Cholesterol 0mg; Sodium 1700mg; Carbohydrate 9g (Dietary Fiber 3g); Protein 2g
% Daily Value: Vitamin A 10%; Vitamin C 22%; Calcium 6%; Iron 14%
Diet Exchanges: 2 Vegetable, 2 1/2 Fat

TOMATO AND POTATO SALAD WITH HERBS
Insalata Estiva alle Erbe

1 pound small red potatoes
 (about 8)

5 roma (plum) tomatoes, cut into
 fourths

1/2 cup chopped fresh basil leaves

1/3 cup chopped fresh sage leaves

1/3 cup chopped fresh mint leaves

1 small onion, finely chopped
 (1/4 cup)

3/4 cup extra-virgin olive oil

1/2 cup red wine vinegar

PREP: 25 MIN; COOK: 20 MIN; COOL: 15 MIN; CHILL: 2 HR
6 servings

1. Heat 1 inch salted water (1/2 teaspoon salt to 1 cup water) to boiling in 2-quart saucepan. Add potatoes. Heat to boiling; reduce heat. Cover and simmer about 20 minutes or until tender; drain. Cool until easy to handle, about 15 minutes.

2. Peel potatoes if desired; cut into 1/2-inch slices. Gently toss potatoes, tomatoes, basil, sage, mint and onion. Pour oil and vinegar over potato mixture; toss gently until vegetables are evenly coated.

3. Cover and refrigerate at least 2 hours to blend flavors but no longer than 24 hours, stirring occasionally. Toss before serving.

1 Serving: Calories 230 (Calories from Fat 110); Fat 18g (Saturated 3g); Cholesterol 0mg; Sodium 10mg; Carbohydrate 17g (Dietary Fiber 2g); Protein 2g
% Daily Value: Vitamin A 6%; Vitamin C 14%; Calcium 2%; Iron 6%
Diet Exchanges: 1 Starch, 3 1/2 Fat

ITALIAN TOMATO AND BREAD SALAD

Panzanella al Pomodoro

4 cups 1-inch pieces day-old Italian or other firm-textured bread

2 medium tomatoes, cut into bite-size pieces

2 cloves garlic, finely chopped

1 medium green bell pepper, coarsely chopped

1/3 cup chopped fresh basil leaves

2 tablespoons chopped fresh parsley

1/3 cup extra-virgin olive oil

2 tablespoons red wine vinegar

1/2 teaspoon salt

1/8 teaspoon pepper

PREP: 20 MIN; CHILL 1 HR
6 servings

1. Mix bread, tomatoes, garlic, bell pepper, basil and parsley in glass or plastic bowl.

2. Shake remaining ingredients in tightly covered container. Pour over bread mixture; toss gently until bread is evenly coated. Cover and refrigerate at least 1 hour until bread is softened and flavors are blended but no longer than 8 hours. Toss before serving.

1 Serving: Calories 185 (Calories from Fat 115); Fat 13g (Saturated 2g); Cholesterol 0mg; Sodium 340mg; Carbohydrate 16g (Dietary Fiber 2g); Protein 3g
% Daily Value: Vitamin A 4%; Vitamin C 46%; Calcium 2%; Iron 6%
Diet Exchanges: 1 Starch, 2 Fat

Italian Tomato and Bread Salad

MARINATED MIXED VEGETABLES
Marinata Mista

2 cups broccoli flowerets
   (1/2 pound)

2 large bulbs fennel, cut into 1-inch
   pieces

4 ounces mozzarella cheese,
   cut into 1/2-inch cubes

1 jar (10 ounces) imported
   Kalamata olives, drained and
   pitted* (1 1/4 cups)

1 jar (8 ounces) marinated
   mushrooms, drained

2 jars (6 ounces each) marinated
   artichoke hearts, drained

1/2 cup extra-virgin olive oil

1/2 cup red wine vinegar

2 tablespoons fresh lemon juice

*1 can (5 3/4 ounces) pitted ripe olives
can be substituted for the Kalamata
olives.

PREP: 20 MIN; CHILL: 2 HR
8 servings

1. Place all ingredients except oil, vinegar and lemon juice in shallow glass or plastic dish. Shake oil, vinegar and lemon juice in tightly covered container. Pour over vegetable mixture; toss.

2. Cover and refrigerate at least 2 hours to blend flavors but no longer than 24 hours. Toss before serving.

1 Serving: Calories 265 (Calories from Fat 200); Fat 22g (Saturated 4g); Cholesterol 5mg; Sodium 660mg; Carbohydrate 15g (Dietary Fiber 6g); Protein 8g
% Daily Value: Vitamin A 8%; Vitamin C 58%; Calcium 20%; Iron 14%
Diet Exchanges: 3 Vegetable, 4 Fat

Parola di Antonio

Olives with pits are almost always served in Italy, a custom that comes down from ancient Roman times. Pickled olives have been served as a snack or after a meal for thousands of years; they should never be confused with plain canned ripe olives. Italians linger over their olives, savoring the last taste of the olive on the pit for as long as possible before they have to relinquish the tasty kernel.

ANTIPASTO PASTA SALAD

Insalata D'Antipasto

1 package (16 ounces) farfalle pasta

Red Wine Vinaigrette (below)

1/4 pound sliced Genoa salami, cut into 1/4-inch-wide strips (3/4 cup)

1 small green bell pepper, cut into 1 1/2-inch strips

1 jar (7 ounces) roasted red bell (sweet) peppers, drained and cut into 1/4-inch strips

1 can (5 3/4 ounces) pitted large ripe olives, drained

1/2 cup chopped drained pepperoncini peppers (bottled Italian peppers)

1/2 cup freshly shredded imported Parmesan cheese

2 tablespoons chopped drained sun-dried tomatoes in oil

1/4 cup extra-virgin olive oil

1/4 cup red wine vinegar

1 tablespoon fresh lemon juice

PREP: 20 MIN; CHILL: 2 HR
8 servings

1. Cook and drain pasta as directed on package. Rinse with cold water; drain.

2. Make Red Wine Vinaigrette. Place pasta and remaining ingredients in large glass or plastic bowl. Add vinaigrette; toss gently until evenly coated. Cover and refrigerate at least 2 hours to blend flavors but no longer than 24 hours.

Red Wine Vinaigrette

Shake all ingredients in tightly covered container.

1 Serving: Calories 365 (Calories from Fat 135); Fat 15g (Saturated 4g); Cholesterol 15mg; Sodium 450mg; Carbohydrate 49g (Dietary Fiber 3g); Protein 12g
% Daily Value: Vitamin A 4%; Vitamin C 52%; Calcium 12%; Iron 18%
Diet Exchanges: 3 Starch, 1 Vegetable, 2 Fat

MARINATED ROTINI AND THREE-CHEESE SALAD
Insalata di Rotini Marinata

1 package (16 ounces) rotini or
   gemelli pasta

Fresh Dill Vinaigrette (below)

1/2 cup shredded mozzarella cheese
   (2 ounces)

1/2 cup shredded provolone cheese
   (2 ounces)

1/4 cup freshly grated imported
   Parmesan cheese

1/4 cup sliced pitted imported
   Kalamata or sliced ripe olives

1/4 cup sliced pimiento-stuffed olives

1/2 cup chopped pepperoni (3 ounces)

1/4 pound salami, cut into 1/4-inch
   pieces (3/4 cup)

1 small red onion, chopped

1/2 cup extra-virgin olive oil

1/4 cup dry white wine or
   nonalcoholic white wine

1 teaspoon red wine vinegar

1/2 teaspoon salt

1/2 teaspoon sugar

1/2 teaspoon chopped fresh dill
   weed

1/4 teaspoon pepper

PREP: 20 MIN; CHILL: 2 HR
8 servings

1. Cook and drain pasta as directed on package. Rinse with cold water; drain.

2. Make Fresh Dill Vinaigrette. Place pasta and remaining ingredients in large glass or plastic bowl. Add vinaigrette; toss gently until evenly coated. Cover and refrigerate at least 2 hours to blend flavors but no longer than 24 hours. Toss before serving.

Fresh Dill Vinaigrette

Shake all ingredients in tightly covered container.

1 Serving: Calories 535 (Calories from Fat 280); Fat 31g (Saturated 9g); Cholesterol 35mg; Sodium 1010mg; Carbohydrate 47g (Dietary Fiber 2g); Protein 19g
% Daily Value: Vitamin A 2%; Vitamin C 0%; Calcium 16%; Iron 16%
Diet Exchanges: 3 Starch, 1 1/2 High-Fat Meat, 3 Fat

Marinated Rotini and Three-Cheese Salad

CHEESE-FILLED TORTELLINI SALAD
Tortellini Freddi in Insalata

1 package (9 ounces) refrigerated or dried cheese-filled tortellini

1 package (9 ounces) refrigerated or dried cheese-filled spinach tortellini

Basil-Caper Dressing (below)

2 medium carrots, sliced (1 cup)

2 medium green onions, thinly sliced (2 tablespoons)

2 tablespoons chopped fresh basil leaves

1 tablespoon freshly grated or shredded imported Parmesan cheese

1/8 teaspoon pepper

PREP: 15 MIN; CHILL: 2 HR
6 servings

1. Cook and drain plain and spinach tortellini as directed on package. Rinse with cold water; drain.

2. Make Basil-Caper Dressing. Place tortellini and remaining ingredients in large glass or plastic bowl. Add dressing; toss until evenly coated. Cover and refrigerate at least 2 hours to blend flavors but no longer than 24 hours. Toss before serving.

1/3 cup extra-virgin olive oil

2 tablespoons fresh lemon juice

2 tablespoons chopped fresh or 2 teaspoons dried basil leaves

2 tablespoons capers

Basil-Caper Dressing

Shake all ingredients in tightly covered container.

1 Serving: Calories 250 (Calories from Fat 155); Fat 17g (Saturated 4g); Cholesterol 70mg; Sodium 140mg; Carbohydrate 18g (Dietary Fiber 1g); Protein 7g
% Daily Value: Vitamin A 36%; Vitamin C 8%; Calcium 8%; Iron 8%
Diet Exchanges: 1 Starch, 1 Vegetable, 3 Fat

CHICKEN, SPINACH AND TOMATO SALAD
Insalata di Spinaci e Pollo Tricolore

1/4 cup olive oil

1 small onion, chopped (1/4 cup)

6 boneless, skinless chicken breast halves (about 1 3/4 pounds)

1/2 cup dry white wine or chicken broth

Herbed Dressing (below)

1 pound spinach leaves

6 medium tomatoes, sliced

1/4 cup freshly grated or shredded imported Parmesan cheese

Fresh rosemary, basil or mint leaves, if desired

PREP: 25 MIN; COOK: 20 MIN; CHILL: 2 HR
6 servings

1. Heat oil in 12-inch skillet over medium-high heat. Cook onion in oil, stirring frequently, until tender. Reduce heat to medium. Add chicken. Cook uncovered about 5 minutes, turning frequently, until chicken is lightly browned.

2. Add wine to skillet. Cover and simmer about 10 minutes or until juice of chicken is no longer pink when centers of thickest pieces are cut. Cover and refrigerate at least 2 hours until chilled but no longer than 24 hours.

3. Make Herbed Dressing. Cut chicken into strips. Arrange one-third of the spinach on large platter. Top with one-third of the tomatoes and chicken; drizzle with about one-third of the dressing. Repeat twice with remaining spinach, tomatoes and chicken; drizzle with remaining dressing. Sprinkle with cheese. Garnish with rosemary leaves.

1/2 cup extra-virgin olive oil

2 tablespoons fresh lemon juice

2 tablespoons chopped fresh or 2 teaspoons dried basil leaves

2 tablespoons chopped fresh or 2 teaspoons dried mint leaves, crumbled

2 tablespoons chopped fresh or 2 teaspoons dried rosemary leaves, crumbled

1/2 teaspoon salt

1/4 teaspoon pepper

Herbed Dressing
Shake all ingredients in tightly covered container.

1 Serving: Calories 445 (Calories from Fat 295); Fat 33g (Saturated 6g); Cholesterol 75mg; Sodium 400mg; Carbohydrate 9g (Dietary Fiber 3g); Protein 31g
% Daily Value: Vitamin A 54%; Vitamin C 68%; Calcium 14%; Iron 18%
Diet Exchanges: 4 Lean Meat, 2 Vegetable, 4 Fat

BEAN AND TUNA SALAD
Fagioli e Tonno in Insalata

2 cans (15 to 16 ounces each) cannellini or great northern beans, rinsed and drained

1 medium red onion, thinly sliced

1/3 cup extra-virgin olive oil

3 tablespoons red wine vinegar

1/2 teaspoon salt

1/8 teaspoon pepper

1 can (6 ounces) tuna in water or oil, drained

2 tablespoons chopped fresh parsley

PREP: 25 MIN; CHILL: 1 HR
6 servings

1. Place beans and onion in shallow glass or plastic dish. Shake oil, vinegar, salt and pepper in tightly covered container; pour over beans and onion. Cover and refrigerate at least 1 hour to blend flavors but no longer than 24 hours.

2. Spoon bean mixture onto serving platter, using slotted spoon; reserve marinade. Break tuna into chunks; arrange on bean mixture. Drizzle with reserved marinade. Sprinkle with parsley.

1 Serving: Calories 320 (Calories from Fat 115); Fat 13g (Saturated 2g); Cholesterol 10mg; Sodium 300mg; Carbohydrate 38g (Dietary Fiber 9g); Protein 21g
% Daily Value: Vitamin A 0%; Vitamin C 4%; Calcium 14%; Iron 32%
Diet Exchanges: 2 Starch, 1 1/2 Lean Meat, 2 Vegetable, 1 Fat

Bean and Tuna Salad

Fresh Fruit Tart,
page 286

CHAPTER SEVEN

Dolci

DELECTABLE DESSERTS

Italian Beverages—Salut!

THE COFFEE BAR

No Italian can do without the daily coffee ritual, which entails starting the day with a cup of piping-hot black coffee. Throughout the day, they will take a few minutes to stop at a local coffee bar to enjoy the pleasure of a cup of espresso or cappuccino. You will find Italians standing elbow to elbow enjoying a quick cup of coffee and conversation. A popular coffee bar can serve as many as five thousand cups of coffee on a busy weekday.

Coffee, or *caffè* in Italian, is a word that represents not only cappuccino and espresso but also means cafè or coffee bar. Since coffee was introduced in Venice in the sixteenth century, Italians have consumed and loved freshly ground, strong, black coffee. They take their coffee very seriously and use only superior-quality coffee beans. The length of time coffee beans are roasted affects the flavor and color. Italian roasted beans are dark brown in color and produce a dark, strong brew that is not bitter and does not leave an unpleasant aftertaste.

ESPRESSO (eh-SPREH-soh), often mispronounced "expresso," is clean and assertive in flavor, with little aftertaste and no bitterness. It is the Italian invention of the espresso machine that brought this beverage to international fame. True espresso must be brewed under pressure so the steam is forced through the finely ground beans. It is served in *tazza*, a small porcelain cup, in one-ounce portions. Italians enjoy espresso throughout the day, but it is not served with the embellishments Americans favor, such as sugar or twists of lemon peel. *Doppio* is a double espresso.

CAPPUCCINO (kah-poo-CHEE-noh) is named after the color of the traditional capes of Italian monks. It is a blend of half espresso and half milk heated with pressurized steam from the espresso machine. The steamed milk gives it a creamy, frothy topping. It is served in a larger cup than is espresso and can be enjoyed with or without froth.

CAFFÈ CORRETTO (kah-FEH koh-REH-toh) is an espresso with a dash of liqueur or grappa that is served after dessert.

CAFFÈ LATTE (kah-FEH LAH-tay) is a blend of one-third espresso and two-thirds heated milk and is served in a cup or a tall glass. There is no frothy cap as with cappuccino. *Latte macchiato* is predominantly milk flavored with coffee.

ITALIAN SODAS

Nonalcoholic beverages are increasingly popular. Italian sodas are sparkling beverages freshly made with soda water and nonalcoholic fruit syrups poured over ice. Soda water, also referred to as club soda or seltzer, is water that has been charged with carbon dioxide to produce effervescence. A wide variety of fruit-flavored syrups are available, and the result is a very refreshing beverage.

WINES AND SPIRITS

The Italian landscape is dotted with lush grape vineyards that produce many fine wines. Italy has a drink for every occasion: wine to better enjoy food; sparkling *spumante* for celebrations; Marsala and sweet wines for dessert or appetizers; *grappa* and brandies to give a sense of warmth; and glowing *sambuca* and *amaretto* liqueurs for romantic and special occasions. Italy offers over two hundred wine and spirit selections, but we've selected the most popular exports to highlight.

AMARETTO (am-ah-REHT-toh) is a popular liqueur that has the flavor of almond but is actually made with apricot pits. Amaretto di Saronno is the original liqueur, hailing from Saronno, Italy.

AMERICANO (ah-meh-ree-KAH-noh) Apéritif made with Campari, sweet vermouth, sparkling water and orange slice.

ASTI SPUMANTE (AH-stee spoo-MAHN-teh) A sparkling white wine with a low alcohol content, similar to champagne, from the Asti region in Piedmont. It has a sweet, fruity flavor and is generally served with dessert or reserved for holiday occasions.

BAROLO (bah-ROH-loh) A full-bodied, aged aromatic red wine from the northern region of Piedmont.

BELLINI (beh-LEE-nee) A cocktail made from fresh white peach juice and *prosecco*, a sparkling white wine. It was created at Harry's Bar in Venice and served in a slender but not very tall glass. Elsewhere it is served in a tulip champagne glass and sometimes made with Asti Spumante.

CAMPARI (kahm-PAH-ree) Trademark name for a bittersweet alcoholic beverage that is served as an apéritif. This brilliant rose-red-colored beverage, created in Milan, is made from herbs, quinine bark and orange peel. It is served with a lemon twist or mixed with carbonated water.

CHARDONNAY (shahr-doh-NAY) A white grape long cultivated in northern Italy but not used for wine until the 1980s. Chardonnay grapes are also used to make *spumante*.

CHIANTI (kee-AHN-tee) One of the best-known Italian red wines, it comes from the Chianti district near Florence. It is excellent with meat dishes.

GRAPPA (GRAH-pah) A colorless, high-alcohol beverage made primarily in northern Italy. It is made from the residue (grape skins and seeds) left in the wine press after the juice is removed. It is mixed with water and distilled, resulting in a fiery spirit that has great depth and character. Grappa may have an added wild-flower seasoning. Some consider it purely an acquired taste.

LAMBRUSCO (lam-BROOS-koh) An Italian wine that may be red, white or rosé. All three can be either semi-sweet (best known by Americans) or dry, which is preferred by Italians. Lambrusco wines are usually drank "young" and are a slightly bubbly wine.

LIMONCELLO (lee-mohn-CHEH-loh) A liqueur of the Amalfi coast and Sicily that is made by steeping lemon peel with alcohol and sweetening slightly with a sugar syrup.

MARSALA (mahr-SAH-lah) A Sicilian fortified wine made with white and red grapes grown around Marsala. It has a rich, smoky flavor that can range from sweet to dry. Sweet Marsala is used as a dessert wine; dry Marsala is used as an apéritif. Marsala is classified by its degree of sweetness: *secco* (dry), *semisecco* (medium-dry) and *dolce* (sweet). This is a wonderful after-dinner drink, or what Italians call a "meditation wine" for sipping with friends after a satisfying meal.

SAMBUCA (sahm-BOO-kuh) A liqueur with the sweet, persistent flavor of anise, usually served with espresso coffee beans floated on top. Traditionally light blue in Italy, this syrupy liqueur is available either clear or in a dramatic transparent black color in America. Generally served after dinner with dessert or espresso.

FRESH FRUIT TART
Tortiera Alla Frutta

2 cups all-purpose flour

1 cup granulated sugar

1/2 cup butter or margarine,
　softened

1 teaspoon freshly grated
　lemon peel

1 teaspoon fresh lemon juice

1 teaspoon vanilla

3 eggs

1/2 cup apricot preserves

1/2 cup raspberry preserves

1 tablespoon amaretto or
　1/2 teaspoon almond extract

Fresh Fruit Topping (such as sliced
　apple, pear, banana, kiwifruit,
　figs, raspberries, blackberries,
　blueberries)

1 teaspoon honey

Powdered sugar, if desired

PREP: 10 MIN; CHILL: 20 MIN; BAKE: 35 MIN
8 servings

1. Mix flour, granulated sugar, butter, lemon peel, lemon juice, vanilla and eggs in medium bowl until dough forms. Place dough on lightly floured surface. Knead about 3 minutes or until dough holds together and is pliable. Shape dough into a ball. Cover with plastic wrap and refrigerate about 20 minutes or until firm.

2. Heat oven to 350°. Butter and flour 11-inch round tart pan with removable bottom or 12-inch pizza pan. Pat dough evenly in pan. Bake about 35 minutes or until toothpick inserted in center comes out clean. Cool completely in pan on wire rack.

3. Heat apricot preserves and raspberry preserves until melted; stir in amaretto. Spread over crust. Arrange fresh fruit on top. Drizzle with honey; dust with powdered sugar. Serve immediately, or cover and refrigerate no longer than 1 hour.

1 Serving: Calories 495 (Calories from Fat 125); Fat 14g (Saturated 8g); Cholesterol 110mg; Sodium 120mg; Carbohydrate 88g (Dietary Fiber 4g); Protein 7g
% Daily Value: Vitamin A 12%; Vitamin C 48%; Calcium 4%; Iron 12%
Diet Exchanges: Not Recommended

Parola di Antonio

The base for this tart is the classic pasta frolla, *a rich, buttery dough. Knead the dough just until it holds together and is pliable, which will take about 3 minutes. If you knead it too long, the butter will soften and the dough will become soft and sticky. Enjoy this dessert all year round using any ripe seasonal fruit.*

BAKED RASPBERRIES WITH BRANDY SAUCE
Mirtilli al Liquore

4 cups (2 pints) raspberries*

1 1/4 cups packed light brown sugar

1/2 cup brandy, amaretto or other
  liquor or liqueur

2 tablespoons honey

1 teaspoon vanilla

1/4 cup butter or margarine,
  softened

*1 1/2 bags (14- to 16-ounce size)
frozen loose-pack raspberries (without
juice) can be substituted for the fresh
raspberries. Rinse frozen berries with
cold water to separate; continue as
directed above.*

PREP: 5 MIN; BAKE: 20 MIN
8 servings (about 1/2 cup each)

1. Heat oven to 350°. Place raspberries in ungreased square baking dish, 9 x 9 x 2 inches. Mix remaining ingredients except butter until smooth; pour over raspberries. Dot with butter.

2. Bake uncovered about 20 minutes or until hot and bubbly. Stir gently, scraping bottom of dish to loosen sugar and stir into sauce. Serve warm.

1 Serving: Calories 240 (Calories from Fat 55); Fat 6g (Saturated 4g); Cholesterol 15mg; Sodium 50mg; Carbohydrate 45g (Dietary Fiber 4g); Protein 1g
% Daily Value: Vitamin A 4%; Vitamin C 12%; Calcium 4%; Iron 6%
Diet Exchanges: 3 Fruit, 1 Fat

Parola di Antonio

A midsummer treat, this warm, buttery berry sauce is often served as an accompaniment to nuptial cakes in northern regions of Italy. In the south, it is used as a topping for ices. You may want to serve it with your favorite ice cream or over thick slices of toasted golden pound cake for a summer dessert. You can leave out the brandy and still enjoy this rich raspberry sauce.

STRAWBERRIES WITH MARSALA SAUCE
Zabaione alle Fragole

4 cups (2 pints) strawberries

2 cups sweet Marsala wine*

1/2 cup sugar

6 egg yolks

*There is no substitute for sweet Marsala wine

PREP: 25 MIN; COOK: 10 MIN
6 servings

1. Remove stems from strawberries. Arrange strawberries, stem ends down, in shallow serving dish, about 10 inches in diameter. Pour 1 cup of the wine over strawberries.

2. Pour just enough water into bottom of double boiler so that top of double boiler does not touch water. Heat water over medium heat (do not boil).

3. Meanwhile, beat sugar and egg yolks in top of double boiler, using wire whisk, until pale yellow and slightly thickened. Place top of double boiler over bottom. Gradually beat remaining 1 cup wine into egg yolk mixture. Cook, beating constantly, until mixture thickens and coats wire whisk (do not boil).

4. Pour sauce over strawberries. Serve immediately.

1 Serving: Calories 250 (Calories from Fat 45); Fat 5g (Saturated 2g); Cholesterol 210mg; Sodium 15mg; Carbohydrate 33g (Dietary Fiber 2g); Protein 4g
% Daily Value: Vitamin A 8%; Vitamin C 90%; Calcium 4%; Iron 6%
Diet Exchanges: 2 Fruit, 3 Fat

Parola di Antonio

The ancient Romans were true gourmets during the height of their empire; often the need to disguise food that was no longer fresh spurred them to create delicious sweet-and-sour recipes or recipes with wine that could preserve fruit. Similar to eggnog, the Marsala sauce on these strawberries may have had its beginnings as a preservative for fruit. Romans also used eggnog as a drink for convalescents, and it is still very popular as a "strengthening" drink.

Strawberries with Marsala Sauce

ITALIAN FRUIT SALAD DESSERT
Macedonia di Frutta

1/2 cup amaretto*

1/2 cup Asti Spumante or sparkling
apple juice

2 tablespoons sugar

2 tablespoons fresh lemon juice

2 cups (1 pint) strawberries, sliced

1 cup seedless grapes

1 medium unpeeled eating apple
(Delicious, Gala, Rome Beauty),
cored and cut up

1 medium unpeeled pear, cored and
cut up

1 medium banana, sliced

1 medium kiwifruit, peeled and slice,
or 1 fig, sliced

1/2 cup Asti Spumante or sparkling
apple juice

Sorbet or sherbet, if desired

*1 teaspoon almond extract mixed with
1/2 cup water can be substituted for the
amaretto.

PREP: 30 MIN; CHILL: 1 HR
8 servings

1. Mix amaretto, 1/2 cup Asti Spumante, the sugar and lemon juice in large serving bowl. Add remaining ingredients except 1/2 cup Asti Spumante and sorbet; toss. Cover and refrigerate at least 1 hour but no longer than 24 hours.

2. Immediately before serving, pour 1/2 cup Asti Spumante over fruit; toss. Top each serving with sorbet.

1 Serving: Calories 130 (Calories from Fat 10); Fat 1g (Saturated 0g); Cholesterol 0mg; Sodium 5mg; Carbohydrate 27g (Dietary Fiber 3g); Protein 1g
% Daily Value: Vitamin A 0%; Vitamin C 60%; Calcium 2%; Iron 2%
Diet Exchanges: 2 Fruit

Parola di Antonio

Asti Spumante is a sweet sparkling white wine from northern Italy that is similar to champagne but sweeter. The pleasant almond flavor of the amaretto marries nicely with the "bubbly" flavor of the Asti Spumante to create a fruit dessert that brings excitement and pleasure to the palate. You will discover that Asti Spumante is excellent in—and with—desserts.

COFFEE LAYERED CAKE
Torta al Caffè

4 egg yolks

1/2 cup granulated sugar

1/2 cup milk

1 cup butter or margarine, softened

2 cups powdered sugar

2 packages (7.05 ounces each)
butter biscuits*

1 cup brewed espresso or very
strong coffee, chilled

2 tablespoons baking cocoa

12 maraschino cherries

*About 36 vanilla wafer cookies can be
used instead of the butter biscuits. Brush
cookie layer with espresso rather than
dipping the cookies. The cookies will
form a layer that is a little softer and
more crumbly because they aren't
glazed and are a little finer in texture
than the butter biscuits.*

PREP: 2 HR 10 MIN; CHILL: 3 HR
12 servings

1. Beat egg yolks and granulated sugar in 2-quart saucepan with electric mixer on medium speed about 30 seconds or until well blended. Beat in milk. Heat to boiling over medium heat, stirring constantly; reduce heat to low. Boil and stir 1 minute. Pour into medium bowl; place plastic wrap or waxed paper directly onto surface of custard mixture. Refrigerate about 2 hours or until chilled.

2. Beat butter in medium bowl on high speed about 5 minutes or until light and fluffy. Gradually beat in powdered sugar. Fold in custard mixture.

3. Dip one-third of the biscuits into espresso, but do not soak. Arrange in single layer, glazed sides up, in ungreased rectangular pan, 13 x 9 x 2 inches. Spread one-third of the filling over biscuits; sprinkle with 2 teaspoons of the cocoa. Repeat layers twice. Cover and refrigerate at least 3 hours to develop flavors but no longer than 24 hours. Garnish with cherries. Store covered in refrigerator.

1 Serving: Calories 445 (Calories from Fat 225); Fat 25g (Saturated 12g); Cholesterol 120mg;
Sodium 260mg; Carbohydrate 52g (Dietary Fiber 1g); Protein 4g
% Daily Value: Vitamin A 16%; Vitamin C 0%; Calcium 4%; Iron 6%
Diet Exchanges: Not Recommended

Parola di Antonio

Mamma Amelia Cecconi, my mother, is credited for this rich coffee-flavored cake. A precursor of the now popular Tira Mi Su, *it combines butter biscuits, the blackest of espresso coffee and a rich, butter cream. Dip the biscuits into the espresso carefully to prevent them from breaking. Surprisingly, this dessert can be made several days before serving and kept frozen. Allow it to thaw several hours at room temperature.*

ENGLISH "SOUP" CAKE
Zuppa Inglese

Sponge Cake (right)

1/2 cup plus 2 tablespoons sugar

2 eggs

3 tablespoons all-purpose flour

2 cups milk

2 ounces unsweetened baking
    chocolate, grated

1/2 cup rum*

1/2 cup cherry-flavored liqueur**

** 1/2 teaspoon rum extract mixed with
1/2 cup water can be substituted for
the rum.*

*** 1/2 teaspoon almond extract mixed
with 1/2 cup water can be substituted
for the cherry-flavored liqueur.*

PREP: 30 MIN; BAKE: 20 MIN; COOK: 2 MIN; CHILL: 4 HR
8 servings

1. Make Sponge Cake.

2. Beat sugar and eggs in 2-quart saucepan using wire whisk until well blended. Gradually beat in flour. Heat milk over medium heat to scalding; gradually stir into sugar mixture. Cook over low heat about 10 minutes, stirring constantly, until thickened. Stir in chocolate. Cook about 2 minutes, stirring constantly, until chocolate is melted. Pour into medium bowl; place plastic wrap or waxed paper directly onto surface of custard mixture. Refrigerate about 2 hours or until chilled.

3. Mix rum and liqueur; sprinkle over cake. Cut cake crosswise into 4 rectangles, 9 x 3 1/4 inches. Place one cake rectangle in ungreased loaf pan, 9 x 5 x 3 inches. Spread with one-fourth of the custard mixture. Repeat layers 3 times. Cover and refrigerate at least 2 hours to develop flavors but no longer than 24 hours. Turn pan upside down to unmold cake. Cut into slices to serve.

continued

1 tablespoon plus 1 teaspoon sugar

1 tablespoon all-purpose flour

3 eggs

1/2 cup sugar

3/4 cup all-purpose flour

1/2 teaspoon salt

Sponge Cake

1. Heat oven to 325°. Grease rectangular pan, 13 x 9 x 2 inches. Line bottom of pan with cooking parchment paper or waxed paper; grease paper.

2. Mix 1 tablespoon plus 1 teaspoon sugar and 1 tablespoon flour; sprinkle evenly over paper in bottom of pan using wire strainer. Beat eggs in medium bowl with electric mixer on high speed about 5 minutes or until thickened. Gradually beat in 1/2 cup sugar. Mix 3/4 cup flour and the salt; fold into egg mixture. Pour into pan.

3. Bake about 20 minutes or until toothpick inserted in center comes out clean. Cool 5 minutes. Turn pan upside down onto rectangular wire rack; remove paper. Cool completely.

1 Serving: Calories 310 (Calories from Fat 80); Fat 9g (Saturated 4g); Cholesterol 135mg; Sodium 220mg; Carbohydrate 47g (Dietary Fiber 2g); Protein 8g
% Daily Value: Vitamin A 8%; Vitamin C 0%; Calcium 10%; Iron 8%
Diet Exchanges: Not Recommended

Parola di Antonio

This cake is an Italian variation on the classic English dessert trifle and is extremely popular in Florence. Trifle, no doubt, found its way to Italy by way of the employees who worked in the London branches of Florentine banking houses.

"LIFT-ME-UP" DESSERT
Tira Mi Su

6 egg yolks

3/4 cup sugar

2/3 cup milk

1 pound mascarpone cheese or
   2 packages (8 ounces each)
   cream cheese, softened

1 1/4 cups whipping (heavy) cream

1/2 teaspoon vanilla

1/4 cup brewed espresso or
   very strong coffee, chilled

2 tablespoons rum*

2 packages (3 ounces each)
   ladyfingers**

1 tablespoon baking cocoa

*1/8 teaspoon rum extract mixed with 2 tablespoons water can be substituted for the rum.

**Sponge Cake (page 293), cut into 10 rows by 3 rows, can be substituted for the ladyfingers.

PREP: 1 HR; CHILL: 5 HR
8 servings

1. Beat egg yolks and sugar in 2-quart saucepan until well blended. Beat in milk. Heat to boiling over medium heat, stirring constantly; reduce heat to low. Boil and stir 1 minute; remove from heat. Pour into medium bowl; place plastic wrap directly onto surface of custard mixture. Refrigerate about 1 hour or until chilled.

2. Add cheese to custard mixture. Beat with electric mixer on medium speed until smooth; set aside. Beat whipping cream and vanilla in chilled medium bowl on high speed until stiff; set aside. Mix espresso and rum.

3. Separate ladyfingers horizontally; brush with espresso mixture (do not soak). Arrange half the ladyfingers in single layer in ungreased baking dish, 11 x 7 x 1 1/2 inches. Spread half of the cheese mixture over ladyfingers; spread with half of the whipped cream. Repeat layers with remaining ladyfingers, cheese mixture and whipped cream. Sprinkle with cocoa. Refrigerate at least 4 hours but no longer than 24 hours to develop flavors. Store covered in refrigerator.

1 Serving: Calories 535 (Calories from Fat 340); Fat 38g (Saturated 22g); Cholesterol 270mg; Sodium 260mg; Carbohydrate 40g (Dietary Fiber 1g); Protein 9g
% Daily Value: Vitamin A 32%; Vitamin C 0%; Calcium 12%; Iron 10%
Diet Exchanges: Not Recommended

Parola di Antonio

"Lift-Me-Up" Dessert takes its name from the ingredients, cream, egg yolks and cheese, thought to be excellent for people in poor health. The addition of rum and espresso are sure to give a lift to those in the best of health!

"Lift-Me-Up" Dessert

ALMOND TORTE FROM PIEDMONT
Torta Alpina Piemontese

1 1/2 cups slivered almonds

2 1/2 cups all-purpose flour

1 cup sugar

2 teaspoons baking powder

1 teaspoon salt

1/2 cup butter or margarine,
    softened

2 teaspoons almond extract

1 teaspoon vanilla

2 eggs

1 tablespoon sugar

Sliced strawberries, if desired

Sweetened whipped cream,
    if desired

PREP: 15 MIN; BAKE: 30 MIN
8 servings

1. Heat oven to 350°. Spread almonds in ungreased shallow pan. Bake uncovered about 10 minutes, stirring occasionally, until golden brown; cool. Finely chop; set aside.

2. Grease round pan, 9 x 1 1/2 inches. Mix flour, 1 cup sugar, the baking powder and salt in medium bowl. Stir in almonds, butter, almond extract, vanilla and eggs until stiff dough forms (dough will be slightly crumbly). Shape into 1-inch balls. Place in pan. Sprinkle with 1 tablespoon sugar.

3. Bake about 30 minutes or until golden brown. Cool on wire rack. Cut into wedges. Serve with strawberries and whipped cream.

1 Serving: Calories 490 (Calories from Fat 215); Fat 24g (Saturated 9g); Cholesterol 85mg; Sodium 510mg; Carbohydrate 61g (Dietary Fiber 3g); Protein 10g
% Daily Value: Vitamin A 10%; Vitamin C 0%; Calcium 14%; Iron 16%
Diet Exchanges: Not Recommended

Almond Torte from Piedmont

RICOTTA-FILLED PASTRIES
Cannoli

1/2 cup slivered almonds

1 cup powdered sugar

1 container (15 ounces) ricotta cheese

1/3 cup miniature semisweet chocolate chips

1 tablespoon amaretto or 1/8 teaspoon almond extract

12 cannoli pastry shells

12 maraschino cherries, cut in half

1 tablespoon powdered sugar

1 tablespoon baking cocoa

PREP: 20 MIN; BAKE: 10 MIN
12 pastries

1. Heat oven to 350°. Spread almonds in ungreased shallow pan. Bake uncovered about 10 minutes, stirring occasionally, until golden brown; cool.

2. Gradually stir 1 cup powdered sugar into ricotta cheese in large bowl. Stir in almonds, chocolate chips and amaretto.

3. Carefully spoon filling into pastry shells, filling from the center out. Place cherry half in filling on one end of each shell. Mix 1 tablespoon powdered sugar and the cocoa; sprinkle over shells. Store covered in refrigerator.

1 Serving: Calories 270 (Calories from Fat 135); Fat 15g (Saturated 4g); Cholesterol 10mg; Sodium 60mg; Carbohydrate 29g (Dietary Fiber 2g); Protein 7g
% Daily Value: Vitamin A 4%; Vitamin C 0%; Calcium 10%; Iron 6%
Diet Exchanges: 2 Starch, 2 1/2 Fat

RICOTTA CHEESECAKE WITH CHOCOLATE
Torta di Ricotta Al Cioccolato

1 tablespoon sugar

1 tablespoon plain dry bread crumbs

1 container (15 ounces) ricotta
   cheese

1/2 cup sugar

2 teaspoons grated lemon peel

4 egg yolks

1/2 cup all-purpose flour

1/2 cup finely chopped candied fruit

3 ounces semisweet baking
   chocolate, grated or very finely
   chopped

2 egg whites

Sweetened whipped cream,
   if desired

PREP: 15 MIN; BAKE: 45 MIN; COOL: 4 HR; CHILL: 4 HR
8 servings

1. Heat oven to 350°. Grease round pan, 9 x 1 1/2 inches. Mix 1 tablespoon sugar and the bread crumbs. Coat bottom and side of pan with bread crumb mixture.

2. Drain any excess liquid from cheese. Mix cheese, 1/2 cup sugar and the lemon peel in medium bowl. Stir in egg yolks, one at a time. Stir in flour, candied fruit and chocolate; set aside.

3. Beat egg whites in medium bowl with electric mixer on high speed until stiff. Fold cheese mixture into egg whites. Pour into pan.

4. Bake about 45 minutes or until set and edge is light brown. Refrigerate about 4 hours or until cool. Run knife or metal spatula around side of cheesecake to loosen; remove from pan. Cover and refrigerate at least 4 hours until chilled. Garnish with whipped cream. Store covered in refrigerator.

1 Serving: Calories 280 (Calories from Fat 90); Fat 10g (Saturated 5g); Cholesterol 120mg; Sodium 125mg; Carbohydrate 39g (Dietary Fiber 1g); Protein 10g
% Daily Value: Vitamin A 10%; Vitamin C 0%; Calcium 18%; Iron 8%
Diet Exchanges: 2 1/2 Starch, 2 Fat

Parola di Antonio

Ricotta cheesecakes have been a Sicilian tradition throughout the centuries. The cheesecakes of today have an impressive variety of flavors for different eating occasions. It's important always to drain excess liquid from the ricotta to ensure proper baking. To infuse a richer chocolate flavor, experiment by adding a tablespoon or two of baking cocoa.

FLORENTINE CHOCOLATE PROFITEROLE
Bongo Bongo Fiorentino

1 cup water

1/4 cup butter or margarine

1/2 teaspoon salt

1 cup all-purpose flour

4 eggs

1 cup whipping (heavy) cream

2 tablespoons powdered sugar

1/2 teaspoon freshly grated nutmeg

4 ounces semisweet baking
  chocolate

2 tablespoons water

1 tablespoon honey

PREP: 30 MIN; BAKE: 30 MIN; FREEZE: 2 HR
6 servings

1. Heat oven to 400°. Grease and flour cookie sheet.

2. Heat 1 cup water, the butter and salt to rolling boil in 2 1/2-quart saucepan. Stir in flour. Stir vigorously over low heat about 1 minute or until mixture forms a ball. Remove from heat; cool 5 minutes. Beat in eggs, one at a time, until smooth. Drop by rounded tablespoonfuls about 2 inches apart onto cookie sheet.

3. Bake about 30 minutes or until puffed and golden brown. Remove from cookie sheet to wire rack; cool. Cut off tops of puffs; reserve. Pull out any filaments of soft dough from puffs.

4. Beat whipping cream, powdered sugar and nutmeg in chilled medium bowl with electric mixer on high speed until stiff. Fill puffs with whipped cream mixture; replace tops. Mound puffs on large serving plate.

5. Heat remaining ingredients over low heat until smooth; drizzle over puffs. Freeze at least 2 hours until chocolate is firm, or serve immediately. Store covered in refrigerator.

1 Serving: Calories 425 (Calories from Fat 260); Fat 29g (Saturated 17g); Cholesterol 205mg; Sodium 310mg; Carbohydrate 35g (Dietary Fiber 2g); Protein 8g
% Daily Value: Vitamin A 20%; Vitamin C 0%; Calcium 6%; Iron 10%
Diet Exchanges: Not Recommended

Florentine Chocolate Profiterole

HAZELNUT MERINGUES
Meringhe alla Nocciola

6 egg whites

1 teaspoon vanilla

1 teaspoon white vinegar

2 cups granulated sugar

1/4 cup powdered sugar

1/2 cup hazelnuts (filberts)

1 cup whipping (heavy) cream

2 tablespoons powdered sugar

1 teaspoon baking cocoa

PREP: 30 MIN; BAKE: 45 MIN; COOL: 1 HR; CHILL: 2 HR
About 12 meringues

1. Heat oven to 275°. Grease and flour 2 cookie sheets, or line with cooking parchment paper.

2. Beat egg whites, vanilla and vinegar in large bowl with electric mixer on high speed until foamy. Beat in granulated sugar and 1/4 cup powdered sugar, 1 tablespoon at a time, until stiff and glossy.

3. Place egg white mixture in decorating bag fitted with star or drop-flower tip. Pipe into about twenty-four 2-inch circles onto cookie sheet. (If decorating bag is not available, drop mixture by 2 level tablespoonfuls onto cookie sheet, and spread into 2-inch circles.)

4. Bake 45 minutes. Turn off oven; leave meringues in oven with door closed 1 hour. Finish cooling at room temperature.

5. Heat oven to 400°. Spread hazelnuts in ungreased shallow pan. Bake uncovered about 5 minutes or until skins begin to crack. Wrap hazelnuts in clean towel; let stand 2 minutes. Rub hazelnuts in towel to remove skins. Chop hazelnuts. Return to pan. Bake about 8 minutes, stirring occasionally, until golden brown; cool.

6. Beat whipping cream, 2 tablespoons powdered sugar and the cocoa in chilled medium bowl on high speed until stiff. Fold in hazelnuts. Put meringues together in pairs with about 3 tablespoons whipped cream mixture. Cover and refrigerate about 2 hours or until firm. Store covered in refrigerator.

1 Serving: Calories 250 (Calories from Fat 80); Fat 9g (Saturated 4g); Cholesterol 20mg;
Sodium 35mg; Carbohydrate 39g (Dietary Fiber 0g); Protein 2g
% Daily Value: Vitamin A 4%; Vitamin C 0%; Calcium 2%; Iron 0%
Diet Exchanges: 1 Starch, 1 Fruit, 2 Fat

ANISE BISCOTTI
Biscotti all'anice

1 cup sugar

1/2 cup butter or margarine,
  softened

2 teaspoons anise seed, ground

2 teaspoons grated lemon peel

2 eggs

3 1/2 cups all-purpose flour

1 teaspoon baking powder

1/2 teaspoon salt

Orange Biscotti (Biscotti all'arancia): Omit anise seed and lemon peel. Add 1 tablespoon grated orange peel to the butter mixture.

PREP: 15 MIN; BAKE: 40 MIN; COOL: 15 MIN
About 3 1/2 dozen cookies

1. Heat oven to 350°. Beat sugar, butter, anise, lemon peel and eggs in large bowl. Stir in flour, baking powder and salt.

2. Divide dough in half. Shape half of dough into 10 x 3 -inch rectangle, rounding edges slightly, on one end of ungreased cookie sheet. Repeat with remaining dough on same cookie sheet.

3. Bake about 25 minutes or until center is firm to the touch. Cool on cookie sheet 15 minutes; move to cutting board. Cut each rectangle crosswise into 1/2-inch slices, using sharp knife.

4. Place slices, cut sides down, on ungreased cookie sheet. Bake about 15 minutes or until crisp and light brown. Immediately remove from cookie sheet to wire rack; cool.

1 Cookie: Calories 85 (Calories from Fat 25); Fat 3g (Saturated 1g); Cholesterol 15mg; Sodium 55mg; Carbohydrate 13g (Dietary Fiber 0g); Protein 1g
% Daily Value: Vitamin A 2%; Vitamin C 0%; Calcium 0%; Iron 2%
Diet Exchanges: 1 Starch

Parola di Antonio

The pleasant anise and lemon flavors contrast nicely with the buttery texture of the biscotti. I keep a coffee grinder just for grinding whole spices. It works great for grinding the anise seeds. Enjoy these biscotti in the traditional way, dipped in a glass of Vinsanto dessert wine, or as is common in America, with a cup of espresso or cappuccino.

HAZELNUT BISCOTTI
Biscotti alla Nocciola

1 cup hazelnuts (filberts), coarsely chopped

1 cup sugar

1/2 cup butter or margarine, softened

1 teaspoon almond extract

1 teaspoon vanilla

2 eggs

3 1/2 cups all-purpose flour

1 teaspoon baking powder

1/2 teaspoon baking soda

Almond Biscotti (Biscotti alle Mandorle): Substitute 1 cup slivered almonds for the hazelnuts.

PREP: 25 MIN; BAKE: 40 MIN; COOL: 15 MIN
About 3 1/2 dozen cookies

1. Heat oven to 350°. Spread hazelnuts in ungreased shallow pan. Bake uncovered about 10 minutes, stirring occasionally, until golden brown; cool.

2. Beat sugar, butter, almond extract, vanilla and eggs in large bowl. Stir in flour, baking powder and baking soda. Stir in hazelnuts. Place dough on lightly floured surface. Gently knead 2 to 3 minutes or until dough holds together and hazelnuts are evenly distributed.

3. Divide dough in half. Shape half of dough into 10 x 3 -inch rectangle, rounding edges slightly, on one side of ungreased cookie sheet. Repeat with remaining dough on same cookie sheet.

4. Bake about 25 minutes or until center is firm to the touch. Cool on cookie sheet 15 minutes; move to cutting board. Cut each rectangle crosswise into 1/2-inch slices, using sharp knife.

5. Place slices, cut sides down, on ungreased cookie sheet. Bake about 15 minutes or until crisp and light brown. Immediately remove from cookie sheet to wire rack; cool.

1 Cookie: Calories 95 (Calories from Fat 35); Fat 4g (Saturated 2g); Cholesterol 15mg; Sodium 45mg; Carbohydrate 13g (Dietary Fiber 0g); Protein 2g
% Daily Value: Vitamin A 2%; Vitamin C 0%; Calcium 2%; Iron 2%
Diet Exchanges: 1 Starch, 1/2 Fat

Hazelnut Biscotti; Anise Biscotti, page 303

SUGAR COOKIE WAFERS
Pizzelle

2 cups all-purpose flour

1 cup sugar

3/4 cup butter or margarine, melted and cooled

1 tablespoon anise extract or vanilla

2 teaspoons baking powder

4 eggs, slightly beaten

PREP: 15 MIN; BAKE: 20 MIN
About 3 1/2 dozen cookies

1. Lightly grease pizzelle iron. Heat pizzelle iron as directed by manufacturer.

2. Mix all ingredients with wire whisk until smooth. Drop 1 tablespoon batter onto each design of heated pizzelle iron; close iron.

3. Bake about 30 seconds or until golden brown. Carefully remove pizzelle from iron; cool on wire rack. Repeat with remaining batter.

1 Cookie: Calories 75 (Calories from Fat 35); Fat 4g (Saturated 2g); Cholesterol 30mg; Sodium 50mg; Carbohydrate 9g (Dietary Fiber 0g); Protein 1g
% Daily Value: Vitamin A 2%; Vitamin C 0%; Calcium 2%; Iron 2%
Diet Exchanges: 1/2 Starch, 1 Fat

Parola di Antonio

These Italian cookies are wafer thin and lightly flavored with anise. They are baked in a special pizzelle iron, which is available in most specialty cookware stores. If you'd like your cookies in a cylinder shape, quickly roll them into a cylinder as soon as you remove them from the pizzelle iron. Work quickly—they cool very fast!

Sugar Cookie Wafers

TRADITIONAL ALMOND COOKIES
Amaretti

3 cups slivered almonds

3 jumbo egg whites

1 1/2 cups granulated sugar

1 teaspoon powdered sugar

1 teaspoon amaretto or
   1/4 teaspoon almond extract

Granulated sugar

PREP: 20 MIN; BAKE: 25 MIN PER SHEET
About 4 dozen cookies

1. Heat oven to 350°. Spread almonds in ungreased shallow pan. Bake uncovered about 10 minutes, stirring occasionally, until golden brown; cool.

2. Reduce oven temperature to 300°. Line cookie sheet with cooking parchment paper, or grease and flour cookie sheet.

3. Place almonds in food processor or blender. Cover and process until finely ground but not pastelike.

4. Beat egg whites in medium bowl with electric mixer on high speed until stiff. Stir in almonds, 1 1/2 cups granulated sugar, the powdered sugar and amaretto. Drop by rounded teaspoonfuls about 2 inches apart onto cookie sheet. Sprinkle with granulated sugar.

5. Bake 20 to 25 minutes or until light golden brown. Cool 5 minutes. Remove from cookie sheet to wire rack; cool.

1 Cookie: Calories 75 (Calories from Fat 35); Fat 4g (Saturated 0g); Cholesterol 0mg; Sodium 5mg; Carbohydrate 9g (Dietary Fiber 1g); Protein 2g
% Daily Value: Vitamin A 0%; Vitamin C 0%; Calcium 2%; Iron 0%
Diet Exchanges: 1/2 Starch, 1 Fat

Parola di Antonio

"A little bitter" is the translation of amaretto, *the almond liqueur of Saronno, as well as the name of these crunchy cookies. Traditionally, Italians use half bitter almonds and half regular almonds to make these cookies. Bitter almonds are harvested before they are ripe, and cooks sometimes make their own bitter almonds from the inner kernel of peaches and apricots. Because bitter almonds are hard to find in America, this recipe uses regular almonds, which give the cookies a slightly different flavor yet make a delicious, crisp-textured almond-flavored cookie.*

STRAWBERRY-ORANGE ICE
Granita All'Arancia e Fragole

2 cups water

1/3 cup sugar

1/2 cup fresh orange juice

12 very ripe strawberries,
    mashed well (1/2 cup)

1 teaspoon vanilla

PREP: 15 MIN; COOK: 3 MIN; COOL: 10 MIN; FREEZE: 35 MIN
About 1 quart ice (eight 1/2-cup servings)

1. Heat water to boiling in 2-quart saucepan. Stir in remaining ingredients except vanilla. Boil 3 minutes, stirring constantly. Remove from heat; stir in vanilla. Cool 10 minutes.

2. Freeze in ice-cream maker as directed by manufacturer. Or cool to room temperature, then pour into ungreased loaf pan, 9 x 5 x 3 inches, and freeze 1 1/2 to 2 hours or until mushy in center. Stir mixture; freeze about 1 hour longer, stirring every 30 minutes, until firm. Stir again before serving.

3. Serve in chilled dessert dishes. Or cut into 1/2-inch chunks and place in serving bowl. Cover and freeze until ready to serve.

1 Serving: Calories 45 (Calories from Fat 0); Fat 0g (Saturated 0g); Cholesterol 0mg; Sodium 0mg; Carbohydrate 11g (Dietary Fiber 0g); Protein 0g
% Daily Value: Vitamin A 0%; Vitamin C 26%; Calcium 0%; Iron 0%
Diet Exchanges: 1 Fruit

Parola di Antonio

Procopio Coltelli, a Sicilian, was a master at making ice cream and ices. In the eighteenth century, he opened an ice-cream parlor in Paris—Europe's first—and popularized Italian ices. His store was a tradition for roughly two hundred years, passed down through generations of the Coltelli family.

LEMON ICE
Granita al Limone

2 cups water

1 cup sugar

1 tablespoon grated lemon peel

1 cup fresh lemon juice

PREP: 20 MIN; COOK: 5 MIN; COOL: 10 MIN; FREEZE: 35 MIN
About 1 quart ice (eight 1/2-cup servings)

1. Heat water and sugar to boiling in 2-quart saucepan; reduce heat. Simmer uncovered 5 minutes; remove from heat. Stir in lemon peel and lemon juice. Cool 10 minutes.

2. Freeze in ice-cream maker as directed by manufacturer. Or cool to room temperature, then pour into ungreased loaf pan, 9 x 5 x 3 inches, and freeze 1 1/2 to 2 hours or until mushy in center. Stir mixture; freeze about 1 hour longer, stirring every 30 minutes, until firm. Stir again before serving.

3. Serve in chilled dessert dishes. Or cut into 1/2-inch chunks and place in serving bowl. Cover and freeze until ready to serve.

1 Serving: Calories 110 (Calories from Fat 0); Fat 0g (Saturated 0g); Cholesterol 0mg; Sodium 5mg; Carbohydrate 27g (Dietary Fiber 0g); Protein 0g
% Daily Value: Vitamin A 0%; Vitamin C 12%; Calcium 0%; Iron 0%
Diet Exchanges: 2 Fruit

Parola di Antonio

Cool down on a hot, steamy day with this beautiful frosty dessert. For an elegant presentation, hollow out fresh lemon halves, and trim a thin slice off the bottom of each half so lemons stand flat. Pile them high with luscious lemon ice, and keep them in the freezer until ready to serve. Fill stemmed wineglasses with crushed ice. Nestle a lemon half in the ice, and add fragrant fresh mint or lemon geranium leaves for the finishing touch.

Lemon Ice; Coffee and Chocolate Ice Cream (page 312); Strawberry-Orange Ice (page 309)

COFFEE AND CHOCOLATE ICE CREAM
Gelato al Caffe e Cioccolato

3/4 cup sugar

1 cup whole milk

1 tablespoon freeze-dried instant coffee (dry)

1 teaspoon baking cocoa

2 eggs

1 cup whipping (heavy) cream

PREP: 20 MIN; COOK: 5 MIN; CHILL: 1 1/2 HR; FREEZE: 35 MIN
About 1 quart ice cream (eight 1/2-cup servings)

1. Mix all ingredients except whipping cream in 2-quart saucepan. Cook over medium heat, stirring constantly, 5 or 6 minutes or until mixture reaches 165°. Cover and refrigerate about 1 1/2 hours or until cool.

2. Beat whipping cream in chilled medium bowl with electric mixer on high speed until soft peaks form. Fold milk mixture into whipped cream. Freeze in ice-cream maker as directed by manufacturer.

1 Serving: Calories 215 (Calories from Fat 110); Fat 12g (Saturated 7g); Cholesterol 90mg; Sodium 40mg; Carbohydrate 21g (Dietary Fiber 0g); Protein 3g
% Daily Value: Vitamin A 10%; Vitamin C 0%; Calcium 6%; Iron 0%
Diet Exchanges: 1 Starch, 1/2 Fruit, 2 Fat

Parola di Antonio

Italians have been in love with ices and ice cream for hundreds of years. In Florence during the Renaissance, special icehouses were built so that cooks would always have access to the ice needed to make their delicious confections. And for many people, a trip to Florence is not complete without a stop at Vivoli's, a shop that has been famous for its ice cream for several generations.

NEAPOLITAN ICE CREAM
Gelato alla Napoletana

1 cup milk

3/4 cup sugar

4 egg yolks

1/2 cup hazelnuts (filberts)

1 cup whipping (heavy) cream

1/2 teaspoon baking cocoa

PREP: 25 MIN; CHILL: 1 1/2 HR; FREEZE: 30 MIN
About 3 1/2 cups ice cream (seven 1/2-cup servings)

1. Mix milk, sugar and egg yolks in 2-quart saucepan. Cook over medium heat, stirring constantly, 5 or 6 minutes or until mixture reaches 165°. Cover and refrigerate about 1 1/2 hours or until cool.

2. Heat oven to 400°. Spread hazelnuts in ungreased shallow pan. Bake uncovered about 5 minutes or until skins begin to crack. Wrap hazelnuts in clean towel; let stand 2 minutes. Rub hazelnuts in towel to remove skins. Finely chop hazelnuts; return to pan. Bake about 8 minutes, stirring occasionally, until golden brown; cool.

3. Beat whipping cream in chilled medium bowl with electric mixer on high speed until soft peak forms. Fold milk mixture, hazelnuts and cocoa into whipped cream. Freeze in ice-cream maker as directed by manufacturer.

1 Serving: Calories 510 (Calories from Fat 305); Fat 34g (Saturated 17g); Cholesterol 300mg; Sodium 60mg; Carbohydrate 45g (Dietary Fiber 1g); Protein 8g
% Daily Value: Vitamin A 30%; Vitamin C 0%; Calcium 16%; Iron 6%

MENUS—BUON APPETITO!

A Special Occasion

Fresh Basil-Wrapped Cheese Balls
(Formaggio al Basilico) 30

Three-Mushroom Risotto (Risotto ai Funghi Selvatici) 54

Grilled Radicchio Salad (Radicchio alla Griglia) 268

Lamb with Sweet Peppers and Garlic Sauce (Agnello
All'Aglio e Peperoni Dolci) 202

Baked Raspberries with Brandy Sauce
(Mirtilli al Liquore) 287

Wines: Red: Barolo; White: Pinot Grigio

A Romantic Dinner

Roasted Red Bell Pepper Toast (Bruschetta Romana) 27

Tagliatelle Pasta with Asparagus and Gorgonzola Sauce
(Tagliatelle Agli Asparagi E Gorgonzola) 116

Chicken Breasts with Tarragon-Mustard Sauce (Petti di
Pollo al Dragoncello e Senape) 214

Fresh Basil and Spinach Salad (Insalata al Basilico) 258

Ricotta Cheesecake with Chocolate
(Torta di Ricotta Al Cioccolato) 299

*Wines: Red: Brunello D'Montalcino;
White: Verdicchio Classico*

A Holiday Tradition

Shrimp with Prosciutto (Gamberoni al Prosciutto) 42

Bow-Tie Pasta Timbale Tower (Timballo di Farfalle) 132

Roasted Beets and Onion Salad
(Insalata di Rape e Cipolle) 264

Grilled Beef Short Ribs with Savory Lemon Sauce
(Costolette Di Manzo Braciato in Salsa Gremolata) 186

Coffee Layered Cake (Torta al Caffe) 291

Wines: Red: Sangiovese Di Romangna; White: Orvieto, Bigi

A Meal on the Run

Sautéed Olives from the South (Olive Saltate del Sud) 38

Spaghetti of the Night (Spaghetti alla Puttanesca) 98

Beans with Sausage (Salsiccia e Fagioli) 200

Hazelnut Biscotti (Biscotti alla Nocciola) 304

Wines: Red: Chianti Classico Riserva; White: Soave Veneto

Dinner with Friends

Spicy Breaded Shrimp (Gamberi Piccantissimi) 238

Four-Cheese Fettuccine
(Fettuccine ai Quattro Formaggi) 110

Chicken Breasts in Lemon-Caper Sauce
(Piccata di Pollo) 216

Savory Zucchini (Zucchine Saporite) 257

*Wines: Red: Vino Nobile Di Montepulciano;
White: Vernaccia Di San Gimignano*

A Meal for the Family

Sardinian Ravioli with Aromatic Tomato Sauce
(Ravioli Sardi al Sugo Aromatico) 134

Roasted Chicken with Walnut-Basil Sauce
(Pollo allo Spiedo con Pesto) 206

Pan-Roasted Potatoes (Patate Al Forno) 254

Almond Torte from Piedmont
(Torta Alpina Piemontese) 296

Wines: Red: Lambrusco; White: Frascati ColliRomani

A Taste of the Islands

Steamed Mussels in Wine Sauce (Cozze al Vino) 44

Linguine with Clam Sauce (Linguine alle Vongole) 108

Grilled Shrimp Kabobs with Fresh Herbs
(Spiedini di Gamberi alle Erbe) 236

Piquant Salad (Insalata Piccante) 263

Fresh Fruit Tart (Tortiera Alla Frutta) 286

*Wines: Red: Corvo Di Salaparuta;
White: Vermentino Di Sardegna*

A Heartwarming Winter Meal

Roasted Garlic and Onion Soup
(Zuppa All'Aglio E Cipolla) 70

Polenta with Sautéed Spinach and Pine Nuts
(Polenta agli Spinaci Saltati e Pinoli) 58

Roasted Loin of Marlin (Trancio di Pesce al Forno) 222

"Lift-Me-Up" Dessert (Tira Mi Su) 294

Wines: Red: Montefalco Rosso D'Umbria; White: Pinot Bianco

A Refreshing Summer Meal

Warm Tomato and Olive Salad
(Olive e Pomodori Saltati) 270

Grilled Swordfish Steaks (Pesce Spada alla Griglia) 226

Vermicelli with Fresh Herbs
(Vermicelli alle Erbe Crude) 102

Coffee and Chocolate Ice Cream
(Gelato al Caffe e Cioccolato) 312

Wines: Red: Biferno Rosso; White: Prosecco Di Conegliano

A Traditional Classic

Basil Toast (Crostini al Basilico) 26

Pork Roast with Rosemary
(Arista Arrosto al Rosmarino) 194

Linguine with Basil-Garlic Sauce (Linguine al Pesto) 105

Rustic Olive Bread (Pane Alle Olive) 166

Asparagus with Parmesan (Asparagi alla Parmigiana) 246

Strawberries with Marsala Sauce (Zabaione alle Fragole) 288

*Wines: Red: Valpolicella Classico; White: Est! Est! Est!
Di Montefiascone*

ITALIAN FOOD AND COOKING TERMS

ABBOCCATO (ah-bo-KAH-toh) "Mouth filling." Descriptive term for a wine that is crisp and palatable.

AGLIO (AH-l'yoh) "Garlic," one of the basic seasonings in Italian cooking.

AL DENTE (ahl DEHN-teh) "Firm to the bite." Doneness test for pasta and risotto denoting that it should be chewy but not hard or mushy.

AL FRESCO (ahl FREH-skoh) "In the fresh air." A picnic or an outside table at a restaurant, café or bar.

AMARETTI (ah-mah-REH-tee) Derived from the term amaro ("bitter"), these traditional bittersweet cookies are prepared with equal amounts of bitter almonds (usually apricot kernels) and regular almonds.

ANCHOVIES Small fish common in the Mediterranean Sea, eaten fresh or as fillets cured in oil or salt. Popular in salads and sauces.

ANTIPASTO (ahn-tee-PAH-stoh) "Before the meal" is the literal translation and refers to appetizers. Antipasti consist of a variety of regional appetizers that can be hot, room temperature or cold that are served before a meal.

ARBORIO (ar-BOH-ree-oh) rice An Italian-grown short-grain rice from Piedmont. The high-starch kernels absorb the cooking liquid but don't become sticky or mushy. Due to these properties, it is ideal for risotto, which is a creamy, moist rice dish.

ARRABBIATA, all' (ahl ahr-rah-bee-AH-tah) "Angry style." A spicy Roman sauce made with tomatoes and chili peppers that has a vibrant character; suitable for short-cut pasta such as penne.

ARROSTO (ah-ROH-stoh) "Roasted," referring to oven roasted, grilled or seared meat or seafood.

ARUGULA (ah-ROO-guh-lah) A curly, mildly bitter green with a peppery mustard flavor. It is very popular with Italians, but many Americans find the flavor too assertive. It is found in most supermarkets and often in organic salad green mix.

BALSAMIC VINEGAR See Italian Vinegars, page 18.

BEVERAGES See Italian Beverages—Saluto!, page 284.

BIANCO (bee-AHN-koh) "White," referring to white wine or a sauce made without tomatoes.

BISCOTTO; pl. Biscotti (bee-SKOH-toh; bee-SKOH-tee) "Twice baked." A dry cookie that often has nuts. The dough is shaped into a long, flat loaf-shape and baked. The baked loaf is then sliced, and the slices are baked again.

BOCCONCINI (boh-kohn-CHEE-nee) The translation is "small mouthfuls" or "morsels." The term applies to small, fresh mozzarella balls about 1 inch in diameter.

BOLOGNESE (boh-luh-NEEZ) A cooking style of Bologna, Italy. It also refers to a traditional meat and vegetable sauce prepared with wine, tomatoes and meats such as beef, veal and pork also known as ragù.

BONGO (BOHN-goh) The Florentine name for profiteroles, small cream puffs filled with whipped cream or ice cream. They are piled high and drizzled with chocolate sauce. Also known as bongo-bongo.

BRODO (BROH-doh) Broth made from chicken, beef and/or vegetables. In brodo is pasta served in broth.

BRUSCHETTE (broo-SKEH-tah) From the Italian word bruscare, which means "charcoal toasted." In ancient Rome, toasted bread slices were used for tasting freshly pressed olive oil. Today it is an appetizer made of toasted bread slices rubbed with garlic and drizzled with olive oil, often with additional toppings.

BUFALA (BOO-fah-lah) It means "buffalo," referring to the water buffalo brought to southern Italy by Romans to produce the renowned fresh Mozzarella di Bufala. Small balls of cheese are called bufaline.

BUON APPETITO (bw'ohn ah-peh-TEE-toh) "Good appetite." A phrase used to begin a meal.

CACCIATORA (kah-chuh-TOH-rah) This Italian word means "hunter" and is used to describe several meat and game dishes in which olives, wine and mushrooms are cooked with meat. These were simple ingredients hunters had on hand to turn their catch into an easy meal.

CAFFÈ (kah-FEH) "Coffee." In Italy, it usually refers to an espresso. See Italian Beverages—Saluto!, page 284.

CALAMARI (kah-luh-MAH-ree) "Squid," a ten-armed member of the mollusk family that is popular throughout Italy. Its meat is firm and chewy and has a mild, slightly sweet flavor. Small squid are often cut into strips or rings, coated with flour and deep-fried. It is sometimes served in its own ink juices in the form of a stew.

CALZONE (kal-ZOH-nay) A foldover pizza stuffed with cheese or with cheese and meat. The Italian name means "stuffed stocking," which a calzone resembles after it is baked or deep-fried.

CANNELLINI (kah-neh-LEE-nee) "Tiny rods." Large, white Italian kidney beans.

CANNOLI (kan-OH-lee) A tubular or horn-shaped, crisp, fried pastry shell that is filled with sweetened ricotta cheese and candied fruit-cream mixture. Originally from Sicily, other regions of Italy include flavors indigenous to the area.

CAPER (KAY-per) The flower buds from the caper bush that are harvested, sun-dried and pickled in a vinegar brine. They are often used in sauces and salads as a piquant seasoning and as a garnish for meat and vegetable dishes.

CAPONATA (kap-oh-NAH-tah) A Sicilian vegetable dish that is made of a variety of ingredients but usually includes eggplant, tomatoes, olives and vinegar. It is most often served at room temperature as a salad, side dish, relish or spread.

CAPPUCCINO See Italian Beverages—Saluto!, page 284.

CAPRESE (kah-PREH-she) "From Capri," a sauce made of tomatoes, basil, olive oil and mozzarella and frequently appearing on menus as an appetizer or salad, insalata all caprese, denoting use of basil, tomato and mozzarella.

CARBONARA (kar-boh-NAH-rah) A Roman pasta dish, usually made with spaghetti, cream, pancetta (or bacon) and Parmesan cheese to which eggs are added and cooked by the heat of the pasta. The name means "coal miner" or "charcoal style."

CARNE (KAHR-neh) The Italian word for "meat."

CARPACCIO (kahr-PAH-chee-oh) Very thin slices of chilled raw meat or fish dressed with such condiments as olive oil, lemon juice, capers, mayonnaise or Parmesan cheese. This appetizer was created at Harry's Bar in Venice.

CARTOCCIO, AL (ahl kahr-TOH-ch'yoh) "In a bag." Food cooked in parchment paper or aluminum foil packet.

CIABATTA (ch'yah-BAH-tah) "Slipper." A bread loaf that is long, flat, dusted with flour and thought to resemble "an old slipper."

CICORIA (chee-KOH-ree-ah) "Chicory." An oval-shaped green used in mixed salads as well as in soups.

CREMA (CREH-mah) Translates as "cream." For soup, it refers to a puree of vegetables. Alla crema refers to a cream sauce. For dessert, it is custard.

CROCCANTE (kroh-KEH-tah) "Crisp" or "crunchy" are the applied meanings, often describing desserts with nuts.

CROSTINI (kroh-STEE-nee) Sliced and toasted Italian bread used as an appetizer and in soups.

CRUDO (KROO-doh) "Uncooked," usually referring to foods that are eaten in their raw state, such as sauces or dressings for salads or meats.

CUCINA (koo-CHEE-nah) "Cooking" and also "kitchen."

DOLCE (DOHL-cheh) "Sweet." Dolci, the plural of dolce, encompasses all types of sweets.

EMILIA-ROMAGNA (eh-MEE-l'yah roh-MAH-n'ya) Region of northern Italy that produces two foods that are fundamental to Italian cooking and widely exported: prosciutto ham and Parmigiano-Reggiano cheese.

ESPRESSO See Italian Beverages—Saluto!, page 284.

FAGIOLI (fah-J'YOH-lee) The Italian word for "beans." There are two basic types: those that are shelled before using (such as cannellini or fava) and those that are eaten with their shells, called fagiolini (such as green beans).

FAVA (FAH-vuh) The highly regarded giant beans of Italy, fava beans are eaten fresh from the pod or dried for use in soups and stocks. They are tan, rather flat and resemble a large lima bean.

FOCACCIA (foh-KAH-chee-ah) A yeast bread that is similar to pizza but thicker. It can be drizzled with olive oil and sprinkled with salt or topped with a variety of savory toppings. It is known throughout Italy in various forms from a flatbread to a filled dough that resembles a stuffed pie.

FRITTATA (free-TAH-tah) The Italian version of an omelet, served open face. The ingredients are usually mixed in with the eggs rather than folded in after the frittata is cooked. The frittata is cooked on one side, then flipped over so both the top and bottom are golden brown, allowing the eggs to set slowly.

GAMBERO (GAHM-beh-roh) "Shrimp." Italians prepare shrimp in many ways, including boiling, frying and mixing with other foods. Gamberetti are very small shrimp; gamberoni are very large.

GELATO (jeh-LAH-toh) Italian ice cream, usually prepared from an egg-based custard using whole milk or cream. An Italian ice-cream parlor is called a gelateria.

GENOA (JE-noh-ah) salami A fine-grind, moderately spiced sausage studded with white peppercorns, generally made from pork but sometimes beef or veal. Originally from Genoa, the popularity of this sausage has spread far beyond its birthplace.

GNOCCHI (NOH-kee) Italian for dumplings that are usually cooked in water or broth or baked. There are two basic types: potato, used mostly in northern Italy, and semolina, made in Rome and the south. Eggs and cheese can be added to the dough, and chopped spinach is another popular addition.

GREMOLATA (greh-moh-LAH-tah) A mixture of chopped garlic, parsley and lemon peel that is sprinkled over dishes to add a fresh flavor.

GRISSINI (gree-SEE-nee) Thin, crisp breadsticks that originated in Turin, Italy.

INSALATA (een-sah-LAH-tah) "Salad." In Italy, salads are made from vegetables or salad greens and are sometimes mixed with grains. Insalata condita is the simplest of

salads, consisting of salad greens tossed with lemon and olive oil. Mista is a mixture of greens and vegetables. Salad is served before the cheese course in a traditional Italian menu plan.

INVOLTINI (een-vohl-TEE-nee) Stuffed rolls of meat or fish. Each region of Italy has its own variation.

KALAMATA olives are plump purplish black, point at one end Green olives. The flavor is balanced and are used in Italian cooking.

MARINARA (mah-ree-NAHR-uh) "Mariner's style." A basic tomato sauce, usually used on pasta, made by sautéing onions and garlic in olive oil, then adding tomato pulp and spices. It is believed that originally fishermen's wives made this fast, fresh sauce when the men returned with the day's catch.

MICHETTA (mee-KEH-tah) Round, crusty rolls, created in Milan, with five slits on the sides that resemble a flower.

MINESTRA (mee-NEHS-trah) "Soup." A light soup with a broth base and pasta or vegetables.

MINESTRONE (mee-neh-STROH-neh) "Big soup." Hearty vegetable soup with ingredients that vary from region to region.

MORTADELLA (mohr-tah-DEH-lah) A sausage made from finely ground pork mixed with spices and usually flavored with peppercorns and coriander. The sausages are quite large, ranging from 3 to 180 pounds each. This sausage originated in Bologna, and is from which the name "baloney" came.

OLIVE OIL See Olive Oils, page 244.

OSSO BUCO (OH-soh BOO-koh) "Pierce bone." A specialty of Lombardy, it is a shank, usually veal, braised in tomato and onion sauce and served with a gremolata, a lemon and parsley mixture.

OSTERIA (oh-steh-REE-ah) Originally the word for a neighborhood tavern, it now refers to a simple inn or eating place.

PANCETTA (pahn-CHEH-tah) Italian cured pork, similar to American bacon, that is cured with salt rather than being smoked. It is generally rolled up, not flat like American bacon.

PANETTONE (pan-uh-TOH-nee) A sweet yeast bread made with raisins, citron and spices and baked in a tall cylindrical shape. This Milan-originated bread is traditionally served during the Christmas season but is also served at other special celebrations. It can be served as a bread or dessert.

PANNA COTTO (PAHN-nah KOH-tah) "Cooked cream." A light egg custard that is served cold and typically with fruit or a chocolate sauce.

PARMIGIANA (pahr-mee-J'YAH-nah) A dish made with Parmesan cheese and prosciutto in the style of Parma. In the U.S., it refers to a breaded meat or eggplant that is topped with tomato sauce, mozzarella and Parmesan cheese, then baked.

PEPERONCINO (peh-peh-rohn-CHEE-noh) The chili pepper of Italy. A small, yellow banana pepper, usually pickled in brine for salads and appetizers. They have a slightly sweet flavor that can range from medium to medium-hot.

PESTO (PEH-stoh) An uncooked sauce found throughout Italy in several versions, but always with the same base of basil, garlic, pine nuts, Parmesan cheese and olive oil. Originally from Genoa, it was a paste made by pounding basil, garlic and pine nuts in a mortar with a pestle and then lacing with cheese, pepper and olive oil. It is excellent served as a sauce for pasta or added to soups.

PICCATA (pih-KAH-tuh) Term indicating a "piquant" spicy sauce used to cook chicken and veal, in which the pungent flavors of capers, lemon juice and wine are combined.

PIGNOLI (peen-YOH-lee) Italian name for pine nuts, extracted from large pinecones. They are used to make sauces, desserts, eggplant salads and other dishes.

POLENTA (poh-LEHN-tah) A staple of northern Italy, polenta is made from cornmeal and traditionally eaten in place of bread or pasta. After cooking, it can be served hot as soft polenta or it can be chilled and fried or baked with tomato sauce and cheese. It can be served as a first course or side dish.

POLLO (POHL-loh) The Italian word for a young chicken.

PORCINI (pohr-CHEE-nee) "Little pigs." Reddish brown-capped Italian mushrooms with a yellow-orange meaty pulp that are added to everything from pasta sauces to stews. They are also available dried.

PRIMAVERA (pree-muh-VEHR-uh), alla "Springtime." Generally refers to any dish prepared with fresh vegetables.

PRIMI (PREE-mee) "First course." The course that follows the antipasto and precedes the main course. It can be pasta, rice, gnocchi, polenta or a soup dish.

PROSCIUTTO (proh-SHOO-toh) The Italian word for cured ham. A lean, salt-cured ham traditionally aged for one year and served in paper-thin slices. Used in several appetizers, it is also excellent with ripe cantaloupe and frequently combined with veal. If aged correctly, it should have a tender texture and minimal salt flavor.

PUTTANESCA (poot-tah-NEHS-kah), alla A spicy tomato sauce made with onions, capers, olives, anchovies and garlic that is served with pasta. It is named after the "ladies of the night" because was quick to prepare between clients.

RADICCHIO (rah-DEE-kee-oh) A small leaf lettuce grown in Treviso in northern Italy. It is available in various colors and degrees of bitterness. The most familiar is the red-purple color with white streaks and a strong, slightly bitter flavor. Radicchio is valued for its digestive properties.

RAGÙ (ra-GOO) A meat sauce serve with pasta that is a staple of Bologna. (Also see Bolognese.)

RISOTTO (rih-SAW-toh) The traditional rice dish of northern Italy, prepared by making a soffritto of vegetables such as onion, garlic and parsley with butter or oil, and then gradually adding liquid, usually broth, while the rice cooks at medium heat until a creamy consistency. (Also see Arborio Rice.)

RISTORANTE (ree-stoh-RAHN-teh) Italian word for a restaurant that is higher class than a trattoria or osteria.

SALTIMBOCCA (sahl-teem-BOH-kah) Literally "jump in the mouth." This term generally refers to a folded-over slice of meat filled with cheese, herbs or other meats that is quickly fried in a pan and eaten while piping hot.

SCALOPPINE (skah-luh-PEE-nee) Cuts of meat pounded thin and usually dipped in flour and sautéed with other ingredients. Two of the most common dishes are made with either wine or lemon juice.

SEMOLINA (she-muh-LEE-nuh) A coarse flour made from milling the whole kernel of durum wheat. This is the flour used for traditional pasta dough and is high in fiber and protein.

SOFFRITTO (soh-FREE-toh) An Italian term similar to sauté, it is a mixture that forms the base of many sauces and gives important flavor to many dishes. Finely chopped onion, garlic and other vegetables and herbs are quickly fried in oil or butter until sizzling.

SORBETTO (sohr-BEH-toh) Sherbet or sorbet made with a various fruit flavors or chocolate.

STROMBOLI (strahm-BOH-lee) A type of stuffed pizza in which the melted cheese and sauce filling flows from the dough similar to the flow of lava from the top of the Stromboli volcano in southern Italy.

SUGO (SOO-goh) A light, mild tomato sauce traditionally prepared with a soffritto of onion, garlic and basil to which crushed tomatoes are added.

TIMBALLO (teem-BAH-loh) An elaborate pasta or rice dish made with meats and colorful vegetables and baked in a mold. It is unmolded just before serving for a dramatic presentation at special occasions.

TIRA MI SU (tee-RAH-me-SOO) "Pick me up." A rich dessert made with layers of ladyfingers or sponge cake, mascarpone and espresso. It was created in a Treviso restaurant in the 1960s and is now a very popular Italian dessert.

TRATTORIA (trah-toh-REE-ah) An Italian eatery that is less elegant than a ristorante and that usually has a limited menu using seasonal ingredients.

VERDE (VEHR-deh) Literally means "green," and is the term used for a sauce with lots of olive oil, parsley, green onions or other greens.

VINEGAR See Wine Vinegars, page 18.

VINO (VEE-noh) Italian word for "wine."

ZABAIONE (zah-bye-OH-neh) A light, airy custard dessert made with whipped egg yolks, Marsala wine and sugar. It is served either warm or cold and often with strawberries.

ZUPPA (ZOO-pah) The Italian word for "soup," zuppa specifically refers to a very thick soup in which vegetables are the main ingredients.

METRIC CONVERSION GUIDE

Volume

U.S. Units	Canadian Metric	Australian Metric
1/4 teaspoon	1 mL	1 ml
1/2 teaspoon	2 mL	2 ml
1 teaspoon	5 mL	5 ml
1 tablespoon	15 mL	20 ml
1/4 cup	50 mL	60 ml
1/3 cup	75 mL	80 ml
1/2 cup	125 mL	125 ml
2/3 cup	150 mL	170 ml
3/4 cup	175 mL	190 ml
1 cup	250 mL	250 ml
1 quart	1 liter	1 liter
1 1/2 quarts	1.5 liters	1.5 liters
2 quarts	2 liters	2 liters
2 1/2 quarts	2.5 liters	2.5 liters
3 quarts	3 liters	3 liters
4 quarts	4 liters	4 liters

Weight

U.S. Units	Canadian Metric	Australian Metric
1 ounce	30 grams	30 grams
2 ounces	55 grams	60 grams
3 ounces	85 grams	90 grams
4 ounces (1/4 pound)	115 grams	125 grams
8 ounces (1/2 pound)	225 grams	225 grams
16 ounces (1 pound)	455 grams	500 grams
1 pound	455 grams	1/2 kilogram

Measurements

Inches	Centimeters
1	2.5
2	5.0
3	7.5
4	10.0
5	12.5
6	15.0
7	17.5
8	20.5
9	23.0
10	25.5
11	28.0
12	30.5
13	33.0

Temperatures

Fahrenheit	Celsius
32°	0°
212°	100°
250°	120°
275°	140°
300°	150°
325°	160°
350°	180°
375°	190°
400°	200°
425°	220°
450°	230°
475°	240°
500°	260°

Note: The recipes in this cookbook have not been developed or tested using metric measures. When converting recipes to metric, some variations in quality may be noted.

HELPFUL NUTRITION AND COOKING INFORMATION

Nutrition Guidelines:

We provide nutrition information for each recipe that includes calories, fat, cholesterol, sodium, carbohydrate, fiber and protein. Individual food choices can be based on this information

Recommended intake for a daily diet of 2,000 calories as set by the Food and Drug Organization

Total Fat	**Less than 65g**
Saturated Fat	**Less than 20g**
Cholesterol	**Less than 300mg**
Sodium	**Less than 2,400mg**
Total Carbohydrate	**300g**
Dietary Fiber	**25g**

Criteria Used for Calculating Nutrition Information:

- The first ingredient was used wherever a choice is given (such as 1/3 cup sour cream or plain yogurt).
- The first ingredient amount was used wherever a range is given (such as 3 to 3 1/2 pound cut-up broiler-fryer chicken).
- The first serving number was used wherever a range is given (such as 4 to 6 servings).
- "If desired" ingredients (such as sprinkle with brown sugar if desired) and recipe variations were not included .
- Only the amount of a marinade or frying oil that is estimated to be absorbed by the food during preparation or cooking was calculated.

Ingredients Used in Recipe Testing and Nutrition Calculations:

- Ingredients used for testing represent those that the majority of consumers use in their homes: large eggs, 2% milk, 80% lean ground beef, canned ready-to-use chicken broth, and vegetable oil spread containing not less than 65% fat.

- Fat-free, low-fat or low-sodium products are not used, unless otherwise indicated.

- Solid vegetable shortening (not butter, margarine, non-stick cooking sprays or vegetable oil spread as they can cause sticking problems) is used to grease pans, unless otherwise indicated.

Equipment Used in Recipe Testing:

We use equipment for testing that the majority of consumers use in their homes. If a specific piece of equipment (such as a wire whisk) is necessary for recipe success, it will be listed in the recipe.

- Cookware and bakeware without nonstick coatings were used, unless otherwise indicated.

- No dark colored, black or insulated bakeware was used.

- When a baking pan is specified in a recipe, a metal pan was used; a baking dish or pie plate means oven-proof glass was used.

- An electric hand mixer was used for mixing only when mixer speeds are specified in the recipe directions. When a mixer speed is not given, a spoon or fork was used.

Cooking Terms Glossary

Beat: Mix ingredients vigorously with spoon, fork, wire whisk, hand beater or electric mixer until smooth and uniform.

Boil: Heat liquid until bubbles rise continuously and break on the surface and steam is given off. For rolling boil, the bubbles form rapidly.

Chop: Cut into coarse or fine irregular pieces with a knife, food chopper, blender or food processor.

Cube: Cut into squares 1/2 inch or larger.

Dice: Cut into squares smaller than 1/2 inch.

Grate: Cut into tiny particles using small rough holes of grater (citrus peel or chocolate).

Grease: Rub the inside surface of a pan with shortening, using pastry brush, piece of waxed paper or paper towel, to prevent food from sticking during baking (as for some casseroles).

Julienne: Cut into thin, matchlike strips, using knife or food processor (vegetables, fruits, meats).

Mix: Combine ingredients in any way that distributes them evenly.

Sauté: Cook foods in hot oil or margarine over medium-high heat with frequent tossing and turning motion.

Shred: Cut into long thin pieces by rubbing food across the holes of a shredder, as for cheese, or by using a knife to slice very thinly, as for cabbage.

Simmer: Cook in liquid just below the boiling point on top of the stove; usually after reducing heat from a boil. Bubbles will rise slowly and break just below the surface.

Stir: Mix ingredients until uniform consistency. Stir once in a while for stirring occasionally, often for stirring frequently and continuously for stirring constantly.

Toss: Tumble ingredients lightly with a lifting motion (such as green salad), usually to coat evenly or mix with another food.

INDEX

Italicized page references indicate photographs or illustrations.